The Mexican Revolution and the Catholic Church

1910-1929

The Mexican Revolution

and the

Catholic Church 1910-1929

Robert E. Quirk

Indiana University Press

Bloomington & London

Published in Canada by Fitzhenry & Whiteside Limited,
Don Mills, Ontario

Library of Congress catalog card number: 73-75399
ISBN: 0-253-33800-X

Manufactured in the United States of America

For Marianne

Contents

Acknowledgment

THE research for this book was made possible by grants from Harvard University, the Social Science Research Council, and Indiana University.

The Mexican Revolution and the Catholic Church

1910-1929

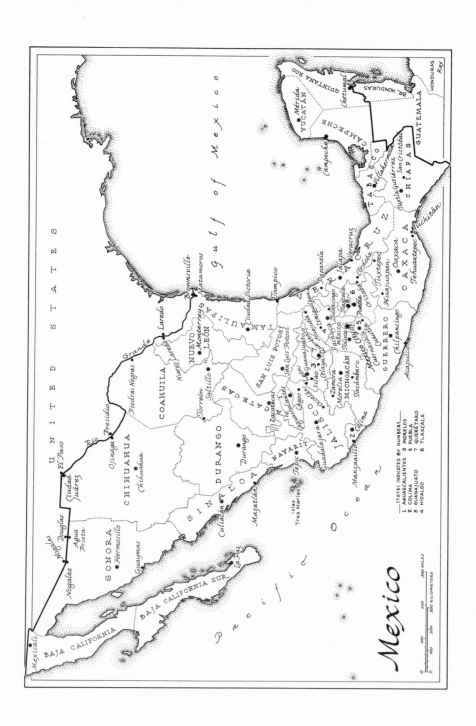

Mexico

STATES INDICATED BY NUMBERS:
1 AGUASCALIENTES   5 MORELOS
2 COLIMA   6 PUEBLA
3 GUANAJUATO   7 QUERÉTARO
4 HIDALGO   8 TLAXCALA

1

Before the Storm

FROM THE EARLIEST DAYS of the colonial period, Mexico has always been a predominantly Catholic country. Yet for more than a century after independence the Church came under periodic and at times violent attack at the hands of various governments, some (in the nineteenth century) liberal, others (during the first third of the twentieth century) radical. From 1926 to 1929 the Mexican bishops ordered all churches in the Republic closed in an effort to force President Plutarco Elías Calles' regime to rescind its anticlerical legislation. The clerical strike failed, in large part because most Mexicans, especially those in the countryside, felt no overwhelming need for Masses and sacraments. Since the Spanish conquest the traditional European practices have played an insignificant part in the religious life of the Mexican people. The Franciscan and Dominican friars who brought Christianity to Mexico sought to impose their own theological conceptions, but the Indians resisted passively until in the end the native ways won out. If the official religion became Spanish and European, the images and the cult practices remained Indian. It was the native, preconquest influences, as manifested at the basilica of Guadalupe and other national and local shrines, that have continued into the last third of the twentieth century to characterize much of Mexican Catholicism.

The cult of the Virgin of Guadalupe is the single most powerful element in Mexican Catholicism. On any day of the year the basilica and the surrounding courtyard are alive with pilgrims who have come to visit the shrine, to drink water from the sacred well and buy maize cakes in the plaza. If the crowds are not too large, many penitents will fall on their knees and shuffle across the courtyard and up the stone steps of the church. Inside they will light candles as votive offerings. Some, to give thanks for a particular miracle, especially a wondrous healing, will leave a silver image of the healed part—a leg, a heart—or even the likeness of an animal who was mysteriously preserved from what seemed to be certain death. (Vendors have permanent stalls outside the courtyard and do a thriving business in these ex votos.) At the great altar, beneath the image of the Virgin, or at one of the side altars, a priest may be offering up the Mass. But few pilgrims pay him heed. Their coming to the basilica has nothing to do with Masses or sacraments, or any of the ordinary rituals of the Church. It is a matter between them and the dark Virgin, and there are no intermediaries at Tepeyac. She appears without the Son, for her powers are immediate, not derivative. Christ the Lord is venerated elsewhere, at other shrines specifically dedicated to His worship. If the well-to-do, usually middle-aged or elderly women dressed in black, kneel in front of the altar and attend to the Mass, the Indians wander in awe about the church, pausing before an image of the Virgin or a saint, then pass their hands over the sacred object and rub their own faces and bodies, as though to transfer to themselves the statue's wondrous powers. They emerge from the church seemingly unaware of the priest or the sacrifice of the Mass.

The great occasion for the basilica, however, is December 12, the anniversary of the appearance of the Virgin in 1531, at Tepeyac outside Mexico City, to a simple Indian, Juan Diego. The Church Universal has never officially recognized or accepted the authenticity of this miracle or of the strange imprinting of the Virgin's image on the mantle of Juan Diego. This oversight does not trouble the Mexicans, for they are certain, whatever learned Vatican theologians might say or do, that the Virgin did indeed appear in Mexico. Skeptics point out that the supposed vision occurred at the site long sacred to Tonantzín, the Aztec mother of the gods, and that the veneration of Mary is only the perseverance of an earlier cult of primeval earth deities. The sacred well and the maize cakes belonged to Tonantzín before they were dedicated to the Mother of the Christian God. And it is true that December 12 sees the annual reenactment of ancient pagan dances within the confines of the basilica courtyard.

Before dawn the participants assemble, and with the first light the dances begin to the eerie accompaniment of primitive flutes and skin drums. Throughout the day the festivities continue, until the entire courtyard becomes a surging mass of dancers and spectators. To the outsider the dances may appear ludicrous, as the feather-clad Indians writhe and stamp in monotonous rhythm, much as their ancient ancestors must have done for Tonantzín before the coming of the Europeans. What the participants think or feel can only be guessed, for their faces betray no emotion. Perhaps they are not thinking—only responding to some inner compulsion.

What relationship is there between the wailing of flutes, the thudding of skin drums, the rattling of castanets, the grunting, and the thrusting of knees, and the sophisticated Christianity of Rome? The answer, in all candor, must be none. But who is to say that one activity is religious in a true sense, hence validly Christian, while another is not? Without doubt the Mexicans at Tepeyac believe that they are venerating the Mother of the Christian God in a way that is peculiarly theirs. Our Lady of Guadalupe is dark skinned; she is a native Mexican. Therefore, Mexico honors her in the ancient ways of the preconquest Indians.

The veneration of the Virgin at Tepeyac is only the strongest and most widespread of many cults to various aspects of the Christian Mother of God, to Christ, and to innumerable local saints. Our Lady of San Juan de Lagos, Our Lady of Juchitán, Our Lady of Zapopan —each has her own special powers and functions. Christ too appears in different guises—Our Lord of the Maize in Michoacán, Our Lord of Ixmiquilpan, and the mightiest of all the Christs, Our Lord of Chalma. Like Mary at Tepeyac, these Mexican Christs are almost invariably native in aspect. The Lord of the Maize is tawny, and he is not the Christ crucified of the New Testament, but a deity of vegetation, the universal corn god. He is seated, holding a stalk of maize. It is the Black Christ, as swarthy as the darkest Indian, who reigns at Chalma.

For the majority of Mexicans, religion is bound up in these extra-sacramental rituals—making a pilgrimage; praying to a favorite saint, in a church, at home, or at a roadside shrine; carrying the saint's image into the fields to bring rain or to ensure fertility; taking food and water to the cemetery on the Day of the Dead. Masses have all too often been poorly attended, and even the most pious feel little need for them or for confession and the Holy Eucharist. Men, particularly, rarely come to Mass. They are baptized in the Church;

some, though not most in the poorer classes, are married in the Church; and at the end they receive extreme unction and are buried as good Christians. But for most of their lives they prefer the traditional cult practices or else, and especially among the educated, they ignore religion entirely.[1]

The villagers call themselves Catholics, but they know nothing of the Church Universal and probably very little of Christian theology. An attack upon a bishop or the persecution of the clergy in the faraway capital means little, so long as the village saint is not molested. They are illiterate, most of them, and have never read the Bible or had it read to them. They remain ignorant even of the most basic catechismal teachings of the Church. Because they focus their religion on the image of the saint, their feelings toward the priest are often ambivalent. In the first place, rural Mexico has never had enough priests to staff the parish churches. Many villages would have no services at all, were it not for the occasional visitations of curates from neighboring parishes. In areas such as Yucatán and Tabasco the people might never see a priest in their village. And too many priests in the past have been insufficiently trained or poorly chosen. They shared the ignorance, the prejudices, and even the vices of their charges. Frequently in the nineteenth century the priest was avaricious and grasping and perhaps immoral. Curates and even bishops had "wives" and "families," whom they flaunted shamelessly to the public view. All the more reason, then, to turn from the priest, who was a "sinner like the rest of us," to the saint, who was compassionate and understanding, and who (above all else) cost nothing. The high fees charged for marriage ceremonies caused most Mexican villagers to prefer free union to a church wedding. Funerals (especially for children) were conducted without the presence of a priest.[2]

Because of the poor quality of Mexico's priests and their insufficiency, great numbers of clergymen came from Europe in the nineteenth century, from Belgium, France, and Italy, and particularly from Spain. But the foreign clergy, more highly educated than the Mexican priests, tended to monopolize the choicer posts in the cities and larger towns, so that the rural areas benefitted little from the immigration. The Church was weakest where it should have found its greatest strength, among the conservative Indian peasants and peons. When it came under attack, it could not count on the strong and united support of the rural majority.

The villagers, if they ignored the priests and the sacraments, had no occasion to attack the Church as an institution. The troubles that beset the priests and bishops came chiefly from the educated sectors of society—from the middle-class liberals and radicals who passed laws and wrote constitutions to restrict or even shackle the activities of the Church. Anticlericalism in Mexico had its origins in the first days of the wars for independence, though its roots are to be found in the influences of the French Enlightenment, in the writings of Voltaire, Raynal, Condorcet, and Rousseau, which stimulated (or corrupted) the minds of a generation of young aristocrats and caused them to take up arms against the Spanish crown and the Church that supported the crown.

In the colonial era, Church and State were one, joined by the *Patronato Real,* the powers of royal patronage granted by the popes in a time of papal weakness and indifference to spiritual matters and by the end of the eighteenth century claimed and exercised by Spanish kings through divine right. The Church was powerful, rich, and conservative, but always under the royal or viceregal thumb. In the 300 years since Cortes' conquest of the Aztecs, the Church had accumulated vast estates that were held in mortmain, hence were untaxable and could never revert to secular ownership. The Spanish government enforced the collection of the *diezmo,* or ecclesiastical tithe, like any other tax, and monastic vows, once taken, were binding under civil as well as canon law. A monk or nun who dared leave the claustral life could be hunted down like a common felon. If the Church educated the young, operated hospitals, asylums, and other charitable institutions, and lent its money to miners, merchants, and landowners for economic expansion in Mexico, it also censored the books, persecuted political dissenters under the Inquisition, and reinforced the conservative tendencies of the Spanish viceregal government. It was this regime, this union of Church and State, that the liberals, after independence, would weaken or even destroy, but which the conservatives wished to preserve intact.

There was much to be said for the conservative position in 1824, when Mexico's first constitution was promulgated. It seemed to promise unity and stability in a country torn by a decade and a half of civil strife. The traditional system offered protection for the rural working classes, the peons, who constituted the largest part of the population in the nineteenth century. Bound to the hacienda much like the medieval serfs, the peons had, nonetheless, a measure of economic security. And they had in their religion the assurance of eternal salvation and happiness. Because almost all Mexicans in 1824 were Catholics, there was no pressing need for toleration of other sects. In any event, the conservatives believed that religious dissidents would breed political disorder and social chaos. In the nineteenth century the Conservative Party counted on the support of the hacendados, the churchmen, and many of the army officers. Military and ecclesiastical *fueros* (special privileges to be tried under martial or canon laws, rather than by civil courts) were made a part of the constitutions fashioned when the conservatives gained power. Under the conservatives censorship and the control of education remained in clerical hands. And the conservatives preferred a centralized regime—the provinces would be dominated by the national government in Mexico City. But as promptly as they were ousted by their political opponents, Mexico reverted to a more liberal document with restrictions on the Church, and to a system of federalism with more powers granted to the provincial governments.

Mexico's liberals continued in the nineteenth century to draw inspiration from the ideals of the Enlightenment, but also looked to the British radical economists, Malthus, Ricardo, and Bentham, and especially to the French novelist, Benjamin Constant. Because no single Mexican theorist synthesized European liberalism for his countrymen or sought to modify it for Mexico's peculiar conditions, the philosophy developed erratically and was often illogical and contradictory—while proclaiming the Rights of Man and individual freedom, the liberals could use state powers to curtail the rights of their opponents. Nor did the liberal leaders achieve a consensus about their program. In general, however, they agreed on certain aspects of European liberalism.[3]

The liberals were secularly minded; they held that man's chief concern was with the here and now; the matter of eternal salvation was an unfathomable mystery, consigned to the realm of the priests and to Sunday mornings. They were optimistic about the future of mankind in general and of the Mexican people in particular. Man was perfectible on this earth and in this life, if he heeded the dictates of his own reason and the teachings of the liberals, rejecting the superstitions of the past (by which the liberal mind usually meant orthodox religious dogma). And because man was perfectible, the liberals believed in the possibility of unlimited progress, but a progress that was material, that could be attained by acquiring earthly goods. Thus they equated happiness with wealth. They looked to a future paradise, not in eternity, not in the Christian sense, but as a temporal state in which all Mexicans would be educated and prosperous. They stressed the basic worth and dignity of the individual, denying the necessity or value of communal organizations. Following laissez-faire doctrines, the liberals rejected government interference in business activities. Individual effort and initiative alone would lead, they believed, to economic well-being.

In principle, then, there was much agreement among Mexico's liberals. In practice, however, they frequently disagreed. The radicals, or *puros*, wished to drive ahead rapidly, often recklessly, toward their goals. The moderates would move more slowly, for they believed that the Mexican people, especially the economically backward Indians, were not ready for rash steps. The radicals were violently anticlerical. They wished to attack the structure of the Church, to curtail the privileges of priests and bishops. They would remove the Church, as a cancerous growth, from the body politic of the Mexican people. They would separate Church and State, would confine the Church to its own sphere, that of spiritual matters. The organization of society would be the concern of the State, not the Church. The radicals would secularize education. Legal marriage would become a civil, not religious, contract. The State, not the priests would keep birth and death records, and cemeteries would be secularized, so that no person, at the whim of a clergyman, could be refused a proper burial. The State, said the radicals, would determine the legal constitution of a family, would declare a man and a woman to be married, would proclaim children to be legitimate and to be members of that family, and would see that the dead were buried with honor.

If men and women wished to be married subsequently by a priest or wanted their children to be baptized, if they preferred to send their sons and daughters to parochial schools, or if they asked a priest to officiate at funerals, that was their own affair. But State functions would take precedence over those of the Church. The radicals deemed all these arrangements reasonable and logical. They would create two spheres in society, the temporal and the spiritual. Each institution would predominate in its own sphere, would be separate and independent from the other.

Though the moderate liberals shared with the radicals of their party the same vision of the future, they would achieve the earthly paradise in a more prudent fashion. They temporized, opposing the more stringent demands of the *puros*. At times the moderates appeared to rest at dead center, paralyzed, refusing to take any action, lest it be wrong. In reality, they seemed closer to the conservatives in their immediate program than to the extremists of the Liberal Party. They opposed separation of Church and State and the toleration of other sects in Mexico.

The moderates controlled the liberal Constituent Congress that met in 1856, and they wrote the constitution promulgated in the following year. Most Mexican liberals in the 1850s were restrained and were not as yet prepared for a violent attack upon religion. Still, even the moderates agreed that some church activities should be curtailed in the constitution and that priests (along with the military) should be deprived of their special status and privileges. They also banned the holding of communal properties by the Church and by the Indian villagers, outlawed compulsory monastic vows, and secularized public education (though private parochial schools were still permitted). The members of the Constituent Congress failed, however, to follow their liberal principles to their logical conclusion —the legal separation of Church and State. Nor could they bring themselves to take a stand on toleration—lest the country see an influx of "Mohammedans, idolators, and even Mormons." In the end, they voted to make no explicit statement in the constitution on either point. At one juncture, with the Congress in complete frustration, the delegates by the narrowest of margins avoided a decision to return to the Constitution of 1824.[4]

Though the moderate view had prevailed, the Catholic clergy still found the new constitution unacceptable, for it sanctioned the expropriation of church lands and ended the traditional privileges of the priests and bishops and their exemption from civil control. In public statements the prelates condemned the constitution and ordered excommunicated any public official who swore to uphold it. No private citizen who supported the liberal government could receive an ecclesiastical burial. And the bishops barred the president and his cabinet from the Mexico City cathedral, unless they retracted their oaths of office. When the conservatives raised the banner of rebellion against the constitution and the liberal government, the bishops threw their support behind the revolutionaries.

The president, Ignacio Comonfort, who was among the more

conservative of the moderates, was inclined at first to bow to the
conservative demands. In the end, however, he resigned and turned
the presidency over to Benito Juárez, liberal head of the Supreme
Court and his legal successor. Because the conservatives gained
control of most of the armies, Juárez was forced to leave the capital
and seek refuge in the port city of Veracruz. Once a moderate, the
new president now turned to the radical liberals, for he could never
forget or forgive the support given his enemies by the priests and
bishops. Beginning in the summer of 1859, Juárez launched a series
of attacks upon the Church—the so-called Reform Laws. Church
and State were now officially separated. All monastic orders were
outlawed, and the regular clergy were obliged to join the seculars.
The provisions of the decree that concerned nunneries were less
severe. These could remain open, but no other novices could be
admitted in the future.

Juárez' sharpest attack on the Church came in the decree that
nationalized all church properties—the buildings, the objects
within, any possession held by the Church as an institution. The
properties would be sold at public auction. These first Reform Laws
were followed in late 1859 and in 1860 by other presidential decrees
to implement the radicals' program. Juárez secularized the cemeteries, made marriage a civil contract, reduced the number of religious
holidays, and restricted public religious processions. He was determined to punish the Church and to assure that in the future clerical
control over the Mexican people would be minimal.

Pope Pius IX denounced both the constitution and Juárez' Reform Laws out of hand. "We raise our Pontifical voice with apostolic
freedom . . . ," he said, "to condemn, reprove, and declare null and
void, and without any value, the said decrees. . . ." In Mexico the
reaction of the Church was equally vigorous. As a result, when
Juárez regained control of Mexico City, he exiled the apostolic
delegate, the archbishop of Mexico, and four other bishops.

Unable to achieve victory with their own military forces, the conservatives, in consort with the bishops, supported the intervention
of the French armies in 1862 and the imperial government of the
Hapsburg Archduke Maximilian. The French withdrawal and the
execution of Maximilian in 1867 signaled the end of the Conservative Party in Mexico. Thereafter there was no effective political
group to support the cause of the Catholic Church. In the 1870s,
during the presidency of Sebastián Lerdo de Tejada, the Reform

Laws were incorporated into the constitution. Though the conserv-
ative-episcopal coalition was irreparably shattered, the Church
steadfastly refused to accept the consequences of the liberal victory
or to recognize the right of the Mexican government to impose
restrictions upon its spiritual and temporal powers. The history of
Mexico in the late nineteenth century and during the first third of
the twentieth century witnessed the resistance of the clergy, usually
passive, though subsequently active, to the Reform Laws.

Catholic theologians in the nineteenth century repudiated the
basic tenets of liberalism, and Pius IX, in his *Syllabus of Errors* (1864),
made clear that no Catholic could, in good conscience, be a liberal.
The Church maintained that man, flawed by original sin, was not
perfectible, that progress, if desirable, could never be an end in
itself. Temporal happiness was only a secondary and incidental
aspiration, for eternal salvation had an obvious priority over the
quality of life on earth. To the Church, individualism and liberal
democracy were unacceptable, because they denied the God-given
right of some men to rule and the obligation of others to follow.
And laissez-faire doctrines, which unharnessed man's economic
appetites, were rejected, because all Christians must bear responsibility for the well-being of their fellow men. Liberalism, with its
deliberate de-Christianization of society, was a cause of, not a cure
for, social disorders. Genuine social reform must come through the
application of Christian principles, through the regeneration of
mankind, through a reform in morals, not through unlimited and
irreligious individual competition.

If man's eternal happiness is of prime importance, then it follows
that the institution that concerns itself with spiritual matters, that is,
the Church, must take precedence over all other human agencies,
such as the secular governments. In an ideal Christian society,
Church and State must remain united, and the government will look
for guidance to the spiritual leaders. All education must be permeated with religion; secular education cannot be admitted in a
Catholic state. Nor could the Church allow the government a role
in marriage, in birth registration, or in the control of cemeteries. As
Catholic principles guided society, so the constitution of the family
would be determined by religious guidelines. Since liberalism was
palpably in error, there could be no toleration for its principles. And
the hierarchy must steadfastly oppose liberals wherever they might
appear, in whatever country of the world. For if Catholicism was the

only true faith, as Catholic writers maintained, then the principles of the Church must prevail everywhere. The pope was superior to kings and to all other secular rulers. Ironically, Pius IX, a politically weak, self-proclaimed prisoner in the Vatican, asserted a papal and religious primacy unenforceable at the apogee of Rome's temporal power—during the reign of Innocent III in the thirteenth century.[5]

Many socially concerned Catholics, particularly educated laymen, recognized that the serious shortcomings of the *Syllabus of Errors* stemmed from its essentially negative character. Society's ills needed a cure, they felt, and it did not suffice to condemn all secular responses to the "Social Question" without providing a Catholic answer compatible with church teaching. This was especially true in the developed Western European countries with the rapid growth of capitalism and modern industry. Out of this concern developed Catholic socialism, which after 1900 became the Social Action movement. Pius' successor, Leo XIII, placed his stamp of approval on the movement in his pathbreaking encyclical "Rerum Novarum" in 1891, and thereafter, though Social Action was seen as primarily a lay endeavor, the Vatican and the bishops assumed control of its direction. It was inevitable that the hierarchy would come to dominate the movement, for only the bishops, according to Catholic principles, could teach the truths of the Church and interpret to the faithful the words of the pope. The laity might organize, might comment, but it was the bishop who instructed. In Mexico, as elsewhere, the prelates guided the movement from the start.

Leo XIII deliberately turned the attention of nineteenth-century reformers back to the Middle Ages, to the magisterial writings of St. Thomas Aquinas. In an age of materialism, science, and skepticism, the pontiff invoked the principles that had guided medieval society (or so it seemed, through the haze of the intervening centuries)— cooperation, communality, and brotherly love. To Leo the liberals portrayed society as little more than a joint-stock company, while the socialists, who appeared as the century ended an ever-increasing danger, saw only hatred and class conflict. More and more Catholic Social Action reacted against the socialist threat, with the result that the movement concerned itself almost exclusively with urban problems—factory conditions, labor organizations, and workers' cooperatives. Western Europe's sturdy peasantry seemed less in need of serious attention by the reformers. And in Mexico, too, because the founders of Social Action looked to Europe, and in fact were often trained in European centers of learning such as the Jesuit University of Louvain, the movement was primarily urban in outlook. It was far easier to promote the formation of labor groups than to effect substantial agrarian reform—a reform that could only shake Mexico's traditional society to its foundations.[6]

The victory of Juárez and the liberals in 1867 brought no peace to Mexico. Nor did it offer social improvement for the depressed masses. Though the liberals had hoped that the lands of the Indian communities and the Church, which had been put up for sale, would be bought by the Indians themselves, almost all went to hacendados, the urban middle class, and members of the government. Even Juárez and his close associates profited personally by gaining rural properties at the expense of the Indian villagers. The liberals looked to eventual social and economic improvement, but only through education and such government actions as road building.

Juárez and his successor, Sebastián Lerdo de Tejada, governed Mexico for nearly a decade. They were hamstrung, however, by the constitution, which had deliberately weakened the powers of the president. The liberals in 1857 had hoped that the federal system would guarantee individual liberties and protect local rights from the tyranny of an all-powerful national regime. Instead federalism promoted anarchy by enouraging local jealousies and the rule of petty caudillos in the various states. The liberals, now without an effective political or military opposition, fell out among themselves and quarreled over the spoils of national and local office.

Both Juárez and Lerdo tried to bring order by strengthening the powers of the presidency, but members of the Congress accused them of aspiring to dictatorial rule and refused to reform the constitution. Elections were as fradulent as under the conservatives, the imposition of the official candidates being inevitably followed by the revolt of the defeated opposition. As a result of the disorder, of the continued civil strife, many responsible citizens became disenchanted with the Liberal Party and called for a system that would protect property. Many erstwhile liberals would accept the rule of a strong man, if he could assure peace and orderly progress. They turned their backs on Juárez and Lerdo and the idealistic principles that had long guided the Liberal Party. Because the Conservative Party had died with Maximilian, they looked elsewhere for inspiration; they found their messiah in the French philosoper, Auguste

Comte, their creed in his scientific positivism, and their leader in General Porfirio Díaz, a politician from the state of Oaxaca.

Díaz, a commander of liberal forces, had served Juárez well, winning battles against the French invaders and against the conservative armies after the French withdrew from Mexico. A candidate for the presidency in 1872 and again in 1876, he lost to Juárez and Lerdo in rigged elections. Both times he revolted. In 1876 his troops defeated the armies of Lerdo, and though he had pledged "No-Reelection" in his Plan of Tuxtepec, he subsequently disregarded his promise. The general permitted his henchman, Manuel González, to succeed him in 1880, but thereafter he maneuvered his own reelection for more than a quarter-century. Díaz' dictatorship brought Mexico for the first time in its history an extended period of peace, free from revolt, free from internal dissension, free from foreign intervention. The president was never a positivist. It is doubtful if he had any political philosophy. But he accepted an alliance with the positivists, because they gave him valuable support with the propertied classes and helped sustain his regime.

Positivism was brought to Mexico during the administration of Benito Juárez, and it came in time to dominate the country's educational system. Because it gave the appearance of being practical and scientific, it appealed to the growing middle class, to the property owners and the professional and business men. Positivism seemed attuned to the materialistic temper of the times. The positivists mixed their creed of Comtism with ingredients from Herbert Spencer and from Europe's Social Darwinists to exalt their class as the country's rightful rulers. They saw themselves as the end-products of a long evolutionary process—the struggle for the survival of the fittest in Mexico. They ignored the Indians as an inferior race who counted for little in their plans for a positivistic future. The positivists did not deny orderly progress, but they believed that no state could be transformed through revolution. The many liberal revolutions had brought only chaos. The positivists admired the Anglo-Saxon nations, the Americans and the British, who were strong and wealthy. To make Mexico vigorous and progressive, therefore, to obtain the material comforts of the United States and Great Britain, the positivists would saxonize their own customs and institutions. In their schools they would turn out replicas of the gringos, white

Mexicans who were fit to follow in the path of their northern neighbors.

With Porfirio Díaz in firm control of Mexico, the positivists (called Científicos by their critics) and the oligarchic class took advantage of the opportunity to enrich themselves and their associates. A leading positivist, José Limantour, became Minister of the Treasury. Friends of the government and even foreigners received large tracts of land, and the Indian villages lost what remained of their communal holdings. Oil fields, railroads, and mines were developed with the aid of foreign capital. The capitalists and financiers of the United States and Britain saw in Díaz' Mexico a "Golden Era"—a period of stability and huge profits. By 1910 Mexico seemed prosperous, and Limantour had set the country's course on an even keel. He had balanced the budget, and the treasury even showed a surplus. With Mexico on the gold standard, the peso achieved a stability unknown in the nineteenth century. Díaz' army and his rural constabulary pacified the country, keeping malcontents in check by means of ruthless terrorism. Through the *jefes políticos* Díaz controlled the state and town governments. Mexico was indeed a safe country for travelers, landowners, businessmen, and foreign investors. Porfirio Díaz had found Mexico in confusion and in danger of falling apart. After thirty years in office, he could boast that it was well on the road to modernization, with a sound, efficient government.

The benefits of modernization went to the select few, however, and the majority of Mexicans were destitute, living in peonage (debt servitude). Robbed of their lands, the Indians were legally tied to the rural estates, and few could ever escape the debts owed the hacendados. For his food, his clothing, his tools, his seeds, his house, even for his church wedding or a family funeral, the peon was in perpetual debt to the landowner. Factory laborers, miners, and railroad workers, if slightly better off than the campesinos, were paid low wages and forced to work long hours under hazardous conditions. When textile and other workers, led by anarcho-syndicalist agitators, sought to organize strikes, the government crushed their movements with considerable loss of life. In the first decade of the twentieth century it had become apparent to concerned critics that Mexico was in grave need of reform.

Díaz, though a dictator who ruthlessly suppressed opposition movements, allowed a surprising amount of criticism, especially in the press. But the criticism dealt with personalities, not institutions. Men could talk and write—but not act—against the government. Andrés Molina Enríquez in *Los grandes problemas nacionales,* published in 1909, pointed to the need for thorough agrarian reform, but he called for evolutionary, not revolutionary, change. A group of young idealists founded a Mexican Liberal Party, not to contest elections, which were always fraudulent, but to suggest prudent reforms. Increasingly, however, they came under the influence of radical syndicalists, such as the Flores Magón brothers, and the Díaz government reacted by jailing the party's leaders. Some went into exile in the United States, where they continued to agitate for revolution in Mexico. And the Catholic Church, in response to Leo's call for a Christian solution to social problems, began its program of Catholic Action to suggest its own answers to Mexico's difficulties.

The Church had no reason to attack Díaz or his government directly, and it would have been indeed imprudent to do so. It is clear that positivism, like liberalism, was incompatible with Catholic teachings. And Díaz, despite his political views, was no conservative. Yet he never enforced the Reform Laws with any consistency, so that monasteries and nunneries continued to operate, and many church properties, through fictitious sales, remained under the control of the bishops. In view of Díaz' tolerant attitude regarding the clergy's activities, the Church adopted a conciliatory "live and let live" policy toward the president and the positivists. The bishops' pastoral letters dealt principally with such politically innocuous subjects as parochial schools and the need for the faithful to tithe regularly. The new social program of the Church was also circumspect in its dealings with the Porfirian regime, criticizing conditions without direct accusations against the president and his associates. Moreover, the movement received little publicity before 1911, never involving more than a handful of clerics and a small group of zealous laymen.[7]

Catholic Social Action had its beginning in Mexico with the formation of a Union of Catholic Men and a counterpart Union of Catholic Women by a Jesuit priest, José Luis Cuevas. This led to the First Catholic Congress, which met in February 1903 in the city of Puebla. Speakers denounced Mexico's chief problems, rural and urban poverty and poor working conditions, and suggested the formation of worker's circles and the promotion of handicraft and commercial schools in the urban areas and especially primary schools in the villages. One delegate, a young layman from Jalisco, Miguel Palomar y Vizcarra, proposed the creation of Cajas Raiffeisen, rural cooperative banks, named for a nineteenth-century German Catholic reformer. Subsequently, Catholic congresses met in 1904 at Morelia, in 1906 at Guadalajara, and in 1909 at Oaxaca. Among the leaders, in addition to Father Cuevas and Palomar y Vizcarra, were a layman, José Refugio Galindo; a Josephine priest, José María Troncoso; a French Jesuit, Bernard Bergoënd; and the bishop of Tulancingo, José Mora y del Río.

In 1905 Galindo founded the Guadalupan Laborers, which published two periodicals, *La Democracia Cristiana* and *Restauración*, and he began to organize workers in the factories and in rural areas. Galindo's group sponsored Agricultural Weeks in various parts of the Republic and petitioned state legislatures to enact social reforms. Father Troncoso proposed in 1907 that the many separate Catholic workers' groups merge to increase their effectiveness and in the following year succeeded in constituting a Catholic Workers' Union, directed by a layman, Salvador Moreno Arriaga. Bergoënd, who was educated in France, worked in Spain before coming to Mexico. In 1907 he organized the first "Spiritual Exercises" among the workers of Guadalajara. There he came to know members of Galindo's Guadalupan Laborers and lay leaders such as Palomar y Vizcarra. The Jesuit priest stressed the need to form a genuine political party, in order to promote the Church's social program. Though a party could serve no useful purpose in the controlled elections of the Porfirian regime and might indeed lead to difficulties for the Catholics, it became a reality when the Revolution toppled the old dictator in 1911.

Mora y del Río became bishop of Tulancingo, in the state of Hidalgo, in 1901. He showed an early interest in Social Action and especially in improving the lot of the campesinos in his diocese. In 1903 he called together the factory owners of Hidalgo to exhort them to fulfill their duties as Christians and to treat their workers fairly, paying them just wages. He had no success, however, for the industrialists needed more than moral suasion to convince them to participate in social reforms. But Mora y del Río's organizational skills attracted the attention of his superiors in Rome, and in 1908 he was named archbishop of Mexico, the chief episcopal post in the Republic. Two years later Pius X designated Mora y del Río president of Mexico's National Episcopate, which was to deal with the growing Catholic Action movement. Still, as long as Díaz remained in the presidency, Social Action could amount to nothing but meetings, speeches, and pious aspirations. It was the Revolution of 1910, led by Francisco I. Madero, that gave the Christian reformers their first real chance to implement their comprehensive program.[8]

Madero, born into an hacendado family from Coahuila had early entered state politics, but without success. In 1908 Díaz told a correspondent for an American periodical, *Pearsons' Magazine*, that Mexico was now ready for democracy, and he promised that the next president would be popularly elected. The article was translated into Spanish and appeared widely in Mexico's newspapers. Taking the octogenarian president at his word Madero published a book, *The Presidential Succession of 1910*, calling for free elections, and launched a campaign for the presidency with a new antireelectionist party. He presented a moderate program in the tradition of Juárez and Lerdo, with no indication that he planned or even favored a revolution. He did not attack the Church, for he felt that the Reform Laws had long ago eliminated the religious question from Mexican politics. The popular enthusiasm generated by Madero's campaign alarmed Díaz, however, and despite the president's promise two years earlier, he ordered Madero jailed until after the elections.

Madero escaped to the United States and turned earnestly to plotting the revolution he had hoped to avoid. He proclaimed his Plan of San Luis Potosí, terming Díaz' victory fraudulent and claiming his own election as president. He called chiefly for political reforms—"Effective Suffrage and No-Reelection" and offered in his plan only a vaguely worded paragraph dealing with the agrarian problem: his revolution would restore lands illegally taken from the villages. But support for Madero mushroomed throughout Mexico; Francisco Villa and Pablo Orozco in the North and Emiliano Zapata in the South led revolutionary bands. Though the rebellion posed no immediate threat to the Porfirian regime, members of Díaz' government decided to force the president's resignation and reach an accord with Madero. Representatives of Limantour met Madero at Ciudad Juárez on the northern border and agreed that Díaz would leave the country, while the Minister of Foreign Relations, Francisco León de la Barra, became provisional president. New elections would take place in late 1911, when, presumably, Madero would be chosen as the new president.

The arrangement at Ciudad Juárez spared Mexico a bloodletting in 1911. But it also assured Madero future troubles. To many, such as the Zapatistas in Morelos, it appeared as though he were selling out their revolution, and they refused his call to give up their arms and turn over control of their state once more to the federal army. Madero erred grievously in his belief that he could halt the military movement, once it had started. Mexico was ready for a genuine revolution, and Madero, a well-meaning, bumbling, utopian dreamer, found no way to manage the wild creature he had un-caged.[9]

The Revolution
of 1910

THE IMPACT OF MODERN scientific discoveries upon the old traditional orthodoxies in the Western world was so destructive that great numbers of men, by the first years of the twentieth century, had lost their religious faith. Millions of these exiles from religion, in Europe and the New World, sought alternative beliefs to replace the old, and they threw themselves with abandon into new causes, followed new messiahs, eagerly embraced new, and usually secular, gospels. Communism, Fascism, and Nazism all owed their success, in part, to this spiritual restlessness, to the needs of people for a cause greater than themselves. This was as true in Mexico in 1910 as in any other place or time in the modern world. The Mexican Catholic Church had long since lost its crusading fervor. The priests were too often ignorant rural curates or sycophantic courtiers in the Porfirian regime. The program of Social Action had made a bare beginning by 1910, and it had as yet only slight influence outside clerical circles. The intelligentsia in Mexico was churchless. Men who would have been in the vanguard when Urban II preached the first crusade at Clermont, or who would have given their lives gladly to drive the Moor from Spanish soil, no longer had a meaningful religion to fight for. They felt that a tired Mexican Catholicism offered them nothing.

The Revolution presented to these people an outlet for their burning zeal, gave them a sense of belonging to a worthwhile cause, inspired them to fight for their fellow man. The crusading spirit in Mexico, forsaking Catholicism (and finding no refuge in drab Protestantism), turned to a secular "religion"—to a native nationalism,

to Indianism, to native socialism, in short, to a movement to remedy
the earthly ills of the Mexican people. The spiritual exiles found a
new homeland of ideas, a dynamic faith that was antagonistic to the
traditional religion and that sought to win converts from the old.
Liberalism in the nineteenth century had been considered by the
Church to be a pact with the devil. The pope and the Mexican
bishops fulminated against the Constitution of 1857 and Juárez'
Reform Laws. But the liberals were, on the whole, content to separate Church and State, to allow each institution relative freedom of
action within its own sphere—so long as the government could
define the spheres. The Revolution of 1910 changed all that. Those
such as Madero who fought in the initial phases of the Revolution
were undoubtedly convinced that their movement was in the liberal
tradition. But the Revolution did not end with the presidency of
Madero. When the fighting was over, many of the rebels became
reformers. They would overturn the old society and create a new
Mexico.

It was the dynamic character of the Revolution that brought it face
to face with the Catholic Church in mortal combat. The liberals who
had sired the revolutionary government found a changeling on their
hands, not the reincarnated philosophy of Juárez and Lerdo, as
Madero supposed, but something that went far beyond mere liberal
notions of separate spheres for Church and State. The crusading
revolutionary spirit would not be confined to its own sphere; or
rather, the Revolution expanded its sphere and crowded the Church
until there seemed to be no place for the Catholic religion at all. The
government in the 1920s began to assume functions that had not
been part of the nineteenth-century liberal State. And it became
exclusive and monopolistic, denying that any other institution had
a right to those functions. The conflict between the government and
the Catholic Church now became a struggle for the souls of the
Mexican people. By the end of the 1910s liberal separation of
Church and State was a thing of the past.

The overturning of the Porfirian dictatorship was then no mere
military coup. It was a total Revolution and resulted in the complete
repudiation of the old regime. Everything that was entangled with
Porfirism was cut off and cast aside. On all levels there was a reaction against the past, against the foreign, and a heralding of the new
and the Mexican. The Científicos and the old regime had hoped to
emulate the Anglo-Saxons, had contemned the Spanish and Indian

heritage of the Mexican people. Now the Revolution proclaimed itself Mexican and for the Mexicans. Nationalism was the new crusading spirit, the gospel of the revolutionary apostles, the inspiration of the new revivalists. It was this intimate relation between nationalistic revivalism and revolutionary socialism that made the Revolution so dangerous to the Church in Mexico. Protestantism was weak, liberalism never the threat the pope had seemed to think it was. But the crusading secularism of the Revolution of 1910 presented a program calculated to win the Mexican people from the only real allegiance they ever had—the Roman Catholic religion. In philosophy, the arts, and music, in social, political, and economic theories, there was a rejection of old ways. The old regime would be destroyed in its totality. The Revolution would create a new society with a new mentality.

Mexicans, especially the writers of recent history, have tended to treat the great Revolution of 1910 as one unified and almost monolithic movement. The official party in the 1970s is still the Party of Revolutionary Institutions. But to view the Revolution in this light is to over-simplify, for it ignores the basic differences that sundered the revolutionaries for nearly a decade and that led Mexico along a via dolorosa, a series of savage wars in which the revolutionaries themselves disputed the course of their own revolution. The Revolution was complex. From the beginning it had no single philosophy; it found no convenient guide posts on the way to peace and stability. The Revolution was pragmatic, changing from year to year, as conditions in Mexico dictated. There was no single source of ideological inspiration. But in general it might be said that within the Revolution ran two main political currents, one liberal in the nineteenth-century sense, and the other radical and more modern. In practice the distinction was not always by any means clear. Rival political philosophies cut across factions, and within any one group considerable differences of opinion might exist. At times it almost seemed as though groupings were made more on the basis of conveniences or of personality than of ideology. But the distinction is a valuable one and helps to explain the enigmatic politics and the factional disputes that wracked Mexico between 1910 and 1920.[1]

The liberal revolutionaries looked backward, beyond the Porfirian dictatorship, to the halcyon days of Juárez and Lerdo. They came mostly from the middle classes—not the businessmen, who tended to support the positivists and the government—but the lawyers, the engineeers, the school teachers, the ranchers, and the small farmers. Most were from the provinces, not Mexico City, and they were federalists, in part by conviction, but also because they reacted against the domination of Mexico by the conservative capital. If the liberals no longer naively held to natural rights, they nonetheless accepted most of the program of Juárez and Lerdo. Like their counterparts in the nineteenth century, they believed firmly in secular education, in separation of Church and State, in a limited government, and in slow and evolutionary social progress. They allowed no place in their system for the rash confiscation of estates or the precipitate encouragement of labor unions or factory legislation. They would preserve intact the Constitution of 1857, including Juárez' Reform Laws. For the liberals there was no "Church problem" after 1910. The issue had long since been settled, they believed, and the priests needed only to obey the constitution and the laws of Mexico to avoid a clash with the State.

Francisco I. Madero was such a liberal. So was Venustiano Carranza, who took up the banner of Madero after the tragic death of the president in 1913. So too were the civilians that surrounded Carranza and helped form his Constitutionalist government. But many revolutionaries found the liberalism of the nineteenth century to be sterile and useless in the new age. Mexico could not afford to wait, they believed, for gradual reforms that might come in some future generation. They looked at the present and found it wanting. They called for even stricter controls over the Church. At the Convention of Aguascalientes in 1914 and 1915 and at the Constituent Congress at Querétaro in 1916 and 1917 the proponents of these rival philosophies clashed in parliamentary debate. The radicals found their champions on the battlefield in Emiliano Zapata and Francisco Villa. The liberals supported Carranza's Constitutionalist armies. Some revolutionaries, such as Álvaro Obregón and Plutarco Elías Calles, took an equivocating stand. Though radical in temperament, they believed that Zapata and Villa were uneducated savages, who stood for rapine, destruction of property, and murder. So they joined Carranza. Thus the Constitutionalists won the battles, but when the new constitution was written, it was much more radical than Carranza would have hoped. Mexico's future belonged to the spirit, if not to the armies of Villa and Zapata. The liberalism of the nineteenth century no longer sufficed to solve the problems of the twentieth. Madero, dead, became an apostle in the greater Revolution; but Madero, alive, could not have brought Mexico the much-needed social and economic reforms. He erred when he believed that his country's ills would respond to solely political reform. Like Madero, Carranza died in 1920 because his political philosophy had become an anachronism in Mexico.

The first problem faced by the Madero government in 1911 after the physical overthrow of Porfirism was that of continuing the stable administration of Díaz. It was a real dilemma for the new president, because that administration had been managed by the chosen few, who clung to their positions and privileges tenaciously. To continue them in office would leave intact the roots of a possible regeneration of Porfirism. Further, it would make likely a consistent sabotaging of the needed and fought-for political reforms. But to oust the Porfiristas completely and precipitously would create chaos, Madero felt, for Mexico lacked sufficient competent and reliable revolutionaries to replace the old bureaucrats. The cautious Madero attempted to steer a middle course between the radical agitation of agrarian reformers and the carping critics of the old regime. He tried to achieve the limited aims of the political revolution—"Effective Suffrage and No-reelection"—while staving off concessions to the Zapatistas. He solved his dilemma by compromising with the old regime.

The middle-class government of Madero preferred to prostitute its principles rather than face the anarchy that might result from a wholesale turning-out of the Porfiristas, and that would inevitably follow the division of lands. His civilian followers wanted only the replacement of the Díaz dictatorship, which centralized authority and privilege in the capital, with a restored federalism to give more autonomy to the provincials. The middle-class political revolution was to be concluded before it set fire to the passions of the masses and spread into a raging social revolution. As a result of the compromise, few Mexicans were satisfied. The Maderistas could not really secure the approbation of the reactionaries. And the radicals, especially the Zapatistas, looked upon the deal with the enemy as treason to the Revolution. In November 1911 Zapata proclaimed his Plan of Ayala and continued his military action, now against the government of Madero. As for the Church, it opposed Madero as a matter of course.

The fall of the Díaz dictatorship signaled the real beginning of the Catholic Social Action program. Although the Catholics had played no part in the Madero revolution—and in fact were largely hostile to it—they took advantage of the freedom offered by the new democratic regime to push their own program of reform—a program that, if successful, would have completely destroyed the liberal system and substituted a polity based on the teachings of Leo XIII.

At a time when the governing clique of Mexico promoted nineteenth-century principles, the Church called for radical (from the liberal viewpoint) reforms: land for the peons, rural cooperatives, labor unions, and factory legislation. The aims, even some of the methods, of Catholic Social Action resembled remarkably those reforms subsequently incorporated by the Revolution in the Constitution of 1917. But the ideologies behind these two programs were fundamentally divergent. The protagonists of each program deemed unilateral action the only possible means of succeeding. Neither considered the desirability or the possibility of cooperation with the other. Thus as two rival ideologies were propagandized and presented to the Mexican people in the second decade of the twentieth century, the seeds of future conflict were sown and nurtured.

The Catholics in 1911, under the leadership of men such as Palomar y Vizcarra, Perfecto Méndez Padilla, and Father Troncoso, but above all of Father Alfredo Méndez Medina, buckled down to the difficult task of organizing the unorganized workers of Mexico, of forming land banks, of assuring land to the vast rural population that had no land at all, and of organizing the Catholic men, youths, and women into groups to implement this reform program. The Catholics continued to draw heavily upon the experiences of priests and laymen in the Catholic Social Action movements in Europe, especially Belgium, France, and Germany.

Méndez Medina, a young Jesuit, had left Mexico before the Revolution to study theology at the University of Louvain in Belgium. There he attended the classes of Arthur Vermeersch in Fundamental Sociology and later went to Rheims and Paris where he heard lectures of Gustave Desbuquois and Martin Saint-Leon on Social Action. After attending Catholic Congresses and "Social Weeks" in England, Holland, and Germany, he returned to Mexico in December 1911 to initiate a course in Catholic Sociology for engineers, doctors, and lawyers at the Jesuit Colegio de Mascarones. In his lectures to the engineers, Méndez Medina dealt with methods of forming workers' syndicates in the construction trades; with the doctors, he proposed a rigorous medical morality; and for the lawyers, he prepared projects for new laws dealing with the social order. His aim was to transport the success of the program in Europe to Mexico. Under the guidance of Méndez Medina, Catholic laymen and priests arranged many more congresses to discuss and thresh out the problems of minimum wages, regulation of the labor of women and children, acquisition of small rural properties, social security, permanent councils of arbitration on labor disputes, and the participation of workers in management profits.

From the beginning, the movement was both clerical and lay. *La Nación*, the leading lay Catholic newspaper of Mexico, explained Social Action to the public as the sum total of all works destined to remedy the evils of society, but stressed that these works must conform to the teachings of the Church. The chief field of these activities, wrote the editors, would be in working out the relation between the workers and their employers.[2] At the same time, in a collective pastoral letter, the archbishops and bishops of Mexico announced that the first aim of the program would be to organize the lower classes into a true family of Christian workers. Thus the unprotected workers would be safe from the onslaughts of socialism. The workers should shun the syndicates and radical trade unions, which espoused class conflict. In the bosom of the Catholic workers' circles there would be no temptation, wrote the prelates, "to depart, even for a moment, from the teachings of the Church."[3]

At Zamora, in January 1913, a month before the overthrow of Madero, the Dieta de los Círculos announced a program of national rehabilitation, in accordance with the papal dictums of "Rerum Novarum." The Diet, which was directed by Méndez Medina, offered assurance that the "honorable and hard-working rural worker" would possess sufficient land to maintain his family—with due respect, it was added, to the legitimate rights of hacendados and freeholders. In his address to the Diet, Méndez Padilla excoriated the socialists and the Zapatistas. The only defense against these assaults on the "rightful fruits of capital," he said, was through Catholic Social Action. Catholic teachings, said Méndez Medina, "say to the employer that he should consider the laborer to be his powerless brother and treat him with charity. They say to the worker that he should respect his boss as a superior, for all authority comes from God; that the rich must love the poor; that the poor must love the rich; and that they must mutually respect each other's legitimate rights; that the industrial worker must respect the property of the capitalist, who must, in turn, respect the personal dignity of the worker; that the artisan must work with honor . . . ; that the capitalist must pay him a just salary. . . . "[4]

Through all of the congresses, all of the pastoral letters, all of the Catholic newspaper editorials dealing with the Social Problem, ran the common skein of fear and dread of the socialists. The socialist movement in Mexico was still minuscule, yet the Catholics had already aligned themselves against socialism, whenever it should appear and under whatever guise. Nor were the Catholics, in their writings, completely clear as to what socialism was. Thus it was possible to lump all radicals in the same category—Marxists, anarchists, syndicalists, Zapatistas, Villistas, anyone who wished to disturb the present hierarchic order of society, anyone who would pit class against class, worker against boss. A collective pastoral letter of the bishops in 1914 warned Mexican Catholics that the Church had "condemned the principles of socialism," and no Catholic could profess them "without incurring the gravest and most lamentable errors." Méndez Padilla said at Zamora: "What else but agrarian socialism in a savage form do these gangs of bandits called Zapatistas represent, they who, proclaiming the partition of lands, despoil the landowners, commit murders, rapes, arson, and every other kind of terrible crime?" The only defense against these socialist attacks upon the rightful fruits of capital, he said, was Catholic Social Action.[5]

The Church also declared itself opposed to the urban radicals in Mexico, the syndicalist Workers of the World, who, said the bishops, "propagandize for the most revolutionary socialism." "Let Catholics know that they cannot, without pain of conscience, attend their meetings, hear their speeches, join the society or its branches . . . or read their publication." The pastoral letter reiterated that only through the Church and its Social Action could the rights of all Mexicans be secured without prejudicing the rights of the few. All other ways were evil and doomed to failure.[6]

In 1911 for the first and last time in Mexico a political party was formed bearing the name "Catholic." Like the program for Social Action, of which it formed an integral part, it was destroyed by the Revolution after Madero's death. But while it was free to act, it seemed to show promise of bringing needed reforms to the Mexican people. In August 1911 the party held its first national convention to choose candidates for the coming presidential election. Bernardo

Reyes, who hoped to enter the political arena against Madero, angled for Catholic support for his candidacy. He intimated to the leaders of the party that he favored modification of the Reform Laws, and he promised that if he were elected he would give two or three cabinet spots to persons designated by the party. Madero, too, sought Catholic support. From El Paso he telegraphed the party president Gabriel Fernández Somellera that he considered the organization of the Catholic Party "the first fruit of the freedom we have won." And as the party was meeting in Mexico City Madero wired from Cuautla his approbation of the program adopted in the convention.

Some of the delegates wished to support de la Barra, while others preferred to abstain from the election, rather than back a candidate who was not a member of the Catholic Party. They knew that no one within the new party had sufficient national stature to attract votes in a campaign against Madero. But one of the young delegates, Eduardo Correa, pointed out that abstention would mean the suicide of the party, for it was obvious that no one, not even the provisional president, de la Barra, could defeat the popular Madero. Persuaded by Correa, the delegates then agreed to give their support to Madero in the election. But when Madero decided to give the second position on his ticket to José María Pino Suárez, this was too much for the Catholics. They asked de la Barra to be their candidate for the vice-presidency, and he accepted. Madero and Pino Suárez won easily, however, and the Catholic Party turned to the congressional elections of 1912 and to the publicizing of their program of Social Action.[7]

La Nación assured Mexicans that the policy of the new party would be one of loyalty to the legally constituted government of Madero, but that its special duty would be to defend the rights of Catholics against the "abuse and persecutions by the impotent fury of vulgar and ridiculous Jacobinism, which in the name of liberty, would try to deprive us believers even of the salt and water of civic baptism." Above all, the party would promote the Social Action program, "conforming to the serene principles" of "Rerum Novarum," and would work to preserve the home through minimum wage laws, regulation of the labor of women and children, workers' accident and sickness insurance, and agrarian reforms "that respect the legitimate rights of property owners." It asked the Madero government to recognize the legal existence of workers' syndicates, to enact laws providing for Sunday rest, to regulate banks, and to make a more equitable distribution of tax loads.[8]

The liberals struck back at the Catholics in congressional debates and in their party newspapers. They charged that the Catholic Party was only a revived Conservative Party, and that it was dominated by the priests and by the hierarchy of the Church. These charges were not without some foundation. The conservative Catholic newspaper, *El País*, had called for the reconstruction of the old Conservative Party, "formed of the intellectual middle class of our society, which without changing the institutions that govern us legally and politically, will fight . . . for the formation of illustrious, circumspect, and dignified governments." Mora y del Río, now Archbishop of Mexico City, favored this suggestion as one calculated to restore order in the country, but he thought that the intellectuals ought to enlist in the ranks of the Catholic Party instead. These proposals brought on new charges by *La Nueva Era*, a Maderista publication, that the Catholic Party and the old Conservative Party were enough alike to affirm their close relationship, since both parties were run by the clerics. But *La Nación* retorted that the Conservative Party had been monarchical, while the Catholic Party was "democratic in its program and its actions." And *El País* attacked these liberal charges as a calumny against the Catholic Party. Its editors affirmed that the Catholics of Mexico did not want a union of Church and State "when the latter was composed . . . of vile rabble." They did not deny, however, that the Party would work subsequently for such a union once the Catholics gained control of the government.[9]

In pamphlets, as well as in the press, the Catholic Party rejected the allegations that it was conservative or reactionary. Nor was its purpose that the upper classes should rule in Mexico, for it accepted the existing form of government. As for the charges that it was controlled by the clerics, the party declared itself free to direct or conduct its own political activities. It was, of course, subject to the bishops' criticism, said one party writer, but only in regard to whether its acts were allowed by conscience or not, as was each individual Catholic in every act of his life.[10]

The bishops, too, made clear that they drew a line between those actions that were officially of the Church and those of the party. Mora y del Río wrote in a pastoral letter that "the Church should never be confused with a political party, even though that party bears the name 'Catholic' . . . ; much less is it just to hold the Church responsible for the acts and doctrines of the parties to which Catholics are affiliated." And later in another pastoral letter he assured Mexicans that "neither we [the hierarchy] nor our clergy have mixed in political affairs."[11]

There is no doubt, though, that the Church and the party walked *pari passu*, even though the bishops disclaimed public responsibility for the party's acts. The party deviated in no way from the teachings of the Church, and the bishops were full of praise for the work of the Catholic politicians. Bishop Ignacio Valdespino y Díaz of Sonora wrote in a Pastoral Instruction to his diocese that "nothing, absolutely nothing, can be found in the program of the Catholic Party that does not accord with right reason. There is nothing it seeks that is not just, nothing that is not in harmony with the most perfect order and that is not worthy . . . , and therefore, there is no reason why the Church should not approve and bless it."[12]

Although they disclaimed all responsibility for the consequences of the party's actions, the bishops were determined to maintain control of its direction. In a circular letter all of the bishops joined to remind Mexicans that "according to the doctrine of the Church, it is the duty of the bishop to determine what political principles are compatible or incompatible with the Faith, what parties the Catholics can conscientiously adhere to, and what political action conforms with or is opposed to morality." As Mexicans prepared for congressional elections in the fall of 1912, Miguel M. de la Mora, Bishop of Zacatecas, advised the faithful of his diocese that it was the duty of Catholics in politics to "take as their norm of conduct . . . the teaching of the Holy See and their respective bishops." Above all, said Bishop de la Mora, Catholics in politics must "observe the prescriptions of the Holy See and obey the bishops who have been sent by the Holy Ghost to rule the Church of God . . . ."[13]

Good Catholics were required, said de la Mora, to aid all those candidates who would give guarantees to the Church that her rights and privileges would be maintained. By nature an indestructible bond linked both religion and politics, whatever the enemies of the Church might say against that truth, and it was the bishops' duty to give counsel to Catholics engaged in politics, especially in the "agitated and dangerous times of elections." He praised the Mexican Catholics for their piety in founding a political party based on Catholic principles. They were to exert all efforts, he said, to protect

Catholic rights under the constitution. He warned the members of his diocese that the Catholic Church did not sanction rebellion against legally constituted authority, for all legitimate authority came from God as the author of natural order. To assume that authority came from the people, as Mexico's liberals affirmed, was to say that the governors had no authority whatever, a doctrine that was both immoral and anarchic, and that had been refuted by the Church. Bishop Mora warned Catholics, therefore, not to affiliate themselves with liberal parties.[14]

The elections of 1912 were without doubt freer than any previous balloting in Mexican history. This is not to say that there was complete freedom, for official pressure was evident in many districts. But the Catholic Party gained a majority in the congressional delegations in the conservative states of Jalisco, México, Querétaro, and Zacatecas, and sent thirty deputies in all to Mexico City. The party controlled the town governments of Toluca and Puebla. In Zacatecas, the interim governor, Rafael Ceniceros y Villarreal, was a leader of the Catholic Party. De la Barra, though never a member of the party, received Catholic support and was elected governor of the state of México. In Jalisco—the most Catholic state in the country—the Catholic Party received 43,000 votes to 12,900 for all the rest of the parties. Because of a law providing for proportional representation in the local legislature, the Catholics gained ten seats, while the opposition was awarded two. The governor of Jalisco, José López Portilla y Rojas, drew strong support from the Catholic Party, though he was ostensibly a liberal.[15]

Jalisco became a testing ground for the Catholic program of Social Action. In the national congress the party, though well organized and disciplined, was always in the minority. When Catholics introduced legislation in the Chamber of Deputies to aid the working classes, the liberal Maderista majority showed no interest. Because the Catholics controlled the state government in Jalisco, however, they were able to enact laws to implement the promises of the many diets and congresses. They made a beginning in the legislative session of 1913, granting labor unions legal status, and licensing cooperatives and mutual-aid societies. The right of a *Bien de Familia* (family estate) was assured by law. Every family had guaranteed possession of a plot of ground and a house, and this land must be cultivated by the family. It might not lie fallow. The property could not be seized or mortgaged, and must not be divided except under unusual circumstances. The land was not given to the families out-right. It had to be paid for—there was no provision for expropria-tion—and the law specified that it must be entirely free from mort-gage before it could be guaranteed as a *Bien de Familia.* Given the assurance of legal status, the Catholic Action groups in Jalisco be-gan to build cooperative stores, theaters, and savings banks. But Catholic Action had no time to succeed. In 1913 the wars of revolu-tion commenced again, the program of Jalisco was destroyed when Álvaro Obregón led his revolutionary troops into Guadalajara in the summer of 1914.[16]

The program of Catholic Social Action proved to be too utopian and was unachievable within the foreseeable future. This was espe-cially true of the proposed agrarian reforms and was due, in fact, to the bishops' insistence upon legality and upon the rights of the hacendados, and to the Catholics' refusal to take precipitous action. The reforms could not have been achieved without action by the federal government, and this was not possible under Madero. Only if the Catholics could gain political control of the country could they effect the needed reforms, and the party attracted only a minority of the voters. Anticlericalism was too strong in Mexico to permit a Catholic party to win national elections. The Catholics constantly emphasized that the foundation of the program would be mutual Christian charity between workers and bosses. But the real solution to the agrarian problem—and in a predominantly rural country like Mexico that was the overriding social issue—was to get land to the landless. Zapata saw that clearly. The Catholics, too, saw that plots must be provided for all those who wanted and needed land. But they condemned confiscation, trusting to the Christian charity of the hacendados to provide the solution. José Mora y del Río, when he had been Bishop of Tulancingo and was pioneering in the Social Action program, tried to persuade the landowners in his diocese to give land freely to their workers from those areas on their estates which were not being cultivated. He found no Christian charity among the hacendados. They laughed at the bishop's naive re-quest.[17]

Palomar y Vizcarra's program for establishing Cajas Raiffeisen, while praiseworthy in its intentions, also had no chance of success in Mexico. It was based upon the demonstrated need for funds by the campesinos, but it provided no sound means of getting those funds. The success of these rural cooperative banks in Germany and

Belgium meant nothing in the Mexican situation. The western European agrarian economy was much more advanced than that of Mexico. The program of Raiffeisen banks was predicated upon an already existing small-landholding economy. With 95 percent or more of the rural population possessing no land at all, and with rural wages depressed below the subsistence level, there was no way that the peons or peasants would have a monetary surplus to invest in the banks. Those who needed to borrow money to purchase land would not, at the same time, be able to deposit the money that was to form the basis for the borrowing. Moreover, most peons were paid in tokens, not cash, on the haciendas, tokens redeemable only at the hacienda store. If the hacendados refused to give land freely to their peons, and the peons had no money to buy the land, the only possible solution was expropriation of the land by government fiat, an impossible procedure in the framework of Catholic Social Action. Therefore, the Catholic agrarian program was handicapped from the start, with too much legality and not enough reality. It was of little comfort to a peon in his miserable hovel, living from day to day, from hand to mouth, to know that his great-grandchildren might have a plot of their own. Yet this was all that Christian charity could promise. The Zapatistas, for all their lack of book-learning, were wiser in things of the soil than the Catholics. And it was their program that became the foundation of the Revolution's reforms. Neither the Catholic party in Jalisco nor Madero in Mexico City could have satisfied the demands of the Zapatistas.

Though Madero received a hero's welcome when he arrived to take charge of Mexico's capital, he proved to be an unfortunate choice as president in a period of crisis. His talents were mediocre; he was weak-willed, a dreamer, rather than a doer. He was a faddist, a vegetarian, and a spiritualist. He had had no previous administrative experience, and he was incapable of giving the Republic the vigorous leadership it needed. He filled lucrative government positions from among members of his large family. His brother, Gustavo, wielded great power in the government. He placed two cousins and an uncle in his cabinet and many other relatives on the public payroll. The newspapers of the capital attacked his obvious nepotism and his equally obvious shortcomings as president.

By early 1913 Madero was sorely beset by his troubles. Zapatistas were in open revolt in Morelos and controlled large areas to the south of the capital. Emilio Vázquez Gómez rebelled at Ciudad

Juárez and had himself declared provisional president of the Republic. Pascual Orozco, piqued at Madero for the latter's refusal to send
him money and supplies for his Colorado forces, declared for Jerónimo Treviño and named a provisional cabinet top-heavy with reactionaries—Francisco León de la Barra, Toribio Esquivel Obregón,
Jorge Vera Estañol, Félix Díaz, and Nemisio García Naranjo. When
factional disputes among the rebels in the north allowed the forces
of the government to gain the upper hand, Félix Díaz, the dictator's
nephew, pronounced in Veracruz against the Madero government.
Científicos in exile intrigued against Madero's administration, trying to bring about American intervention. The Díaz adherents still
remaining in the government used every opportunity to hinder the
president. The senate was still made up largely of Porfiristas, hold-
overs from the old regime, and the Chamber of Deputies, which
was controlled by a Maderista coalition of Liberals and Progressive
Constitutionalists, effected to counter the strength of the Catholic
Party, had split apart at the seams. The Catholics, inside and outside
the Congress, opposed Madero. The American ambassador, Henry
Lane Wilson, undermined Madero and his government in dispatches to the Secretary of State. By February 1913 the opposition
newspapers of Mexico City were calling for the president's resignation.

In October 1912 Félix Díaz launched his military revolt. It proved
to be a fiasco, however, and he was taken prisoner by the government troops. Instead of acting energetically and ordering the trial
and execution of the rebel, Madero was lenient and allowed Díaz to
live. The president ordered him to Mexico City to be imprisoned.
But from his cell he continued his treasonable activity against the
government, conspiring with Generals Manuel Mondragón and
Bernardo Reyes—both prominent members of Porfirio Díaz'
regime—to overthrow Madero and install Félix Díaz as president.
The proposed revolt, and the events that followed hard upon another in the succeeding days of February 1913, represented a re-
crudescence of Porfirism, the reaction of the old regime against
Madero's liberalism. Brute force and dictatorship were to replace
parliamentarianism, order to replace chaos once more.

The conspirators expected the rebellion to be a walkover. They
met with surprising resistance at the National Palace, however, and
Reyes was killed by gunfire. Madero then unwittingly signed his own
death warrant by naming General Victoriano Huerta to direct the

defense of the government. While the government forces at the National Palace and the rebels in the Ciudadela aimed shells in the general direction of the enemy—causing thereby considerably more damage to the city than to the military installations—Huerta and Díaz, under the aegis of the American ambassador, Henry Lane Wilson, arranged to double-cross Madero. At 9:30 P.M. on February 18 Díaz and Huerta met to draw up plans for a government to replace that of Madero. They agreed that Huerta would become provisional president, as Díaz remained outside the cabinet (while giving it his support), so he could be free to campaign for the presidency in the coming election. There was a tacit assumption that Huerta would not be a candidate, since Mexican law forbade a provisional president to succeed himself in office. Madero and Pino Suárez were then forced to sign their resignations, leaving Pedro Lascuráin, the Minister of Foreign Relations and head of the cabinet, as provisional president. Lascuráin immediately named General Huerta Minister of Gobernación, then resigned himself, leaving Huerta as legal president of Mexico. The conservative Catholic periodical, El País, expressed pleasure at the change of administrations. Speaking for those elements that considered Madero's continuation in office the chief obstacle to the restoration of law and order, the editors indicated their belief that Huerta was the man capable of giving the nation the peace for which it was crying.[18]

Madero's captors were less kind—and perhaps more realistic—than he. The president and Pino Suárez met death at the hands of the reimposed dictatorship. During the night of February 22, a group of Huerta's supporters murdered Madero and his vice-president at the penitentiary, according to the official version, when a gang "tried to free them." El País, in an editorial, lamented the deaths of the martyred president and vice-president and called for an investigation. But the Catholic and conservative press found it difficult to accept the accounts as revealed in the American newspapers—that Madero had been killed by the agents of the new government. For, reasoned the editors, men such as de la Barra, García Granados, and Esquivel Obregón, who now became members of Huerta's cabinet, would not have allowed themselves to associate with murderers. The official version had more air of probability, said El País, for the excitement of the rabble "could easily explain the events as related by the government."[19]

With the cruel assassination of Madero, the enemies of democracy flocked to Mexico City to the side of Huerta. Pascual Orozco, the onetime revolutionary of the North, came to make his peace with the government and give military support to Huerta. De la Barra showed little compunction about entering the cabinet of the usurper. He had presided at the birth of the liberal, democratic Republic in 1911; he was there to act as pallbearer two years later. Ceniceros y Villarreal, Catholic governor of Zacatecas, made haste to Mexico City to confer with Huerta about the best methods of pacifying his state, which was menaced, he said, by revolutionary armies. Rodolfo Reyes, son of the dead conspirator, became Huerta's Minister of Justice.[20]

One seeks in vain in the columns of La Nación, El País, La Tribuna, the Mexican Herald, or any of the other newspapers of the capital for any criticism of the Huerta coup. On the contrary they wrote most obsequiously of the general. La Nación referred to him as "don Victoriano." In contrast to this cordiality, Venustiano Carranza, soon to revolt against Huerta, was always the "rebel chief." The editors, who had long sounded the tocsin against the liberals, remained silent about the obvious iniquities of the Huerta administration. In an editorial of February 25, 1913—three days after Madero's death—La Nación opposed further revolutionary activity, now that the initial bloodletting of the Huerta coup had ended. The editors said that the road to true peace was through the religion of Christ, not rebellion. They did not condemn Huerta for his part in the murder of Madero: "To discuss certain matters at present would be to throw fuel on the flames, and we do not think such a proceeding is either prudent or patriotic." El País called for strong-arm methods against those who would not accept Huerta's government. According to the newspaper, the ideal polity was that which brought material strength, wealth, and justice. The "estimable" government of Porfirio Díaz provided the first two, but forgot the third. Huerta must now bring about all three. The editors saw the necessity of the new government's using a mailed fist to establish the peace, of being implacable, even cruel, "with those who have made of anarchy a way of living. Let the scourge of brute force fall upon them, without pleasure, but also with no feminine timidity. . . . When legality is not sufficient, long live the dictatorship!"[21]

The Church and the bishops made no official reaction to the new government. Yet there is little doubt that the clerics preferred Huerta to Madero. They were under no illusions regarding the character of the usurper. But Huerta in the spring of 1913 seemed to promise the restoration of order and stability, an end to the many revolts throughout the Republic. The Congress continued to meet. The burgeoning Catholic Social Action movement continued to grow, as new organizations were formed, new congresses planned. In the capital, the archbishop heralded the restoration of peace by singing a *Te Deum* in the basilica of Our Lady of Guadalupe. Thousands of Catholics marched as pilgrims from the center of Mexico City to the shrine at Tepeyac. The Spanish Virgin of Los Remedios was brought into the capital and paraded through the streets for the veneration of the faithful. It is true that the manifestations were in celebration of the supposed end of hostilities, but they followed so hard upon the heels of Madero's death that many Mexicans believed the Church was rejoicing in his assassination. When war subsequently broke out against Huerta, the prelates of Mexico issued a joint pastoral letter in which they solemnly warned the Catholics that rebellion against the "legitimate government" would not be permitted. Mora y del Río, when the situation seemed most dire for Huerta, lent money to his government to pay the troops in the capital. It was a paltry amount—25,000 pesos—but it is worth noting that less than a year later the Church refused a similar demand from the Constitutionalist forces of Obregón. In a sense the Church was trapped by its own unalterable principles: if liberalism and radicalism, Madero and Zapata, were equally condemned, there was no choice in 1913 for Mexico but Huerta.[22]

Catholic Social Action ultimately disappeared in the maelstrom of the revolution against Huerta and the subsequent wars among the revolutionary chiefs, and all that was left of the program was the intransigence of the Church against radicalism. The Catholics compromised themselves by choosing the wrong side when Huerta ousted the Maderistas. They committed the unpardonable sin—in the eyes of the revolutionaries—of being identified with military reaction, with the terrorism and debauchery of Huerta. The strides made toward social reform in Jalisco were forgotten, because they were ephemeral and because the Catholics seemingly feared radicalism more than they detested dictatorship. Increasingly in the 1910s the fulminations of the Church were directed against the radicals—to defeat socialism became the aim of the priests, not to aid the oppressed. With the fall of Huerta the last prop of the Church disappeared. From the Catholic viewpoint there was little to choose among the Carrancistas, Zapatistas, and Villistas. The Church chose none, chose to oppose indiscriminately every faction of the Revolution and, as a consequence, suffered from all. It was not until the twenties, when Álvaro Obregón imposed peace upon the Republic, that the Catholics received another opportunity to vindicate themselves and their program, and Social Action became once more a reality in Mexico.

Via Dolorosa

WITH THE RESIGNATION and assassination of Madero, General Victoriano Huerta became the legal president of Mexico.[1] Many responsible Mexicans acclaimed his seizure of power, because they now saw hope for the restoration of peace throughout the Republic. They preferred even a military dictatorship to the inept government of Madero; brute force, despite the loss of political liberties, was better than the chaos and destruction of the Revolution. And so most of the public officials hastened to offer their support to the new president. State governors came to Mexico City to assure Huerta of their allegiance. The Senate and the Maderista Chamber of Deputies continued to meet, thus seemingly giving tacit approval to the military coup. In March 1913 Huerta appeared to be master of most of Mexico. The federal army supported him. If the Zapatistas were worrisome gadflies in the mountains of Morelos, an effective military campaign by the federal forces would soon bring that area under control. The Catholics took hope when Huerta, in addressing the opening session of the Congress, announced: "We are in the presence of God." Huerta was strong, vigorous, and—so it seemed to the Catholics—pious, as well.[2]

Yet many Mexicans refused to accept Huerta's usurpation of power, among them Emiliano Zapata, Francisco Villa, and Venustiano Carranza. Zapata, who in his Plan of Ayala had given his support to Pascual Orozco, now emended his plan to declare his opposition to both Huerta and Orozco. His Army of the South would continue to fight for the Zapatista ideals—"Land and Liberty," and his men would not lay down their arms until each peasant received his plot of ground. In the North the opposition to Huerta coalesced around the person of Venustiano Carranza, the governor of the state of Coahuila. At first Carranza hesitated, evidently hoping to work out a deal with the new president. Like Madero before him, Carranza was a reluctant revolutionary. But on March 26, 1913, Carranza proclaimed his own Plan of Guadalupe denying recognition to Huerta. He created a revolutionary force and designated himself First Chief of the Constitutionalist Army in Charge of the Executive Power. Carranza laid no claim to the provisional presidency, for under the constitution—and his movement was, above all, "constitutionalist"—he had no right to do so. Further, if he did become provisional executive, he could never be elected the legal president, and even at this early date it was obvious that Carranza intended to be the constitutional president of Mexico. The plan contained no hint of social or economic reforms. Carranza did not think them necessary. He intended solely to restore the constitutional regime of Madero, and, like the martyred president, he felt that political freedoms were all-important. Social and economic improvements would come in time, and in a legal and orderly manner. But because of the failure of the Plan of Guadalupe to specify land reforms, Zapata and his Army of the South found it incompatible with their own revolutionary aspirations. At no time would Zapata accept the plan or acknowledge the leadership of the Constitutionalist First Chief.

Yet Carranza's plan was sufficiently vague to gain adherents in all the northern states. In Sonora a revolutionary force was recruited under Álvaro Obregón, a rancher. Carranza designated Obregón's troops an Army Corps of the Northwest and named him a division general. An Army Corps of the Northeast was created in Tamaulipas and Nuevo León under the command of Pablo González, also a division general. In the state of Chihuahua a third force assembled under the leadership of Francisco Villa. While Villa accorded Carranza grudging recognition as First Chief of the revolutionary forces, he remained skeptical of the Plan of Guadalupe. Like Zapata, Villa fought for social reforms, not for middle-class politicians. Villa was a difficult subordinate. He did what he pleased without consulting Carranza or any other revolutionary chief. So long as Huerta was in power, Villa and Carranza united against the usurper. But when Huerta was defeated and left the country, the two leaders fell out, and the victorious Revolution split asunder.

Carranza, Villa, and Zapata were a study in contrasts. Both Zapata and Villa were of lower-class origin. Both were illiterate; Villa learned to read and write, but only in a crude fashion, as an adult. Zapata loved the soil passionately—the soil, that is, of his native state of Morelos. He fought against Díaz, against Madero, against Huerta, and—ultimately—against Carranza, because he wanted to restore to his people the lands unjustly seized under the Ley Lerdo. Beyond this simple act of land restitution, his Plan of Ayala had no ideological content. Like his followers, Zapata was naive and parochial. For him, justice consisted in taking from the rich and giving to the poor. He saw no need for laws, courts, or public officials. From 1911 to 1919, while he controlled Morelos, the state had no government, no administration, and no schools. Nor was an army necessary in peacetime, he felt. Rather each man would carry his own weapons as he worked the fields; if an enemy came, the men would march off to repel him. Zapata had no concern for the greater world outside Morelos. If other states wanted land reforms, let their people rise in arms, seize the estates, and distribute them to the poor. Zapata was too simple to be an anticleric. He could shoot a priest without compunction, if he considered the priest an enemy of the people. But the Church no longer had lands in Morelos, and so Zapata had no interest in political intrigues against a national or universal Church.

Like Zapata, Villa too was a rustic. But he was neither simple nor naive. By the end of 1913 Villa, as a brigadier, commanded a large Division of the North (Carranza in his petulance refused to designate it an Army Corps or give Villa the rank of division general) and handled large and complex problems of supply, movement, and attack. Where Zapata was shy, Villa was bluff, hearty, and, at times, unbelievably cruel. A man of passion, he could threaten a man with death at one moment, and clasp him in an *abrazo* in the next. He was earthy, virile, given to coarse language and scatological humor. He hated the middle classes (especially the civilians around Carranza), despising them as weak and effeminate. "I don't fool around with those chocolate drinkers," he once said. He distrusted the politicians who would "feather their own nests," and forget the needs of the poor. Villa was also a deep-dyed clerophobe—he hated all priests, especially the Spaniards. Of all the revolutionary chieftains, Villa was the most hostile to the clerics. He told an American correspondent: "I believe in God, but not in religion. I have recognized the priests as hypocrites ever since, when I was twenty, I took part in a drunken orgy with a priest and two women he had ruined. They are all frauds—the priests and their cloth, which is supposed to be a protection, they use to entice the innocent. I shall do what I can to take the Church out of politics and to open the eyes of the people to the tricks of the thieving priests."[3]

Villa's army consisted largely of men like himself, uneducated peasants and cowboys with little moral sense or self-discipline. They stole, they looted, they raped. The Villista leaders were crudely mischievous, full of pranks, and completely uninhibited. For as long as men could remember the peasants had been ground under the heel of the landowners. Now through the eloquence of their rifles, they gained mastery over their former oppressors. They revenged themselves for wrongs, real or fancied, by destroying property ruthlessly and with abandon. Any city captured by the Division of the North could expect drunken orgies, licentious living, and a thorough sacking, for the Villistas respected neither property nor person.

If Villa was almost feral in his appetites, Carranza was austere, aloof, and cultivated. A landowner and a long-time politician, he had been a senator under Porfirio Díaz and a governor during the regime of Madero. He was older than most revolutionaries—Villa, Zapata, and Obregón were all in their thirties, while Carranza was twenty years their senior. A nineteenth-century liberal whose ideals were those of Madero, Juárez, and Lerdo, he believed firmly in middle-class, civilian control of Mexico, and he surrounded himself with lawyers, teachers, and engineers. He himself was insufferably dull; his public speeches were filled with platitudes; he said little that was important or worth hearing. Others composed his political documents, lawyers such as Juan Natividad Macías or engineers such as Félix Palavicini. Carranza was also an anticleric, though he never attacked the Church publicly. For him, as with Madero, there was no longer a religious problem in Mexico, because the constitution and the Reform Laws must of necessity be enforced. Church and State were separated, and the priests were now excluded from politics. They would not be persecuted if they obeyed the laws. Public education would remain secular, though the priests were free to conduct their own parochial schools, if they chose. Carranza regarded the religious question as he looked at all other problems in Mexico—from an Olympian height of serenity and dispassion. He was insufferably conscious of his own eternal rectitude. Mexico need only restore the legal regime of Madero and the liberal constitution, and all its problems would be resolved.

Huerta might have weathered the storms of revolution raised against him if his enemies had been solely internal. Unfortunately for him, he gained also the implacable opposition of Woodrow Wilson, the new president of the United States. Wilson and Huerta came to high office almost simultaneously, but their roads to the presidency were widely divergent. Where Wilson had been elected by the free vote of the American people, Huerta had become president through bloody revolution and assassination. Wilson never forgot the difference. To the idealistic American, Huerta was a murderer and a usurper who could not be recognized by the United States. For more than a year the Mexican policy of Woodrow Wilson turned upon the elimination of Victoriano Huerta. The Constitutionalists bought arms freely (if clandestinely) in the United States, while the American government sought to deny weapons and supplies to Huerta. In April 1914 Wilson ordered the seizure of Veracruz, ostensibly to vindicate American honor when Huerta's men arrested American sailors at Tampico, but actually to prevent a shipment of arms to Huerta and to hasten his downfall.[4] The opposition of Wilson proved to be too much for Huerta, and by July 1914 he was forced to resign the presidency and flee the country, leaving Mexico to the Constitutionalists.

In early 1913, however, the rebels of the North were still weak. Carranza could not even hold his own state capital of Saltillo, and he took refuge in Sonora with Álvaro Obregón. Through 1913 the Constitutionalists suffered reverses, as they recruited armies, supplied and trained them, and made ready for the march to the south and to Mexico City. Of the three forces Francisco Villa's Division of the North became the most powerful. Villa had ready access to a source of wealth unobtainable in the areas controlled by Obregón and González—the mines and ranches of Chihuahua. Villa taxed the American mine companies, and his men rounded up the cattle and sold them across the border in the United States. In this way he obtained dollars with which to purchase his war supplies. By the first month of 1914 he was ready to attack the federal bastion at Torreón, which blocked the route of the Constitutionalists to Mexico City.

As the revolutionary movement grew in the North, Victoriano

Huerta through 1913 sought to solve the legal problem of remaining in the presidency by means of an election—an unconstitutional procedure—while at the same time maneuvering to secure American recognition. In the field his armies occupied key railroad points to hold off the Constitutionalists until he could get more arms abroad. When Huerta and Félix Díaz deposed Madero they agreed that Díaz would become president through a special election in July 1913. As a result, Felixista clubs were organized (there were still no true parties in Mexico) in the expectation of Díaz' assured candidacy. The vice-presidency was assigned to and accepted by Francisco León de la Barra, who discovered that he could stomach the role of Felixista as easily as that of Porfirista, Maderista, or Huertista. But Huerta was determined by now not to yield the presidency so easily. A week after de la Barra announced his willingness to be a candidate, both he and Díaz were summoned to the president's office for a conference. The subject of their conversation was not made public, but on April 24 both Díaz and de la Barra renounced their candidacies. *La Tribuna,* directed by Nemisio García Naranjo, which had ardently championed the candidacy of Díaz since the overthrow of Madero, was forced to change its editorial staff. Until then it had been assumed in Catholic circles that the Catholic Party would support both, since the party had backed de la Barra in the previous election, and the Catholic leaders were known to be sympathetic to Félix Díaz. With the withdrawal of Díaz and de la Barra, the national Congress voted to postpone the elections until the fall. Meanwhile, Huerta remained in office as provisional president.[5]

Despite the decisions of Díaz and de la Barra, rumors persisted in the capital that both would receive support at the polls. More conversations took place with Huerta, and in July de la Barra resigned as Minister of Foreign Relations to accept a lesser post in Paris. Huerta named him special representative of Mexico in the controversy with France over the possession of Clipperton Island, which was being adjudicated by King Victor Emmanuel of Italy. And the president appointed Félix Díaz special ambassador to Japan to thank the Mikado for the Japanese delegation sent to Mexico three years earlier during the centennial celebration. Thus both de la Barra and Díaz would be far from Mexico when the elections finally occurred. To replace de la Barra, Huerta selected Federico Gamboa (the novelist-diplomat), who was a prominent lay Catholic, though not actually a member of the Catholic Party.[6]

In early August the government of Huerta announced that elections for president and vice-president would take place on October
26. As a result, the Catholic Party held its nominating convention
in Mexico City on August 5. The delegates heatedly discussed the
international situation, the mission of Félix Díaz to Japan, and the
general political situation of Mexico. Francisco Elguero, vice-president of the party, proposed that the Catholics name no candidate
until the political air had been cleared. He insisted that Félix Díaz
was the only logical selection for the Catholics, and Díaz had been
exiled by Huerta. The younger members of the party opposed Elguero, maintaining that their failure to place a candidate in the field
would prejudice the interests of the Catholics in politics. They proposed that the party select a military man who would be both a
strong campaigner and a vigorous president. But Elguero replied
that there was no "eminently popular" man in the Catholic party at
that time whom they could nominate. Manuel de la Peza also spoke
against Elguero's resolution. He said that unless the Catholics
named a candidate, they would lay themselves open to the charge
that they were afraid to enter the campaign. He feared that the party
might destroy itself unless it found and supported a candidate. Lazo
Herrera said that it was the general wish of the Mexican people that
Huerta continue as head of the government. He admitted that there
was no legal way to accomplish that end, but said that the Catholic
Party could give proof of its courage by nominating Huerta for the
presidency. The convention voted to support Elguero's resolution,
however, and the decision on a Catholic candidate was postponed.[7]

As newspapers announced the date of elections, Félix Díaz was
traveling to Japan by way of the west coast of the United States and
Canada. In Vancouver he got an urgent telegram from Gamboa
notifying him that the Japanese emperor had not yet given permission for the mission; since the Mikado would not receive Díaz, the
Foreign Minister ordered him to proceed to Europe, and subsequently to Japan, by way of the Suez Canal. But on September 21,
Díaz had word in London from Mexico City to proceed to Japan "as
rapidly as possible." The Mikado had finally consented to receive
his mission, said Gamboa. Díaz replied obliquely: "Please inform
me if the Congress has changed the date of the elections." He
remained in Europe, visiting England and Germany.[8]

In Mexico City, meanwhile, the Felixista clubs renewed their activity on behalf of Díaz. On September 24 his leading supporters

went to the National Palace to ask Huerta if their candidate could return. Under Mexican law a candidate was not eligible for election unless he was on Mexican soil on the day of the balloting. Huerta replied: "Very well, gentlemen, I shall give an order that General Díaz return to the country. But I warn you that I shall hold you personally responsible for any disturbances." As the Felixista delegation left his office, he ordered an aide to take their names and addresses. On the following day, Gamboa cabled Díaz to cancel his mission and return to Mexico. De la Barra, he said, would go to Japan in Díaz' stead to fulfill the mission to the Mikado.[9]

During August and September 1913 the way seemed clear for the peaceful replacement of Huerta. John Lind, Woodrow Wilson's special representative to Mexico, had been working to persuade Huerta to retire and to hold free elections. On August 27 Lind telegraphed Wilson that his mission had succeeded, for Gamboa had advised him that the Mexican constitution barred the provisional president from succeeding himself. And in September Huerta announced his "ardent desire to turn the government over to a constitutional successor." Now free to present their candidates, the pro-Díaz groups united to choose José Luis Requena, who had organized the first Felixista club, as their candidate for vice-president. On September 21 the Catholic Party met once more in Mexico City to determine their choice of candidates. The chances of the Catholics seemed bright, for they had the best organized political party in Mexico. Because the disagreements and bickering of the earlier convention had been aired in the newspapers of the capital, the representatives of the press were barred from the proceedings. After several days of discussion the delegates named Federico Gamboa and General Eugenio Rascón as their candidates.[10]

Gamboa, a novelist and diplomat, had gained national attention as Minister of Foreign Relations by conducting negotiations with the American government on recognition of the Huerta regime. Rascón was one of the oldest officers in the federal army. During Madero's administration he had served as Minister of War, and was Governor of Yucatán under Huerta. His selection was a concession to the younger members of the party, who had hoped to support a military man for the presidency. On September 25, Gamboa resigned his post in the cabinet and officially accepted the candidacy of the Catholic Party. The way was now seemingly open for a contest between Félix Díaz and Federico Gamboa. The prospect of a free election pleased the American government. Secretary of State William Jennings Bryan told Wilson: "I feel that we have nearly reached the end of our trouble." The State Department announced that it would recognize Gamboa if he were elected.[11]

A storm was brewing in the Congress, however, that was to make free elections impossible. On September 18 Eduardo Tamariz, a leader of the Catholic Party and a member of the Chamber of Deputies, was named by Huerta as his Minister of Public Education. The possibility that a Catholic would take control of Mexico's educational system delighted the Catholics in Congress, and the twenty deputies of the party united behind Tamariz. The Liberal deputies were appalled, however, at the prospect of a Catholic in charge of public education. They took advantage of a technicality in the rules of the Congress and voted to refuse Tamariz a leave of absence from the Chamber to accept the portfolio in Huerta's government. Despite pleas, and even threats, from Huerta, the majority in the Chamber remained adamant. In the end, the issue was resolved when Tamariz resigned his position in the government and returned to the Congress. Later he received a less sensitive post as Minister of Agriculture and Development. But by that time the Chamber of Deputies had been reorganized and was a pliant tool of the dictator Huerta.[12]

The action of the contentious Chamber still rankled with Huerta, who did not take opposition lightly, when the deputies met on October 9 to discuss the mysterious disappearance of Senator Belisario Domínguez of Chiapas. Domínguez had delivered an inflammatory address in the Senate attacking Huerta and had the temerity to print his speech and distribute it to the public. Although he had congressional immunity to arrest, Domínguez was spirited away by Huerta's police and murdered. In a stormy session the lower chamber voted unanimously to name a committee to investigate Domínguez' disappearance. Huerta's Minister of Gobernación, Manuel Garza Aldape, attempted to persuade the deputies to retract their action on the ground that they had "invaded the rights of the judicial power." Moreover, complained Garza Aldape, several bills introduced by the Executive had not yet been acted upon by the Congress. When the deputies refused to back down and continued to defy the Executive, Huerta ordered the arrest and imprisonment of all the Liberals in the chamber. The Catholics who had supported Tamariz were not molested. The president dissolved the Congress and ordered new elections for the Senate and Chamber of Deputies.[13]

The approaching elections, which had seemed auspicious only a few days earlier, now took on a foreboding air. Though he could not be a candidate, and publicly disavowed any support, Huerta now seemed the only possible victor in the campaign. His name was coupled with that of Aurelio Blanquet, the Minister of War, as an official ticket. The Catholic party leaders met to reconsider the situation with the dissolution of Congress and Huerta's apparent determination to maintain himself in office. Although they expressed their distaste for Huerta's use of force against the Congress, the Catholics decided to stick in the campaign to demonstrate that the party did not accept the Huerta-Blanquet ticket. The supporters of Díaz, too, pressed their campaign, despite orders from Huerta's government to local officials to suppress the Catholics and the Felixistas and to promote the candidacies of Huerta and Blanquet. Up to the day of the election, however, there was no mention in the press of the official ticket. The reaction of Woodrow Wilson to the affairs in Mexico was understandable, given his insistence upon legal and democratic government. He termed the action of Huerta "lawless" and threatened that he would not recognize the results of any election while Huerta still held power in Mexico.[14]

Félix Díaz arrived in Veracruz on October 23, three days before the election. Members of his party met him in the port city and advised him of the danger of lingering in the country. But he was determined to stay at least until the balloting was completed. He received a telegram from Blanquet, advising him that Huerta had placed a train and a military guard at his disposal. Blanquet directed him to come to Mexico City. But Díaz mistrusted Huerta's seeming cordiality and decided to remain in Veracruz, where he had many partisans, to have legal proof that he was in the country on the day of the election. Díaz called in three notaries to attest to his presence in Veracruz. When Huerta was informed of this, he became enraged and sent orders to Gustavo Maass, the military commandant in Veracruz, to arrest and shoot Díaz. The radiogram from the capital was intercepted by the American battleship, *Louisiana,* however, which was in the Veracruz harbor. The Americans had a copy of Mexico's official code and easily broke the cipher. The American Consul, William W. Canada, warned Díaz that his life was in danger. In the early morning hours of October 27, while it was yet dark, Díaz climbed across the rooftops of the buildings between his hotel, the Alemán, and the American consulate. An American newspaper correspondent then took him to the United States cruiser, *Wheeling*. Later he moved to a Ward Line steamship and, with the help of the American navy, was able to escape the country. Díaz came to the United States subsequently and lived for many years in exile, still dreaming of ultimate victory and spinning gossamer plans for revolutions against a succession of Mexican governments. For more than a decade he remained to many Catholics the ideal candidate for the presidency.[15]

The election of October 26 passed quietly and without incident. The public was apathetic, and few persons bothered to go to the polls. Huerta reiterated that he was not a candidate and that votes cast for him would not be counted. But the newspapers of Mexico agreed that the Huerta-Blanquet ticket had gained a majority of the few votes cast. When the new Congress met on November 18, all cordiality between the Catholic Party and Huerta had evaporated. Eduardo Tamariz became president of the Chamber of Deputies, but his selection by the Huertista legislature led several of the Catholic deputies to resign in protest. In December 1913 the government suppressed the Catholic newspaper, *La Nación*, and Enrique Zepeda, the director of the periodical, and Gabriel Fernández Somellera, the party's president, were arrested and deported to Yucatán. Both went before a district court to obtain judgments against the action of the government and were able to return to Mexico City. But they found it difficult to live in the capital with the oppressive Huerta regime, and both left the country ultimately.[16]

In the early months of 1914, as the northern revolutionaries began to win battles against the federal troops and to press inexorably upon Mexico City, and as the American forces in Veracruz shut off supplies to his government, Huerta became increasingly irascible. Always a heavy drinker, he now drank incessantly. He never came to his office, but spent his days—and nights—with army cronies in disreputable restaurants and bars. On May 11 Archbishop Mora y del Río sought an interview with the president, hoping to persuade him to resign for the good of the country. The next day a messenger from Huerta came to the archiepiscopal palace with an order for the prelate to leave the country. Huerta was determined to maintain control of his government, whatever the consequences. Though Mora y del Río did retire from Mexico, coming to the

United States for the next four years, he held no animosity toward the president. If called upon to choose between the revolutionary factions of Carranza and Villa or the authoritarianism of Huerta, he still preferred the dictator. As the revolutionary armies moved south to capture city after city, the Church began to suffer attacks and spoliations hitherto unknown in Mexico's history.[17]

On December 8, 1913, the Division of the North captured Chihuahua City, forcing the federal garrison to flee to Ojinaga, a small town on the Texas border. Villa's first act in Chihuahua was to order the expulsion of all Spaniards. Francisco Villa had a passionate hatred of the Spanish and Chinese in Mexico, and whenever his armies captured a city these foreigners suffered cruelly at his hands. In Chihuahua, as elsewhere in Mexico, many of the priests were Spaniards. Villa did not exempt them from his decrees; rather he tried in every way to demean and humiliate them for what he fancied to be the wrongs inflicted upon the Mexican people in previous centuries by the Spanish clergy. Three days after the capture of Chihuahua, Villa sent written orders to every priest in the city demanding a payment of one thousand pesos. Because they could not get the money together on such short notice, the priests came to Villa, asking him to modify his demands. Instead he abused and insulted them, calling them oppressors of the people. One priest was lodged in the penitentiary—in order to intimidate the others. The priests then begged from door to door through the city until they had collected 3,300 pesos. Villa accepted the money and then ordered the priests from the country. As their train left the Chihuahua station (they were forced to ride in a boxcar), Villa stood on the platform and jeered at them. "We are going to have only Mexican priests," he said.[18]

Villa also ordered the expulsion of Spanish nuns from Chihuahua. The Siervas de María, a Spanish order, conducted a girls' school in the city. They were turned out of their houses and the school, and when they had left the city Villa set up public brothels in the former nunneries. Although his ire was directed principally against the foreigners, other priests and nuns thought it prudent to flee also. As Villa headed south, capturing cities from the federals, his reputation for savagery (and especially the reputation of henchmen such as Rodolfo Fierro) preceded him to strike terror into the hearts of the Spaniards and the Chinese, and all the priests and nuns.[19]

On April 2, after three days of bloody fighting, Villa captured
Torreón, the important railroad junction with lines running south
to Mexico City and east to Saltillo and Monterrey. It was the greatest
conquest of the revolution against Huerta, and there was no federal
garrison short of the capital strong enough to hinder the Division
of the North. As Villa made plans to march on Mexico City, he was
cock of the walk. He ignored Carranza completely, appointing his
own state governors and local officials in the area under his military
control. His impertinence was intolerable to the First Chief, who
held firmly to the principle of civilian control of political offices.
Moreover, Carranza was determined to control the national government himself. To do this he must divert Villa to allow González or
Obregón to reach the capital first. Both of these generals were
completely loyal to the First Chief, and they, like Carranza, had
become suspicious of Villa's manifest insubordination. In May Carranza came to Torreón with the hope of persuading Villa to turn
east against the federal garrison in Saltillo—the remnants of the
troops from Torreón had taken refuge there. Villa twisted and
turned, but in the end he capitulated. "All right," he said, "we'll do
it for the Chief." Carranza had won his point, and Villa's chance to
take control of the revolution was lost. The First Chief ordered
Obregón and González to make all haste toward Mexico City.

During the evening of May 20 the rearguard of Huertista General
Joaquín Maass pulled out of Saltillo without a fight, leaving the city
to the advancing Villistas. On the same night the first troops from
the Division of the North—the forces of Severino Rodríguez and
José M. Robles—entered Saltillo. Except for some routine looting
of houses, the occupation proceeded smoothly, and the soldiers did
not molest priests in the city. But on May 21 Villa arrived with the
"Doraditos," his elite cavalry guard. Early the next morning, he
dispatched officers to scour the city with orders for the priests to
appear at his headquarters at 3 P.M. Eighteen priests answered the
summons, six of them Jesuits. As they were ushered into his presence, Villa reviled them: "You have deceived the people. You have
the people's head tied up in rags, while you have been drinking
chocolate. But this must stop, and I do not know with what conscience you have been acting thus."

Villa asked if any were Spanish. Only one replied, Father Juan
Diego Martínez, but the group also included three Frenchmen and
an Italian. Villa turned to the foreigners: "You are not wanted here.

You will go and make a living elsewhere, won't you? You have lived on our people and sucked our wealth long enough and enough." The priests thought it prudent not to antagonize Villa, and one, a Frenchman, said: "We will leave by the first train, General, and as soon as possible—tomorrow if you will." The priest showed Villa a certificate from John W. Silliman, an American consular agent, that he was French and that he did not concern himself with Mexican affairs. Villa brushed it aside impatiently. "I don't know how to read," he said. "When I go to Torreón and Chihuahua you will come along. In the meantime you will stay here."

Villa demanded that the Jesuits and the parish priests (the curates were Mexican) pay a ransom of one million pesos. A French Jesuit offered to pay 9,000 pesos, but Villa pocketed the money and reiterated his demand for the million pesos. The Mexican priests then went from door to door in the city, but failed to collect more than a few thousand pesos. When they returned, Villa turned upon them angrily: "There is no remedy for it. It is necessary to put you to the guillotine and to execute all the fathers. Neither more nor less than this, and I am the man to do this." As he talked he cracked nuts with his teeth, spitting out the shells and punctuating his tirade with vile oaths against the clergy.

For three days the priests remained prisoners in the house Villa had commandeered for his headquarters. They had little food and were forced to sleep on the bare floors. At midnight on May 25 they were awakened by Colonel Fierro. "Get up," he said. In two minutes they were ready to go, thinking they would be taken to the train. "Leave your blankets," Fierro said. "You won't need them." Instead, they were taken to another house—presumably Fierro's headquarters—and thrust into a dark room. They would all be shot, Fierro said. He threw a horsehair lariat about the neck of one priest —a Jesuit—and dragged him from the room. In the next room Fierro ordered the priest to reveal where the Jesuits kept their buried treasures. The priest insisted that they had no treasure. Fierro tightened the noose until the priest fainted. When he revived, Fierro was standing over him with a gun. Fierro repeated his question. The priest was silent. Fierro fired his pistol.

In the next room the other priests could hear the noises plainly —the rattling in the throat, the gasping for breath, and finally the single shot and the eloquent silence that followed. As death loomed large in their hearts they prayed for the departed soul: "Requiem

aeternum dona ei domine, et lux perpetua, luceat eio. Requiescat
in pace." Without hope, they knelt on the wooden floor and made
their absolutions and Acts of Contrition. One after another, they
were led from the room, and the succession of noises was repeated.
As the last priest was dragged into the adjoining room, he found all
the priests, not dead, as he expected, but huddled silently together.
Fierro had perpetrated a cruel joke in order to extort money from
the supposed victims. All returned to their rooms in Villa's house,
but the Jesuits were kept apart from the parish priests.

After holding the priests for six more harrowing days, Villa told
them that he was leaving the city and that they would come with him.
One of the priests was weakened by an illness. Villa taunted him:
"You are so thin and feeble because you drink too much chocolate.
It is necessary for you to go somewhere else and eat roots." The
priests were taken to the railroad station in Saltillo by Fierro and
shipped off to Torreón like cattle in a freight car. As they were
herded to the station, some of their parishioners brought carriages
for them to ride in. But Villa refused: "I do not wish enemies in my
country, and because of this I am going to send these gentlemen to
the United States to eat ham. Out of the way with those carriages!
Let them go on foot between soldiers to the station." Though
drunken soldiers insulted the priests and threatened them many
times with death on the long ride to Torreón and from there to the
American border, they were not molested physically again. Despite
the threats of Villa, he did not kill any priests, then or later. He
would rob them, insult them, terrorize them, wring money from
them, exile them, but he did not shoot them. The murders of priests
in his territory were committed by his subordinates.[20]

Wherever the revolutionary forces went, these attacks upon the
clergy and upon the churches were repeated. When Francisco Mur-
guía took Piedras Negras in April 1914 his troops seized and burned
parish church records and drove the priests from the city.[21] In the
same month the Carrancista soldiers of Antonio I. Villarreal captured Monterrey. They demanded a "loan" from the clergy of
500,000 pesos, and when it was refused all the priests were jailed. Villarreal's troops ransacked the churches, as well as the residence of
Archbishop Francisco Plancarte y Navarrete. The wooden confes-
sionals were torn loose and dragged to the public plaza, where they
were burned. Without reason and indiscriminately, the soldiers
ravaged or stole church properties. The archbishop was a student

of early Mexican history with an international reputation. His library, which he had collected over a forty-year period, contained some 75,000 volumes and seven hundred manuscripts, some of them priceless and dating back to the sixteenth century. All of these were destroyed or scattered. The archbishop had a handwritten manuscript, which he had been working on for forty years, ready for publication. It too disappeared in the sacking. In the archiepiscopal archives the soldiers found records of priests in the diocese who had been charged with various crimes and dismissed from their posts. Villarreal had these published in a Constitutionalist periodical, *El Bonete*, to prove the truth of the stories about clerical corruption.[22]

Villarreal, one of the more radical of the Constitutionalist generals, had a checkered history before and during the Revolution. A schoolteacher and an early adherent to the Liberal Party of Flores Magón, he had spent several years in jail under Díaz for the murder of a fellow schoolmaster. Because of his support for Madero's revolution, he was rewarded with a diplomatic post in Barcelona—where he came under the influence of Catalán syndicalists and anarchists. Villarreal was not a doctrinaire syndicalist, but throughout his revolutionary career he supported radical causes. And he was a rabid anticleric. The crude Villa stole from the priests and threatened them with death, but Villarreal punished and restricted them with legal decrees. As military commander in Monterrey, and later as Constitutionalist governor of Nuevo León, he issued edicts to hinder the effective operation of the clergy. "During the life of the nation, the Church has been a pernicious factor in disruption and discord and has entirely forgotten its spiritual mission," he said. The priests had allied themselves with "conservatives, reactionaries, and foreign invaders," and had been the "implacable enemy" of every liberal and progressive movement in the country. The supposedly celibate priests were evil and dangerous, he said, for they lived "in contradiction with nature," and carried in them the "seeds of corruption." For Villarreal "the confessional and the sacristy [were] to be feared as the anteroom of prostitution." And in the Catholic schools, he felt, "truth [was] perverted; the pure soul of childhood, the idealistic burning spirit of youth [were] deformed."[23]

Villarreal ordered the expulsion of all foreign priests from the state, and every Jesuit of whatever nationality. Other priests who could not demonstrate their "complete abstention from politics"

would also be excluded. Churches were to be opened solely from
6 A.M. to 1 P.M., and only priests who asked permission of the
governor could officiate at services. He banned confessions, as well
as all bell-ringing, except for "civic holidays and triumphs of the
Constitutionalist armies." All Catholic schools were required to
conform to the official texts and programs used in the state. Infrac-
tions of these decrees would be punished by fines or imprisonment.[24]

Through the intervention of American representatives in Mexico
Carranza moderated Villarreal's attacks on the Church. When several prominent Catholic women in Monterrey came to William C.
Hanna, the consul-general in that city, to ask him to use his influences with the First Chief, he wrote to Carranza requesting him to
permit the churches to be reopened. When Silliman in Tampico
made a similar request, Carranza ordered Villarreal to allow services. But though the churches in Monterrey did reopen, only one
priest remained in the city, and he was ill in a hospital. Villarreal
refused to alter his restrictions, and these remained in effect as long
as he was governor of the state.[25]

South of Torreón lay Zacatecas, an important station on the main
rail line to Mexico City. After the fall of Torreón to Villa, the federal
garrison in Zacatecas was reinforced, and as Villa captured Saltillo,
Carranza gave the task of assaulting the other city to a group of
revolutionary forces under Generals Martín Triana and Pánfilo Na-
tera. It was soon obvious that these forces were incapable of capturing Zacatecas without aid—aid which could come only from Villa.
But Carranza mistrusted Villa and, hoping to prevent the Division
of the North from moving directly to Mexico City, he decided to
break up the division. On June 11 he ordered Villa to send 5,000
men to aid the attack on Zacatecas. Villa refused to destroy his
division, however, and when Carranza persisted, the Chief of the
Division of the North impetuously offered his resignation. Unex-
pectedly Villa had provided the means to eliminate a dangerous
rival, and the First Chief quickly accepted the resignation. But Villa's henchmen, despondent at the prospect of fighting on without
their beloved leader, prevailed upon him to reconsider his resignation. Villa agreed at once. In one of the most fateful acts of the
revolution, Villa chose to move on Zacatecas with his entire division,
in defiance of Carranza's orders. Carranza reacted to Villa's breach
of discipline by shutting off all coal and supplies to the Division of

the North. Though there were no immediate hostilities between the two chiefs—Huerta was still the greater enemy—thereafter a dangerous schism remained in the ranks of the revolutionaries.

On June 23, after two days of fighting against federal troops and Benjamín Argumedo's Orozquista soldiers, Villa took Zacatecas. Villa detested all his enemies, but he reserved his deepest hatred for the followers of Pascual Orozco. The Orozquistas had been among the first to revolt against Villa's hero, Madero, and they continued to dispute the control of the state of Chihuahua with the Division of the North. In Zacatecas every captured Orozquista was shot without mercy. Nor did Villa spare the federal prisoners. The unfortunate city of Zacatecas endured a pillaging unparalleled in the Revolution, as though Villa were taking out his spite against Carranza and the soldiers of Huerta upon the hapless population. The Villista soldiers shot their enemies and then began a prolonged drunken orgy through the streets, smashing windows and looting shops, while the people of Zacatecas cowered behind their barred doors. The house of Bishop Miguel M. de la Mora was gutted, and its rich furniture and paintings were destroyed or carried away. Villa had brought a safecracker from the United States to travel with the Division of the North, and he broke open the bishop's safe and removed the money and valuables. Three priests—two of them French—were shot in Zacatecas.[26]

The account of this affair is unclear, and the Mexicans later denied that any priests had been killed. But the most probable explanation is that General Manuel Chao, Villa's lieutenant, ordered the executions as a favor for one of his officers. The priests were associates of the Christian Brothers Community in Zacatecas, which operated a school for boys. The sons of Miguel Macedo, one of Villa's most vicious henchmen, had been students earlier at the school, but had been expelled by the priests as incorrigible. Macedo asked that the priests be killed, and Chao acquiesced. Human life, even of a priest, meant nothing to the Villistas. But this was an isolated incident. The other priests in Zacatecas were rounded up and held for ransom. Villa demanded one million pesos. As in other places occupied by the Constitutionalists, the priests went through the city, collecting money from their parishioners. They got only 100,000 pesos, and were then held as prisoners for several days, before Villa sent them to Torreón and thence to Juárez, where they were exiled into the United States.[27]

As Villa captured Zacatecas Obregón moved with little difficulty down the Pacific coast of Mexico. Though his force was smaller than that of Villa, the federal garrisons on the west coast were also correspondingly smaller. But there was a gap in the rail lines of one hundred miles through the mountains, and the advance of Obregón's men was slowed, despite Carranza's orders to proceed with all haste to Mexico City. Not until the first week of July did the Army Corps emerge upon the plain before Guadalajara. On July 8 the Constitutionalist forces entered Mexico's second largest city, after defeating the federal army on the previous day at Orendáin. The way was now clear to Mexico City. Villa was closer. His army was more powerful. But he could not move without fuel for his trains, and Carranza still would not give him coal. Carranza was assured of a loyal army in Mexico City when he arrived to take charge of the national government.

Of the various revolutionary generals Obregón was the most moderate. He lacked the personal vices of Villa, and he was a better commander of troops than Pablo González. Nonetheless, his men in Guadalajara acted much as other revolutionaries had in other parts of Mexico. In all times and in all places it is difficult for soldiers to maintain high standards of personal morality during wartime. In war one must commit the greatest of crimes, the most heinous of sins; he must kill his fellow-man. And if murder is sanctioned, what of stealing or rape? The soldier finds it easy to slough off whatever vestige of morality he possessed when he donned his uniform. He blurs "mine" and "thine" and takes what he wants or needs. In Guadalajara the soldiers confiscated every automobile they could find. Beginning with the sumptuous residence of the archbishop, Obregón's men took Francisco Orozco y Jiménez' carriages and horses, his furniture, his table service and linens, and his clothing. The generals and officers occupied the best homes, confiscating wine cellars and food stores. The soldiers took for their own barracks the schools and other public or religious buildings. And the camp followers moved in with their men.

During Mexico's wars women traditionally marched with the soldiers. In the field they cooked for and slept with the troops. If a man were killed, his woman—who might be but usually was not his legal wife—moved in with another soldier. An army, then, consisted of soldiers and their women and children, all moving across the countryside like a swarm of locusts. Many of Obregón's soldiers were

uneducated Yaqui Indians from Sonora. Little burdened with the
deterrents of modern civilization, these troops made fine soldiers
on the battlefields, but poor garrison troops. In Guadalajara most
occupied the Jesuit college. A not unprejudiced resident described
the advent of the Yaquis: "It is a mass of human bodies, filthy men,
women, and children who cook their meals, make their beds, wash
their clothes, and bathe themselves in view of all. They live with
their instruments, arms, playthings, and animals heaped around
them." In the College of the Sacred Heart, a girls' school, they
destroyed the library and the furniture. "Soldiers, and their shame-
less women, went to bed in the rooms of the sisters and the pupils,"
said the observer.

When Obregón went on to capture Mexico City, taking most of
his troops, he left behind a garrison under the command of Manuel
Diéguez. General Diéguez was a convinced enemy of the Church,
and one of his first acts as military governor of Guadalajara was to
order the arrest and detention of the priests in the city, in all 47.
Archbishop Orozco y Jiménez had gone to Mexico City before the
arrival of the Constitutionalists, but the Bishop of Tehuantepec,
Ignacio Placencia y Moreira, who happened to be in the city, was
jailed. After the priests had spent several days in police cells,
Diéguez ordered their expulsion from the country, along with all the
nuns in Guadalajara, and he closed the church buildings. Although
the federals still held Manzanilla on the coast, the priests and nuns
were shipped to that port, where they remained until Diéguez' men
took it also. Then the priests and sisters were put aboard a Peruvian
ship crowded with Chinese coolies, which was heading for San Francisco. The city of Guadalajara remained for many months without
priests or Catholic schools.[28]

As city after city capitulated to the revolutionaries, the priests
were abused, imprisoned, held for ransom, or expelled from the
country, for each commander and his troops took personal revenge
upon the Church because of its supposed complicity in the usurpation of Victoriano Huerta. In Aguascalientes the Villista governor,
Alberto Fuentes D., expelled Archbishop Ignacio Valdespino y Díaz
and many of his priests. General Gertrudis Sánchez captured Morelia on July 31, and on the following day he summoned all the
clergy to ask for a forced loan of 500,000 pesos. Although the
Catholics in the city gave Sánchez 100,000 pesos and promissory
notes for the rest, the general was not satisfied. He decreed the

expulsion of all foreign clergy (most of them Spanish) from his state. In September Cándido Aguilar, military governor of Vera-cruz, ordered the foreign clergy deported and limited the number of native-born priests to from one to four for each town, according to its size. But in addition to these official harassments of the military commanders against the Church, there were many stories of atrocities of a baser nature. It was said that the revolutionaries had profaned churches and violated nuns.[29]

An exiled nun described her observations later to Archbishop James H. Blenk of New Orleans: "I have seen the chasubles, scarfs, maniples, cordons, pluvial capes, and altar cloths used for housing the horses, while women wore the copes and albs and used the corporals as handkerchiefs. The sacred vessels have been profaned in a thousand ways. After drinking from them they have used them as night vessels and then thrown them into the street in the utmost contempt. In some towns they have burned the monstrance with the sacred Host. They have thrown the Sacred Hosts on the ground; they have eaten them sacrilegiously, and others they have fed to their horses. They have shot down the saints with their bullets."[30]

There is no doubt that priests and nuns suffered at the hands of the soldiers. The extent of the violence, on the other hand, is not so clear. Tales ran like wildfire before or followed after the armies —tales told by hysterical women, tales embroidered upon, tales vouched for by supposed eyewitnesses, tales told and retold until they were believed implicitly. Today it is impossible to separate the fanciful from the real. In any event, the truth of the stories is less important than the fact that they were believed, and that men acted accordingly. Especially were they believed in the United States. Most of the refugees either came to the United States or passed through the country on the way to Spain, France, or Italy. The relations of their ordeals were collected and publicized, and because of the outrages, the Church problem, which had been a purely Mexican concern, suddenly took on international implications. American Catholics used the stories to seek American intervention against the revolutionaries. Some Catholics, who were at the same time Republicans, used the stories in a partisan attempt to demonstrate the failure of Woodrow Wilson's Mexican policy.

In the United States two priests were particularly energetic in publicizing the plight of the Mexican Catholics, Francis C. Kelley, editor of *Extension*, the monthly magazine of the Catholic Extension

Society, and Richard H. Tierney, chairman of the Federation of Catholic Societies and editor of the Jesuit periodical *America*. Both worked tirelessly, and with great zeal, writing letters to the president, publishing editorials, and making public addresses throughout the country. Because they were so busy and noisy it seemed at times as though Father Kelley and Father Tierney were the Catholic Church in the United States. Still there were other spokesmen for outraged American Catholicism. Bishop James A. McFaul of Trenton and Bishop Joseph Schrembs of Toledo worked with Kelley and Tierney to prepare public statements on the position of the Church in the United States. Father John Cavanaugh, president of the University of Notre Dame, complained of Wilson's policies: "A simple millionaire could get us into war tomorrow for money," but the violations of Sisters of Charity "by the incarnate devils of Mexico" were ignored.[31] The Knights of Columbus passed resolutions condemning the Mexican revolutionaries. Not all American Catholic leaders reacted as vehemently as Kelley and Tierney. James Cardinal Gibbons of Baltimore was a solid rock of moderation. Now an octogenarian, Gibbons had fought for many years to liberalize the Catholic Church in America. While he did not approve of Villa or Carranza, he thought that the First Chief should be given an opportunity to bring peace in Mexico and to fulfill the promise he had made to end the attacks upon the Church. Gibbons' hopes for peace faded, however, when he received a letter from Bishop de la Mora in August 1914, indicating that the defeat of Huerta and the conclusion of hostilities had not ended the persecution of the Church. De la Mora said that neither he nor his priests had been permitted to return to Zacatecas. All the churches in the city were still closed, he said. Gibbons wrote to President Wilson on August 18, enclosing de la Mora's letter. "I feel sure," the cardinal wrote, "that just one word from you to the Constitutionalist leaders would have a great effect and would relieve the sad conditions of affairs." Secretary of State Bryan acknowledged Gibbons' letter and said that for some weeks his department had advised the Constitutionalist authorities "to exercise justice and moderation in their treatment of persons and properties belonging to religious organizations."[32]

Wilson replied to Gibbons on August 21: "Alas, I am sorry to say that it is not true that 'one word from me to the Constitutionalist leaders would have a great effect and would relieve the sad conditions of affairs' in Mexico with regard to the treatment of the priests, for I have spoken that word again and again. My influence will continue to be exerted in that direction, and, I hope, with ever increasing effect. For the present, apparently we shall have to await the subsidence of the passions which have been generated by the unhappy condition of the country."[33]

Although Wilson had intervened militarily to ensure the defeat of Victoriano Huerta, and American troops still occupied Veracruz, the policy of the government in Washington toward Mexico's religious question remained one of strict nonintervention. Wilson and Bryan sent notes to Carranza, cautioning him against the effect of continued persecution on public opinion in the United States, but the American government took the position that attacks upon Mexican nationals or upon Spaniards or other Europeans were not an occasion for direct American action. Unless the Catholics could demonstrate that American citizens had been injured, or their rights abridged, the United States would remain aloof.

Diplomatic relations between the United States and Carranza's Constitutionalist regime were complicated by the continued presence of American troops in Veracruz, even after Huerta's resignation and flight to Europe. These forces had been sent to Mexico to attack a government that was no longer in existence. Wilson hoped that Carranza, upon occupying Mexico City, would convoke national elections to form a legal government. At that time the United States would grant recognition to the new regime and return the port to the Mexicans. But Carranza had no intention of holding elections until he had brought both Villa and Zapata to heel. Further, he felt that a preconstitutional, extralegal government could deal better with the Huertistas still in the country. Consequently, in August and early September 1914 he maintained his role as First Chief, governing Mexico—or rather those parts of Mexico not controlled by the Zapatistas or Villistas—by decree, with no courts and no Congress. Because the American occupation was becoming an embarrassment to Washington, Wilson directed his representatives in Mexico to initiate negotiations to turn over Veracruz to the Constitutionalists.

No sooner had the American government announced that the occupation would end, however, than anguished protests came from Veracruz. General Frederick F. Funston, commander of army troops in the port, told his superiors that the Constitutionalists intended to punish those Mexicans who had collaborated with the military government and to collect duties on all goods brought into Veracruz, even though duties had already been paid to the Americans. This threat offended Wilson's sense of fair play and decency. He warned the Mexicans that the United States would not relinquish the port until Carranza had made a public avowal neither to collect double duties nor to punish the Mexicans in Veracruz. But Carranza, as stubbornly self-righteous as Wilson, refused to give the guarantees, even to gain the valuable port facilities of Veracruz. Through September and October 1914, the American government and the Constitutionalist regime, both with diplomatic hackles raised, refused to back away from their positions. In the end Carranza gave way, not because he believed Wilson was right, but because he suddenly needed Veracruz as a refuge. War had broken out between the Villistas and the supporters of Carranza. When the First Chief was driven out of Mexico City there was no place for him to go but to Veracruz. So he capitulated, offering the required guarantees, and in the last week of November the American soldiers and marines boarded waiting transports to sail back to the United States. Behind them came the Constitutionalist soldiers of Cándido Aguilar. The port was once more in Mexican hands.

While the Americans occupied Veracruz a great number of Catholic priests and nuns had come to the city to escape the Constitutionalist troops. Some were foreigners who had been expelled; others were Mexicans who feared to remain in areas controlled by the various revolutionary factions. A few had taken ships to the United States or Europe, but most remained, hoping that a fortunate change of governments would permit their return to their posts. As the American troops prepared to leave, there were nearly four hundred priests and nuns in the city. It was inconceivable that they would stay to face the Constitutionalist soldiers, but the problem was how to bring them out. Few had any money, and when they raised the question of using United States government funds to provide for their transportation, the State Department replied that this was impossible, since they were not American citizens. Anthony Matre, National Secretary of the American Federation of Catholic Societies, told William Jennings Bryan that if the American government failed to provide transportation, the Catholics of the United States would. But he made it clear that the Catholic Church expected the government to do so. "Please advise," he wrote, "whether the government has assumed the responsibility, as we expected it would, or whether it expects the Church Extension Society, which is solely and purely a charitable organization, to assume the burden." In the end, the State Department found that it could use American facilities to transport the priests and nuns, and all were brought safely to the United States before the troops evacuated Veracruz. But the exchange of letters was symptomatic of the growing rift between spokesmen for the Catholic Church in the United States and the Wilson government.[34]

When in the last week of September 1914 the American Federation of Catholic Societies met in its annual convention at Baltimore, the principal topic of discussion was the Mexican religious problem. In an address to the delegates, Bishop Schrembs described the tribulations of the Mexican Church and criticized the Department of State for its failure to help the suffering Catholics. Schrembs, Bishop McFaul, and Father Tierney prepared a report protesting "the outrages perpetrated against bishops, priests, and religious men and women in Mexico." And they asked that the American government withhold aid and recognition for any regime in Mexico that did not guarantee religious liberty. They showed a copy of their statement to Cardinal Gibbons, who advised them to withhold publication of the protest until President Wilson had a chance to reply. Robert Lansing, the acting Secretary of State, acknowledged the protest of the convention, but assured the delegates that his government had "repeatedly used its good offices in behalf of persons and the properties of religious orders in Mexico."[35]

Though many Catholics continued to critize American policy in public statements, Gibbons preferred to maintain his more moderate position. On October 16 he wrote to Bishop McFaul: "The effect of this ceaseless harassing might probably result, not in securing any assistance in our cause, but in setting the entire Administration against us." His admonition had no effect on Tierney and Kelley, however, and the two priests kept up their agitation on behalf of the Church in Mexico. Father Tierney sent the Department of State a long letter in which he listed the many kinds of attacks against Mexican Catholics. The revolutionaries, said Tierney, had confiscated properties, tortured and murdered priests, violated nuns, desecrated churches, and turned convents into brothels. The rebels, he charged, had attempted to "discredit the priests by dressing a soldier in Mass vestments and photographing him standing by a nude woman"; had garbed a "prostitute in sister's attire and sent her into the street to preach against Catholicism"; and had placed "a nude woman on the altar of the Chapel of the Jesuit Colleges in Saltillo and Puebla."[36]

Father Kelley had not attended the convention in Baltimore, for he had gone to Cuba and Texas to collect statements and affidavits from refugees on the persecution of the Mexican Church. With Archbishop Blenk he interviewed priests, nuns, and laymen. Later he was to publish these statements in his *Book of the Red and the Yellow* as a stinging indictment of Wilson's Mexican policy. Kelley had come to Cuba ostensibly to aid the refugees, but he was also interested in collecting ammunition for the Republicans in their attacks on the Wilson administration. He was in communication with Theodore Roosevelt, who wanted information for an article he was writing for the New York *Times*. When Kelley returned to New York, he was met by Roosevelt's private secretary and driven at once to Oyster Bay. Kelley showed Roosevelt a number of the affidavits. But the former president impatiently pushed them aside. He wanted something more salacious. "These are all right," he said, "but I have heard that convents have been broken into and nuns ravished. Have you anything to prove that such things happened?"[37]

Father Kelley slipped a paper from the bottom of the pile of documents, saying: "I was going to keep that back for reasons which you can guess." "Of course I understand quite well," Roosevelt replied, "but I don't believe in keeping back any of the truth. The whole thing is damnable, and I intend to let the American public know it. You had better let me have that paper also." And so the former president wrote the article, and it appeared in the *Times* and a great many other newspapers throughout the country. What had been primarily a humanitarian problem in Mexico became inextricably meshed with partisan politics in the United States, for Roosevelt, as well as some of the Catholic spokesmen, placed the responsibility for conditions in Mexico squarely on the shoulders of Woodrow Wilson.[38]

Roosevelt wrote: "The simple fact is that thanks to President Wilson's actions—and at times his inaction has been the most effective and vicious form of action—this country has become partially (and guiltily) responsible for some of the worst acts ever committed even in the civil wars of Mexico." When the United States interfered in Mexican affairs to aid the Carranza faction, it "thereby made itself responsible for the frightful wrongdoing, for the terrible outrages, committed by the victorious revolutionists on hundreds of religious people of both sexes." The government Wilson had been supporting, said Roosevelt, was "looting and defiling Churches and treating ecclesiastics and religious women with every species of abominable infamy from murder and rape on down."[39]

Father Kelley echoed Roosevelt's thunder in *Extension* editorials: "Who has brought this state of things about?" he wrote. "Ourselves! Who insisted upon the non-recognition of a government lawfully in charge, according to the Constitution of Mexico? Ourselves! Who upheld the hand of Carranza or Villa? Ourselves!" It was not too late, he said, for the United States government to redress the wrongs suffered by the Church in Mexico by insisting that the Catholics there should enjoy free exercise of their religion and by demanding the restoration of all seized ecclesiastical properties. In effect, Kelley asked that Mexico turn the clock back to the days before Benito Juárez' promulgation of the Reform Laws in 1859.

Cardinal Gibbons was becoming increasingly exercised with the intemperance of Kelley and other Catholic leaders. When he read the editorial in *Extension* he wrote to Kelley: "This is a serious charge and one that has been felt keenly at Washington. It is one that can be made only after very careful investigation and with sufficient proof." Kelley assured the cardinal that he meant no disrespect toward the president, but insisted that he was in possession of so much "irrefutable evidence" from Mexico that he felt sure of his position. If in October 1914 the propaganda subsided, it was not because the situation in Mexico had improved or because the Catholics in the United States had come to accept the policy of Woodrow Wilson. Rather it was because Father Kelley went to Rome to carry his campaign to the pope, and while he was out of the country, the noise and furor died down. When he returned from Rome in the last week of November, the pot began to bubble over again.[40]

Though the State Department had received no dispatches from Mexico to confirm the charges made by Kelley and Tierney, Wilson and Bryan wished to determine the validity of the many stories retailed in the press and in public addresses. On January 14, 1915, the department sent telegrams to all the consular officials in Mexico asking for details of the religious persecution in their areas, and especially for verification of the reports on the outraging of nuns and the desecration of churches. The replies of all the consuls were most conclusive: Though priests and nuns had been expelled and properties had been confiscated, there was no truth in the accounts about the raping of nuns. John R. Silliman, the department's representative in Mexico City, interviewed Msgr. Antonio Paredes, the vicar-general of the archdiocese of Mexico, and obtained a written statement from him categorically denying the stories. The Zapatistas had shot two priests, Paredes said, and one church in the capital suburbs had been profaned, but no nuns had been violated in his archdiocese. Nor did he believe such rumors coming from other areas of Mexico.[41]

When the State Department made public the substance of the consular reports, which were at variance with the statements of American Catholics, Kelley and Tierney turned savagely on Paredes to impugn his veracity. They charged that he was a Carrancista, a toady of the revolutionaries, who owed his ecclesiastical position to the First Chief. They maintained that they had unimpeachable proof of their charges, citing the documentary evidence collected from exiles in Texas and Cuba. And Archbishop Mora y del Río, in San Antonio, backed them up, asserting that he thought the affidavits should be believed. Inquiries from Bryan about Paredes brought confirmation from Mexico City that he was friendly with Carranza. But J. M. Cardozo de Oliveira (the Brazilian Minister), who represented the interests of the United States in Mexico, replied that Paredes was considered honorable and was not a man who would "disvirtue" the truth. Silliman, too, supported Paredes. The vicar-general had been, said Silliman, a "faithful and true priest and at the same time a patriotic Mexican," who had chosen to remain in Mexico to work with his people, and "to suffer and share the sorrows and the afflictions of his own country," rather than flee and seek refuge in a foreign country. Silliman had put his finger on a sore point with many Mexican Catholics. Too many of the priests and bishops had deserted the country to avoid persecution, instead of remaining with their flocks to aid and protect them. The exiled priests maligned Paredes "at a distance of 3,000 miles," said Silliman, while he was at his post in the "great, beautiful, humiliated, plague-stricken capital."[42]

Father Kelley continued through 1915 to mount his attacks upon the revolutionaries in Mexico and upon the Mexican policies of the Wilson administration. He wrote to Wilson on February 23 a long, rambling letter filled with excerpts from his *Book of the Red and the*

Yellow. "The destinies of Mexico are in your hands," he told the president, "and it is because we know this that we have troubled you." He confessed that he was a Republican, but avowed that he had not "allowed his politics to interfere with his duty." If mistakes had been made by the administration, if the president had been "deceived by his advisors," the mistakes could be "rectified," he said. Kelley opposed any move by the American government to grant recognition of the Constitutionalist regime.[43]

Wilson referred Kelley's letter to Bryan for a reply, but indicated to his Secretary of State what he wished to say to the priest. It was an indirect answer that did not really address itself to the main points in Kelley's letter. Wilson and Bryan stressed the need in Mexico for land reforms. The American government, said Bryan, could not "dictate laws or the forms of government in Mexico." But it could and would bring to bear upon Mexican affairs, wherever it might legitimately do so, "the pressure of American opinion and American example." "The Mexican leaders will certainly know that in order to command the sympathy and moral support of America, Mexico must have, when her reconstruction comes, just land tenure, free schools, and true freedom of conscience and worship. We know of no other foundation stones upon which to build the economical and spiritual life that makes political freedom a reality and a blessing.[44]

Father Kelley waited nearly a month before replying to Bryan's letter. He agreed that Mexico needed land reforms and education, but he attributed the difficulties to the liberal revolutionaries of the previous half-century, who "took the land from the Indian pueblos," and "tried to destroy religious education." He asked that the American government stipulate that any revolutionary faction receiving recognition must guarantee religious freedom "as it exists in the United States."[45]

More and more the Catholics in the United States turned toward a policy of championing a nonrevolutionary regime for Mexico. Kelley lauded the exiled Huerta in his writing and in his speeches as a man who could have brought peace to Mexico. And even Cardinal Gibbons, by the spring of 1915, was having misgivings about any government that emanated from the Constitutionalist armies. The aged prelate spent the winter of 1914–1915 with his brother in New Orleans, and met and talked with Mora y del Río and other refugees who gave him firsthand information about the atrocities in Mexico.

When he returned to Baltimore in March, he told the press that Villa and Carranza were a "disgrace to their country." Gibbons hinted that there was another candidate for the Mexican presidency, "who is most worthy and the one who can bring lasting peace." While he did not identify the candidate, it is probable that he meant Félix Díaz. Although earlier he had opposed the demands of many Catholics for American intervention in Mexico, by August Gibbons had changed his mind. The cardinal told reporters that "some form of intervention by this country is the only solution to the reign of anarchy that has existed there for several years."[46]

American Catholicism, then, to judge by its most vociferous spokesmen, was by the middle of 1915 solidly opposed to the recognition of any revolutionary regime in Mexico. Some preferred Victoriano Huerta, others Félix Díaz or Eduardo Iturbide (the Huertista governor of the Federal District), but none would accept Carranza, Villa, or Zapata. Wilson was peppered with letters and telegrams—often couched in identical words, indicating that the campaign was organized by the American clergy—repeating the old charges and insisting that the United States must refuse to recognize Carranza.

Yet in the opening months of 1915 the currents in Mexico seemed to run strongly against the First Chief. His enemies controlled the largest and most important parts of the country. Villa had the most powerful army in the Republic, and maintained interior lines of communication from Ciudad Juárez in the north to Mexico City. Zapata's Army of the South, though inexpertly led and poorly armed, could harry the rear of the Constitutionalists, while Villa dealt them a crushing blow from the front. But Villa and Zapata failed to cooperate, and the Constitutionalist forces gained the precious advantage of time—time to recruit and train men, time to import weapons from the United States. And above all Carranza had the loyalty of Mexico's finest revolutionary general, Álvaro Obregón. Although the Constitutionalist forces contained elements under Pablo González and other Carrancista generals, Obregón was primarily responsible for the defeat of Villa—and the defeat of the government of the Convention, which supported Villa.

The origins of the Convention were to be found in the bitter quarrel between Carranza and Villa in early 1914 and in the Pact of Torreón, signed by the representatives of the Division of the North and González' Army Corps of the Northeast in July of that year.

Carranza had never recognized the right of the revolutionary generals to make legislative plans, but nevertheless in September 1914 he
issued a summons for a meeting of revolutionaries and civilians in
Mexico City. He did not call it a Convention, for to apply that term
would indicate that it had powers that Carranza preferred to reserve
for his civilian advisers. To the First Chief it was always a "junta."
But the generals took the bit in their teeth and moved the Convention—as they called it—to Aguascalientes as a gesture of reconciliation to Villa, who had sent no representatives. Because its early
meetings were held in that city, the assembly was subsequently
known as the Revolutionary Convention of Aguascalientes, though
it moved to Mexico City again in January 1915, when Villa took the
capital, and even to Cuernavaca and Toluca. Led by Obregón, the
generals in Aguascalientes voted to replace Carranza with Eulalio
Gutiérrez, a man of little distinction in the Revolution—which was
precisely why he was chosen. He had done nothing to incur any
man's anger and so was the ideal compromise choice for provisional
president of Mexico.

Carranza refused to recognize Gutiérrez or the Convention that
elected him and ordered the withdrawal of the Carrancista delegates
from the assembly. On November 9, 1914, the Convention voted
Carranza in rebellion against the "legitimate" revolutionary government, and the hostilities that Obregón had so desperately sought
to avoid became a reality. On one side stood the Constitutionalist
forces loyal to Carranza, on the other the Conventionist troops of
Villa and Zapata. In the end, Obregón chose to remain with the First
Chief, and with this decision of Obregón lay the ultimate salvation
of Venustiano Carranza.

Because Villa had the immediate advantage of strong and united
forces, Carranza was forced to abandon Mexico City to the armies
of the Convention, finding refuge in the port of Veracruz. In Mexico
City, Gutiérrez formed a government and tried to provide—in his
bumbling way—an executive for the Conventionist regime. But
there could be no order in Mexico City so long as Villa remained.
He did what he pleased, paying no attention to the complaints of
Gutiérrez. And the Convention, now consisting of Villistas and
Zapatistas, looked upon the provisional president as a Carrancista.
On January 16, Gutiérrez fled from the capital, taking with him the
treasury and a few loyal followers. The Convention then assumed
the executive powers itself and designated Villa's representative,

Roque González Garza, as the presiding officer "in charge of the executive power."

The Convention in Mexico City proved to be much more radical than the Constitutionalist leaders. There were differences of opinion, however, among the delegates on matters of revolutionary reform, and in general the Villista leaders resisted the more radical pressures of the Zapatistas. From March until May 1915 the Convention met in Mexico City and Cuernavaca to work out a revolutionary Program of Government. When Villa removed his troops to the north, the Zapatistas came to have a majority in the assembly, and their views on reform prevailed. The Convention accepted Zapata's Plan of Ayala as the basis for land reform. The delegates voted to support labor and factory legislation and to pass laws recognizing the juridical personality of the syndicates. Though moderate Villistas, led by González Garza and Federico Cervantes, opposed many of these measures, most of the Conventionists were as one on the question of religion. Almost without exception they were anticlerics.[47]

In supporting the measure for secular education, Villista Federico Cervantes represented the predominant revolutionary viewpoint inside and outside the Convention: "The school must be kept apart from anything religious. The role of the teacher is to educate the student in the purest morality, not religious morality. The priests inculcate the child from his first years with lies, such as the lies that we should fear the dead, and they fill him with ideas that confuse him and place hindrances in his development . . . ; I would a thousand times rather that they give preferences to philosophical and sociological concepts, and not to religious education." Cervantes was supported by the Zapatista Cuervo Martínez: "Until now, the hand of the clergy has had three claws—the confessional, the pulpit, and the school. We cannot form the national character while the priests control education, for they have made their teaching a means of propaganda." Overwhelmingly the Convention voted to eliminate all religious education and to permit only secular public schools to operate.[48]

This was the extent of the antireligious legislation of the Convention. The main concern of the majority was with land reform, not national policies of state, and the Convention's Plan of Government, as it emerged from the debates of the delegates, reflected the Zapatista domination. Even as the debates continued, however, it was increasingly apparent that unless the Conventionist forces won a smashing military victory over Carranza the Plan would never see fruition. The success of the Convention's program depended upon the armies of Villa and Zapata, and by April 1915 Obregón had proved himself to be the master of both. The Zapatistas were confined to their enclave in Morelos, while the Villistas were driven north in a series of decisive victories by the main Constitutionalist army.

As the Convention debated the plans for revolutionary reform, Carranza in Veracruz showed, for the first time, a similar interest in radical legislation. While he was still fighting Huerta there had been little need for a program of social reform. All the armies of the Revolution were united against the usurper. The First Chief told an audience at Hermosillo in 1913 that the Plan of Guadalupe, while not utopian, was the plan of all patriotic Mexicans, because it gave promise not of the division of land or the construction of schools, but of something "more sacred"—the establishment of justice. But when the forces of the Revolution split down the center at the Convention, it became apparent that the aims of the revolutionaries were divergent, and that the interests of the masses lay with the Convention, with the men of Villa and Zapata. To gain support it behooved the Carrancistas to make a gesture toward the masses, and in this moment of crisis the Veracruz decrees of January 6, 1915, were born.

In December 1914, nearly two years after the Plan of Guadalupe, Carranza hammered out a reform program for the Constitutionalist armies. It provided for the development of small farm properties, the equalization of tax loads, improvement in the working conditions of the peons and urban workers, municipal liberty, electoral reforms, an independent judiciary, revision of the laws of matrimony, reform of legal procedures, and the destruction of monopolies. Carranza was to continue as First Chief and would issue decrees, he said, to implement this program.

The job of filling in the details was given to Luis Manuel Rojas and José Natividad Macías, both liberals and both former Maderista legislators. Just before Christmas 1914 they sent the projected agrarian reforms to the First Chief. They proposed that Carranza void all confiscation of ejidos carried out under the Ley Lerdo, decree the formation of new pueblos from expropriated lands, and grant five hectares of land to each Constitutionalist soldier at the

end of the war. On January 6, 1915, Carranza signed the famous
Veracruz decrees, which many Mexicans subsequently saw as the
basis for Article 27 of the Constitution of 1917. But these decrees
had more window dressing than real substance. In reality they offered little more than Madero's Plan of San Luis Potosí. The First
Chief declared that all lands taken by the *jefes políticos* or any other
government officials in contravention of the Law of 1856 would be
returned to the rightful owners. But it would have been difficult to
establish that land was taken illegally, for the Ley Lerdo specifically
banned landholdings by corporations such as the pueblos. If the
burden of proof were put on the claimant—as it was—no large
turnover of land could be expected as the result of this legislation.[49]

When Carranza promulgated the Veracruz decrees he was
penned up in the port city, and the Villistas and Zapatistas had
control of most of the Republic. The liberal First Chief was more
than willing to snatch at any radical straw to gain support for the
Constitutionalist armies. But by June 1915, with Obregón's defeat
of Villa at Celaya and León, the military situation brightened considerably for the Carrancistas, and the liberal leadership began to
renege on even the mild reforms promised by Carranza. The First
Chief hedged his program around with restrictions by added decrees that increased the difficulties of securing land. In a "Manifesto
to the Nation" Carranza told the Mexicans that "the solution to the
agrarian problem would not involve confiscations," but rather the
equitable distribution of government lands, the restoration of illegally held properties, and the buying by the government of large
plots, if it should prove necessary. By 1917—the end of the preconstitutional period—the Carranza government had fulfilled none of
its promises. But by that time the wars were over, and Carranza was
the president of Mexico. There was no longer any need to woo
public opinion in support of the Revolution.[50]

Much more important to the Carrancistas was the political legislation of the First Chief. The civilian Constitutionalists aimed to re-
create the liberal republic, and other decrees of Carranza during the
preconstitutional period were all steps in that direction. He decreed
municipal independence by ending the noxious *jefatura política;* promulgated a divorce law—the first in Mexico; and freed the judicial
branch of the government from the domination of the executive,
thus effecting a balance of authority among the three branches.[51]

The touchstone of the Carrancistas' liberalism was their attitude toward education. By the first months of 1916 the Constitutionalist cause was assured, and Carranza began consolidating the gains of his liberal revolution. In February of that year he published a decree granting complete independence to the ayuntamientos in all matters concerning education. The local governments would take over the responsibilities of the curricula, of hiring teachers, and—most important—of paying salaries. His objective, said Carranza, was a laical education in the public schools, free of prejudice, based upon rational principles. Commenting on the decree, *El Pueblo,* the leading Constitutionalist newspaper, found it "the fundamental basis for democracy." "Without doubt," the editors wrote, "the future of the people's education has been safeguarded by the decree of the First Chief."[52]

In religious matters the Carrancista regime was also guided by the liberal principles of the nineteenth century. The maximum demands of the Carrancistas upon the Church were separation of the State from the Church and liberty for all faiths. They promised to enforce the Constitution of 1857 and the Reform Laws. All those who spoke with authority for the First Chief were unanimous in denying that there was a religious problem in Mexico. Yet the Mexican and American Catholics were equally unanimous in their condemnation of Carranza's government as a persecutor of religion. Archbishop Mora y del Río saw in the assaults upon the Church the conniving of the Constitutionalists with Masons and "certain Protestant corporations in the United States." The Catholics denounced Carranza because they held him responsible for the individual attacks on priests and on church property. The fact was that Carranza deprecated these attacks as much as the leaders of the Church. But Carranza was First Chief only through the sufferance of his generals, notably Obregón and González, and he had little or no control over them, much less their subordinates. Plutarco Elías Calles, for example, the Constitutionalist governor of Sonora, expelled all Catholic priests from his state in March 1916, alleging that Bishop Ignacio Valdespino y Díaz, at that time in exile in the United States, had written to a friend in Mexico expressing the hope that a new reactionary revolution would break out.[53]

The sharpest Constitutionalist attack upon the Church came at the hands of General Obregón, however, the one man upon whom the Carrancistas depended most for victory and the least amenable to civilian control. When he captured Mexico City from the Convention in January 1915, he found the capital in straits because of the ravages of war and the frequent seizures and evacuations of the city and because the fighting had decimated the food supplies. Zapata's men ranged at will through the countryside surrounding the capital, shutting off food for the city in an effort to weaken Obregón's armies. Prices in the city soared, and the poor were caught in a vise between the high costs of food and their own absolute lack of money. Obregón, ostensibly to alleviate the suffering of the poor, levied a "contribution of war" of 500,000 pesos upon the clergy of the city. Other revolutionary chiefs had sought even larger sums from the clergy, but in no other instance of an attack upon the Church was there so much notoriety.[54]

Obregón summoned all the priests of the capital to the National Palace to hear a message from his headquarters. They were immediately taken prisoner by the soldiers guarding the palace and told that they would be held as hostages to insure the payment of the levy. Included in the catch were 116 Mexican clergy and a number of foreign priests, mostly Spanish and Italian. When the foreign embassies protested the seizure of their nationals, Obregón turned the foreigners loose on condition that they leave the country at once. The vicar-general, Paredes, and Gerardo Herrera, dean of the cathedral chapter, offered to raise money among the several parishes of the diocese for charity, because, they said, the parish priest would presumably know better the needs of their people. Paredes proposed to sell the "last chalice," if necessary, for the sake of the poor, but insisted that the Church could not pay 500,000 pesos, for it had no money. On Sunday, February 21, the Catholic women of Mexico City organized a protest demonstration, while the radical workers in the capital countered with their own manifestation before the monument of Benito Juárez on the Alameda. The two rival demonstrations ended in a clash in which many were injured and two persons were killed.[55]

When the American embassy reported the arrest of the priests to the Department of State, Bryan directed Silliman in Veracruz to make representations to Carranza, calling for their release. Bryan wrote: "Say to him that the employment of such methods for the collection of money are so unusual and so unjustifiable, that they will arouse world-wide disapproval." He told Silliman to present the matter with "all possible earnestness, for it is a very grevious [sic] mistake and will be sure to arouse resentment in Mexico, as well as here and in other countries." The First Chief paid no attention to the American protest, for he considered such matters the concern of the Mexicans, not of foreigners. Moreover, he was not prepared for a showdown with Obregón on the matter of their respective powers, and he preferred to avoid trouble wherever possible. He said nothing, either to Obregón or in reply to Bryan's note.[56]

Meanwhile, in Mexico City the priests had been removed to jail cells, and the ransom was lowered day by day until a mordida of five pesos was considered enough to permit the freedom of a priest. Because a few refused on principle to pay even a nominal sum, 33 priests remained in custody when Obregón's troops evacuated the city in March 1915. Though Obregón announced that he was leaving the capital because of its "unfitness as a military base," in truth the pressure from the armies of the Convention made the city untenable. On March 5 the remaining priests were ordered to appear early the following morning at the Buena Vista railroad station. Obregón told them that they might write to their families for anything they needed for the journey. At dawn the next morning a large crowd gathered near the military headquarters to bid farewell to the prisoners. Those priests who were over 70 were called out and sent home, but the 26 who remained did not leave until March 10. Late at night—it was Obregón's wish to avoid a public demonstration—the priests were taken to the station and herded into a dark and dirty freight car, together with 25 Yaqui soldiers as guards. For several days, and without any explanation, the car was shuttled back and forth among several small railroad stations in the vicinity of Mexico City. On the morning of March 17 the train finally left Tula for Veracruz. At 3 P.M. the priests arrived at Téllez and were ordered to dismount and march into a field. Certain they would be shot, they fell to their knees to make their acts of contrition and to receive absolution. There was a carload of syndicalist workers from Mexico City, on their way to join Carranza's forces in Veracruz, and they laughed and jeered at the plight of the priests. As it turned out, it was simply a practical joke of their captors. After a few minutes, the priests were ordered back into the train once more. At 6:40 P.M. on March 18 the priests arrived in Veracruz, to be taken to a jail where they spent the night sleeping on the stone floors of their cells. The next day Carranza ordered their release, and most, ultimately, made their way back to Mexico City.[57]

Through 1915 the depredations against the Church in Mexico

lessened, not so much because the revolutionaries changed their attitudes, but because most of the priests and bishops, as well as the nuns, had left the country. The generals turned to their principal business—the fighting and winning of battles. Though Villa still controlled large areas in the North and the position of Zapata in the mountains of Morelos seemed impregnable, it was apparent by late summer of 1915 that Carranza and his Constitutionalist armies would win. On October 27 the American government gave Carranza *de facto* recognition as the head of the Mexican State. Eliseo Arredondo, Carranza's representative in Washington, pledged that his government would "respect everybody's life, property, and religious beliefs, without other limitation than the preservation of public order and the observation of the institutions in accordance with the laws in force and the Constitution of the Republic."[58]

The Catholic spokesmen in the United States reacted with vehemence to the announcement of Carranza's recognition, and a cascade of letters from irate Catholics throughout the country poured in on the White House and the Department of State. Even Cardinal Gibbons spoke bitterly of the American action: "Let a Protestant missionary be threatened and the United States will send a gun boat to see that American lives are protected. Yet there are many lives being snuffed out in Mexico, and we take no action." To counter this criticism the administration released the text of a letter from Wilson's secretary, Joseph Tumulty (who was a Catholic), to a prominent layman, Dr. James J. McGuire. Tumulty minimized the extent of the attacks on the Church. He told Dr. McGuire that the files of the State Department failed to disclose "a single proved case of outrages upon nuns" in Mexico. He enclosed a copy of Paredes' statement denying the substance of rumors that nuns had been assaulted. Tierney and Kelley turned angrily upon Tumulty, questioning his veracity and renewing their attacks on Paredes. The vicar-general, said Tierney, was a Carrancista, "appointed to his office by Carranza," and he sought to place the blame for the murder of the priests on the Zapatistas instead of the Constitutionalists. In a signed editorial in *America* Tierney said Dr. McGuire had asked Tumulty how conditions were in Mexico. "He did not get an answer," said Tierney. "I shall answer him. It is plain hell, just plain hell, ruled by demons of cruelty and bestiality, and will remain plain hell until the hand of God smites the demons who have devastated unfortunate Mexico, the land of weeping children and mistreated

women." Kelley told the press that he had signed affidavits proving
the attacks on priests and nuns. The worst atrocities had not yet
been made public, he said. "Mr. Tumulty may not perhaps have
heard that nuns were forcibly taken from trains and sent into the
revolutionary army. The number of nuns who reached Cuba or the
United States safely is negligible. How many of them will never be
heard from?"[59]

Despite the propagandizing of Kelley and Tierney, the Constitutionalists had won recognition, not because the government of the
First Chief was necessarily better or more moral than the leadership
of the Zapatistas and Villista factions—though it probably was—but
because Obregón and González and the other Constitutionalist
generals had won military victories over their enemies. Whatever
the American Catholics might say or do, the political and military
trends in Mexico were irreversible. Woodrow Wilson turned a deaf
ear to the pleas for intervention or withdrawal of recognition to the
Carrancista faction. The American Catholics' attacks on the president merged into the general criticism of the Wilson administration
being made by the Republicans in anticipation of the presidential
election of November 1916. The president's Mexican policy and his
failure to aid the Church in Mexico became major issues in the
campaign of Charles Evans Hughes.[60]

In Mexico the First Chief faced formidable problems still. He
must pacify all of Mexico and win the presidency in a legal election.
He must give sanction to his preconstitutional decrees by incorporating them into Mexico's legal structure. While state governors
decreed legislation in 1916 that restricted the operations of the
Church, the First Chief serenely, and (it seemed) obliviously, prepared for a constitutional convention that would give Mexico a new
instrument of government, which would be grounded—he planned
—firmly on the principles of nineteenth-century liberalism. But the
delegates ignored Carranza, and from the Constituent Congress of
1916–1917 at Querétaro came the most severe attacks on the
Church in Mexican history.

4

The Constitution
of 1917

SINCE MARCH 1913 Venustiano Carranza had been governing Mexico—or rather those parts of Mexico occupied by his revolutionary forces—as First Chief of the Constitutionalist Army. By the fall of 1915 he had gained control over most of the Republic. If Villa still held sway over his northern bailiwick of Chihuahua, and if Zapata remained holed up in the mountains of Morelos, it was clear that Carranza and the Constitutionalist forces had won the day. The American diplomatic recognition accorded his regime in October 1915 was President Wilson's reluctant acknowledgment of that fact. Most Mexicans believed that Carranza would finally declare himself provisional president, so that regular constitutional government might be restored. But Carranza was determined to be president for a full term, and under the constitution if he occupied the office of the provisional presidency he could not legally succeed himself. He refused to accede, therefore, to the demands of various revolutionaries that he become provisional president and instead prolonged his tenure as First Chief through 1915 and 1916. In this so-called "preconstitutional" period the forms of legal government (courts and Congress) did not exist, and the extralegal character of the national revolutionary regime was duplicated in the various states, where Carranza appointed provisional governors with wide powers, including the right to decree legislation. The First Chief in turn issued decrees, as they were needed, on a wide number of subjects, including the proposed agrarian reforms at Veracruz in January 1915. But this fiat legislation would have no legal sanction once constitutional government was restored. It was necessary, therefore, in order to give permanence to the enactments of the First Chief and the provisional governors, to reform the constitution by incorporating into it the substance of the decrees.

Carranza did not desire wholesale changes in the constitution. The amended document of 1857, which represented the political philosophy of Benito Juárez and Sebastián Lerdo de Tejada, mirrored the First Chief's own nineteenth-century liberalism. But it was widely recognized that the constitution contained flaws that had made possible the dictatorships of Díaz and Huerta. Carranza proposed to eliminate the defects while maintaining the basic structure of the 1857 Constitution. As early as January 1915, with the Carrancistas still in precarious straits, Carranza began his campaign to prepare Mexico for a new constitution. He asked Félix Palavicini, a member of his civilian staff, to direct the propaganda campaign in the Constitutionalist press. Palavicini, an engineer by profession, wrote articles in the revolutionary newspapers, made public speeches, and published pamphlets and books during the next year in which he stressed the necessity of assembling a Constituent Congress as soon as the fighting should end. The Congress, said Palavicini, would be elected when a majority of the town and city governments in Mexico could hold free elections. Thus the new constitution would be the work of the people through their own elected representatives. The election would demonstrate Mexican grass-roots democracy, he thought, and the resulting constitution would be a Carrancista, hence liberal, document.[1]

Through the spring and summer of 1916 the Constitutionalist military successes gave administrative control of the largest part of the Republic to the First Chief. With the imminent restoration of peace and the return of legal government the need for constitutional reform became apparent. On September 19, 1916, Carranza decreed elections for a Constituent Congress, which would meet in Querétaro, he said, to avoid the "reactionary influences of Mexico City," during the last week of November. The elections would take place on October 26, and the delegates to the Congress would have a two-months period in which to carry out the mandate of the First Chief to give Mexico a new constitution. Once assembled, the Congress would receive from Carranza a "projected constitution" for its consideration, approval, or alteration.[2]

Whatever their professed political ideals, the Carrancista liberals did not intend that the election be completely free. Only those who had not opposed Carranza's revolution could come as delegates to Querétaro. There would be no Porfiristas or Huertistas, no Catholics, no Zapatistas, no Villistas, no supporters of the Convention. It would be, in short, a highly unrepresentative body. The advisers of the First Chief believed that the delegates would represent their own philosophy, and that the liberals would control the convention. They were betrayed by their own utopianism. They considered the Mexicans ready for elections and believed that the people would share their own ideals and express those sentiments by sending liberal delegates to the Congress. If the Carrancistas desired a compliant congress, however, it was necessary to dominate the balloting from the capital, rigging the election to secure a safe liberal majority. This was precisely what Mexico's federal system made difficult. Through insisting upon local autonomy, the liberals, by default, allowed the domination of the elections on the state and municipal levels. The result was the imposition of local candidates, often regional caudillos and revolutionary leaders in the district, who were men of the people and much more radical than the civilian members of Carranza's regime. The Querétaro Congress was intended as an instrument of the liberals. In actuality it heralded the radical social revolution.

Nowhere was the political naivete of the Carrancistas more amply demonstrated than in the simple act of announcing an election to be held in a month's time and then expecting that the electorate would rally around Carranza and the liberals. They thought that calling the election would somehow cause large and coherent political parties to be formed, political parties in the mold of the American system. But Porfirio Díaz had killed off all attempts to form true parties, while the revolutions had prevented attempts at revivals. It was not to be expected, then, that parties in the Anglo-Saxon sense —and that was the Carrancistas' frame of reference—could be brought to maturity within the space of a month. Instead Mexico saw the mushrooming of a great number of small parties, formed locally and spontaneously, and with no intention of subordinating their own principles or candidates to the discipline of a national party. Most were either liberal or radical; all were Constitutionalist. Too often the parties had a personalistic base, depending upon the local leader for their character.

The Constitutionalist press decried this proliferation of factions. Heriberto Barrón, editor of *El Pueblo,* wrote that while most parties seemed to share identical ideals, they had taken to fighting among themselves, and he advocated the establishment of a central directorate to coordinate the activities of all Carrancistas and mold them into a Gran Partido Liberal Constitucionalista. It was true, he admitted, that Carranza had called for the formation of political parties, but the First Chief meant two parties as in the United States, not the factionalism of small local, uncoordinated clubs. Barrón organized a meeting in the capital of several factions who agreed to support a single slate of candidates for the Congress. But despite the protestations of the Mexico City newspapers, the elections in most areas favored radical candidates, men who were closer to Villa and Zapata and to the Aguascalientes Convention in their political philosophy than to their own First Chief.[3]

In the preliminary sessions of the Congress, beginning on November 2, it became disconcertingly clear that a cleavage was taking place among the delegates. The liberal body, which the Carrancistas had expected, did not take shape. Instead, the splintering of parties at the hastily convoked elections had sent to the Congress many small independent groups, and these groups met in various buildings in Querétaro to formulate their programs before the regular sessions commenced on December 1. As the meetings progressed these groups found their way into two camps, one distinguished by its adherence to the principles of the First Chief, the other by its radical intransigence against any compromise with the aims of the Revolution. The former were designated *rojos*, because they voted on red slips of papers. Led by civilians close to the First Chief, many had had previous legislative experience in the Madero and Huerta years as senators or deputies. Their chief spokesmen were Luis Manuel Rojas, Manuel Aguirre Berlanga, José Natividad Macías, Alfonso Cravioto, and Félix F. Palavicini. These delegates supported the cause of the First Chief in brilliant legalistic declamations. Because of their knowledge of parliamentary matters, the *rojos* gained technical control of the assembly, and Luis Manuel Rojas was elected president of the body. But two generals became vicepresidents, Cándido Aguilar and Salvador González Torres, and the selection of these two soldiers gave evidence that the majority of the Congress, the *blancos,* were radical. The *blancos* were more poorly organized than the liberals. Many were inarticulate and often at a loss to express their deeply felt convictions that Mexico needed social and economic reform even more than political changes. They reacted instinctively, rather than rationally. Emotional, pugnacious, prejudiced, and intolerant, they had little patience with legalistic quibblings. They would move directly to their desired goals without too much concern for traditional constitutional principles. The radicals found their most ardent champion in General Francisco Javier Múgica, a delegate from the state of Michoacán.

At the age of 32 Múgica reached the peak of his revolutionary career. More than any other delegate at Querétaro he directed the shift in the direction of the Revolution by which the liberal Carrancistas were thrust aside by the radicals. It was through Múgica, aided by General Heriberto Jara in the assembly, and with the strong backing of Álvaro Obregón in the government of the First Chief, that the ideals of the social revolutionaries, of the absent Zapatistas and Villistas, of the Convention of Aguascalientes, became warp and weft of the Constitutionalists' program, and the Mexican Revolution—with a capital "R"—was born. The subsequent history of Mexico was shaped in large part by the reforms written into the constitution at Querétaro by Múgica and his associates.

As early as 1915 Múgica had been recognized as a radical by the Carrancistas. A brigadier general in the Constitutionalist armies, he had been made collector of port revenues at Veracruz and then sidetracked by the First Chief as military governor of far-off Tabasco. Before coming to Querétaro, Múgica expressed his dissatisfaction with Carranza's government in a letter to General Salvador Alvarado, the socialistic governor of Yucatán. He told Alvarado that, in his opinion, the regime was filled with Huertistas, that Carranza's cabinet had done nothing to solve Mexico's problems, and that the various departments were stagnant and obstructionist.[4]

His fellow delegate, Juan Bojórquez, wrote later of Múgica's work in the assembly: "No lawyer, he knew how to legislate as no one else; no polished orator, he drew the longest and most thunderous ovations; no hygienist, he understood problems of health; and no school master, he could lecture on systems of education. . . . No one worked more than he. No one studied as he did. No one surpassed him in the tribunal defending the highest ideals of the Mexican people. Champion of the most radical left, he was followed enthusiastically by the majority and respected by the men of the right. . . ."[5]

Nonetheless, the making of a constitution is primarily a legal problem. Whatever abilities Múgica—along with the other leaders of the *blancos*—might possess, he could not create a constitution from thin air. Moreover, the delegates had been allotted only the short period of two months to complete their labors. (The constitution writers in 1824 and 1856–1857 had taken more than a year.) It was inconceivable that unguided they could carry out the task set them. Nor did the First Chief intend that the delegates themselves write the constitution. He had seen the rancor, the quibbling, the pulling and hauling that characterized the Convention of military men at Aguascalientes, and he was determined that the new constitution would conform to safe, sane, and tested principles. The delegates received the constitution ready made, the product of the best legal minds in the First Chief's government.

Early in 1916 Carranza named Cravioto, Macías, and Juan N. Frías to a legislative section in his government to work through the Constitution of 1857, eliminating some parts, refurbishing a few, and making additions here and there. Subsequently, Macías revised the document prepared by the committee, and, in the main, the proposed constitution reflected his work.

Macías epitomized the politics and philosophy of the Carrancista regime. He was older (59) than the other delegates at Querétaro, for most of the revolutionaries were men in their thirties. Macías had had a long and distinguished legal and political career. A deputy and a senator under Díaz, he had become a close friend of Carranza in the Porfirista Senate. After Madero's revolution, Macías was elected once more to the Chamber of Deputies and served in the Congress until its dissolution by Huerta in October 1913. In 1915 Carranza named Macías rector of the National University and sent him to the United States to study American democratic institutions in order to adapt them to Mexican conditions. Many of the revolutionaries distrusted Macías, as they distrusted the other Maderista legislators who had remained in the National Congress after Huerta's usurpation in 1913. But the young soldiers also suspected his liberal philosophy. They had not fought against Díaz and Huerta to see the perpetuation of nineteenth-century social and economic conditions.[6]

The projected constitution, as written by Macías and his committee, did bear a superficial resemblance to that of the United States. It provided for a federal system of government with many powers reserved to the various states. But the obvious parallels in the constitutions did not mean that the Mexicans had simply copied the

American document. In one sense, all written constitutions are alike in that they set forth the system of government for the country (executive, legislative, and judicial branches) and delineate the rights of the citizens. In a free Western society these systems and rights will all appear similar, for the various countries have reached a consensus on the basic ideals of government. Like the American Constitution, the Macías document guaranteed freedom of assembly, speech, and the press, and the right to bear arms. The agrarian problem received scant attention; Article 27 made provision for expropriations in the public interest, but did not specifically provide land for the peasants. The proposed constitution certainly did not fulfill the pledges made by Carranza in his Veracruz decrees. Andrés Molina Enríquez was highly critical of the manifest evasion of Mexico's land problems. Macías' project, he said, appeared to demonstrate "the indisposition of the First Chief to fulfill the obligations of the Revolution expressed in detail in the decree of December 12, 1914."[7]

The Macías document continued the traditions of Juárez and Lerdo in matters concerning Church and State. The Reform Laws were embodied in the new code, while the individual churches came under the jurisdiction of the government. Article 129 separated Church and State and stipulated that Congress would enact no laws establishing any religion. Matrimony would be a civil contract, and a simple promise to tell the truth replaced court oaths. Article 3, which dealt with education, provided for free, laical schooling in public institutions, but did not prohibit the Church from founding and operating its own school system.[8]

This was the constitution that Carranza, Macías, and all the civilian members of the First Chief's government expected the Congress to endorse. In effect, the delegates were asked to affirm the principles that had guided Mexico in the nineteenth century. Except for the incorporation of the Reform Laws and the extralegal decrees of the First Chief, an article by article comparison between the Constitution of 1857 and the proposed Carranza constitution shows the two documents to be virtually identical in spirit and meaning, if not in wording.

The Constituent Congress at Querétaro, controlled by the radicals, was of no mind to swallow the legal pabulum offered by Carranza. The delegates were determined to fulfill the social aims of the Revolution, bringing land to the landless, protecting the workers, both urban and rural, asserting the national patrimony over foreign exploiters of Mexico's resources, and above all shackling the Church. The delegates had no time to rewrite the charter handed them by Carranza. Until they came to Querétaro and exchanged ideas with fellow delegates, many were not even certain what they wanted to do. Not one had been to such a convention before; few had been legislators or public administrators. Most were soldiers in Carranza's armies. The Congress accepted the largest part of the constitution—the sections on government structure and citizens' rights—with little ado, and the delegates spent most of their time in committee sessions and in long and rancorous debates in the assembly on a few key articles. In these articles, as rewritten in the committees headed by Múgica and Jara, are seen the fruition of the social revolution. In Article 3 on education, Article 27 on land reforms, Article 123 on labor legislation, and Article 130 on the Church, the spirit of the new replaced the obsolete. Liberalism gave way to a militant nationalism and to a native, but non-Marxian, socialism. Because of the way the constitution was put together, and because of the inexperience of most of the delegates, the result was a hodgepodge of liberal and radical provisions, often illogical and contradictory. Rights proclaimed in one article were blatantly denied or curtailed in another. The delegates embraced the liberal principle of federalism, for to champion centralism in 1916 and 1917 was to align oneself with the Porfiristas and Huertistas. Yet the provisions written into the most radical articles presupposed a Leviathan in Mexico City to implement them. If the constitution were to be enforced, the nineteenth-century ideals must give way to the new and the dynamic—to the spirit of the radical revolutionaries.

The sessions between November 21 and 30 were consumed with the discussion and approbation or rejection of credentials. The most vexatious question concerned the presence of the Renovadores—former Maderista legislators, such as Macías and Rojas, who had remained in the Congress when Madero was deposed and assassinated. The military men, who considered themselves the true revolutionaries, would exclude these delegates peremptorily. Not only were they tarred with the brush of usurpation, but they were civilians who had stayed safely with the First Chief, while the soldiers risked their lives for the Revolution on the field of battle. Carranza intervened in the debates by sending the Congress a letter in which he alleged that he had advised the legislators in 1913 to stay in Mexico City and to oppose the government of Huerta by hampering the passage of legislation. Though the radicals were by no means convinced or placated by Carranza's explanation, they acquiesced to his desires and voted to accept the credentials of all of the Renovadores who had come to Querétaro. By the end of the month, however, it was abundantly clear that the control of the Convention had passed into the hands of the radical faction.[9]

At 4 P.M. on December 1 Venustiano Carranza mounted the rostrum to address the delegates and open officially the sessions of the Constituent Congress. He was old for a revolutionary—nearly 57 years of age—and old enough to remember, however faintly, the last days of Benito Juárez. He had grown to manhood under Lerdo and Porfirio Díaz, had served Madero, and was now a venerable relic of a bygone age. He spoke to the young delegates through his grey Olympian beard in the language of other years. Carranza's speech was serene, prolix, and wearisome. He seemed oblivious of the ideological magma boiling up among the delegates. He ignored the need for social reform or advanced thinking. Instead, he uttered platitudes about the "primordial duty" of the government being to "facilitate the necessary conditions for organizing the law." He insisted that the first responsibility of the Constituent Congress was to guarantee human liberty. The First Chief dwelt at length upon the achievements of his revolution in creating the free municipality and stressed the necessity of a balance of power among the three branches of government in order to ward off a dictatorship. He concluded his address to great applause from the delegates who signified that they respected their First Chief if they did not uphold his principles.[10]

The liberal press, like Carranza, seemed to have no doubts that the Congress would approve the constitution offered by Carranza. In an editorial for *El Pueblo*, Heriberto Barrón praised the address of the First Chief extravagantly and noted that the "wisdom of the Congress" would insure the acceptance of the liberal document— "guided by the most noble of impulses."[11]

After the address of the First Chief, the delegates marked time for several more days awaiting the constitution that Carranza had promised. On December 5 Rafael Martínez, liberal editor of *El Demócrata*, announced that he had received word from his printing company that the projected constitution was in press and would be in Querétaro within 24 hours for distribution to the members of the assembly. On the following day, the Carranza constitution was read to the Congress, article by article, and then the real work of the delegates began. They now had only 57 days to complete their labors and to give Mexico a new charter.

Through the session of December 6 the delegates debated the composition of the committee to study the constitution, and the Congress showed its tenor by rejecting Carrancistas Macías, Guillermo Odorica, and Gerzayn Ugarte as members of the committee. Several delegates expressed the opinion that Macías and his projected constitution were not revolutionary or radical enough. But the official reason for his exclusion was that, as the chief author of the proposed constitution, he should not be permitted to study its reform. Gerzayn Ugarte, like Martínez a Carrancista editor, told the Congress that only lawyers should be named to the committee, because "in matters of constitutional law, a lawyer knows more than a cobbler." After a heated debate, however, the delegates in a secret ballot elected a radical commission. General Múgica was designated chairman, while Enrique Colunga, Luis G. Monzón, Enrique Recio, and Alberto Román served with him as members. Later in the month, when work piled up for this commission, another committee was created to review the last part of the constitution. This second committee was responsible for rewriting Article 129 (130 in the final draft of the constitution), but the more radical introductions into the constitution were the work of the five delegates of Múgica's committee.[12]

The two lawyers on his committee, Enrique Colunga and Enrique Recio, were by no means liberals. They were overshadowed by the more vociferous members, especially the chairman, Múgica, and Luis G. Monzón. Monzón was the most uninhibited reformer on the committee, and certainly one of the most radical members of the Congress. He dissented from many of the committee's proposals, because he felt that they did not go far enough. A primary school teacher in Sonora during the Díaz regime, Monzón was exiled from Mexico as a Floresmagonista and jailed in Douglas, Arizona, in 1906 as a syndicalist agitator. Though many of the revolutionaries tempered their radicalism in their later years, especially as they enriched themselves at the expense of the Mexican people, Monzón remained a staunch radical all his life. In 1923 he joined Mexico's nascent Communist Party as one of its first members. The constitution, as it was finally adopted, represented primarily the work of Múgica and his committee, superimposed upon the Macías-Carranza document. The Congress debated the proposals article by article, but voted to accept the recommendations of Múgica's committee virtually unchanged. The important decisions concerning key articles were made in committees before the articles were submitted to the floor. The committees and the Congress had been offered a constitution in the liberal tradition, and they deliberately distorted it.[13]

The proposed charter contained 129 articles. The first dealt with the rights of the Mexican people, the last with the Church. The committee of Múgica and the Congress took up the articles consecutively and adopted the first two without a flurry. The third article, which concerned education, proved to be a stumbling block. The liberal Constitution of 1857 had stipulated that public education be free, with no strings attached to that freedom. The article in Macías' draft paralleled the liberal provisions of the earlier constitution. Because the Church would be free to conduct its own schools in Mexico, the article was completely unacceptable to Múgica and his associates. For several days the committee labored over the rewriting of the article and on December 11 reported to the Congress. At this point, early in the sessions of the Congress, the delegates were forced to choose between the liberalism of their First Chief and the heady radicalism of the committee they had elected. This was the most important moment for the assembly, because once the decision was made to uphold the committee's recommendations, the liberal delegates ceased to put up any real fight. With the adoption of Article 3 the reform of the other key articles followed as a matter of course.

In his report to the Congress on Article 3, Múgica frankly admitted that it contravened rights supposedly guaranteed to the Mexican people in other articles. He wrote: "The committee holds the theory that the mission of the public power is to procure to each citizen the greatest liberty compatible with the rights of all; and from that principle, applying the deductive method, it reaches the conclusion that it is just to restrict a natural right when its free exercise would endanger the preservation of society or hinder its development. Religious education, which seeks to teach the most abstract ideas, ideas that the intelligence of the child cannot assimilate, hinders the child's natural psychological development and tends to produce a deformation of his spirit, similar to the physical deformation brought about by a faulty course in gymnastics. As a consequence, the State should proscribe religious education in all the private schools, either official or private."

"In the history of our country, studied impartially," he said, "the clergy appears as the most cruel and tenacious enemy of our liberties. The doctrine of the clergy has been the interests of the Church before the interests of the people. . . . It is necessary to exclude the priests from any part in primary education."

For Macías' article the committee substituted its own emended version, which would permit only laical education in the primary schools. To guide the Congress it defined such education as being "void of every religious belief, the education that transmits the truth, free from error and inspired by a rigorously scientific attitude." The Church was not banned completely from education, for the article implied that priests and nuns might operate secondary schools. The committee felt, however, that by the time the child reached secondary schools, religious influence would be attenuated. (It should be noted, too, that there were very few secondary schools in Mexico in 1917, so the question of Church-affiliated institutions of higher learning did not seem important to the Congress.) Enrique Monzón dissented from the committee report with a vigorous separate opinion in which he asked the Congress to substitute the word "rationalism" for "laical education."[14]

Reports from Querétaro of the radical temper of the Congress alarmed Carranza and his cabinet, and debate on the article began on the afternoon of December 13 with the First Chief looking on. Carranza hoped that his presence might intimidate the delegates, causing them to reject the revised article. Aware of the significance of the moment and conscious of the First Chief's displeasure, Francisco J. Múgica took to the lists as the champion of radicalism. He did not quail. Speaking firmly and with conviction, he made clear to the world his unequivocal hatred of the Catholic Church. "Gentlemen," he said, "I am a foe of the clergy, because I consider it the most disgraceful and perverse enemy of our people." "What has the clergy given our children, our workers, or our Nation? The most absurd ideas, the greatest contempt for our democratic institutions, the most unrelenting hatred for the very principles of equity, equality, and fraternity taught by the first democrat, Jesus Christ. Are we going to commend to the clergy the formation of our future, to surrender to them our children, our brothers, the children of our brothers, so that they can educate them in those principles? Frankly, I think not. For what sort of morality, gentlemen, will the clergy teach our children? We have seen it—the greatest corruption. . . ."

"If we permit absolute freedom of education," he said, "and allow the clergy to come in with their outdated and retrogressive ideas, we shall not form new generations of intellectual and cultivated men. Instead, those who come after us will receive an inheritance of fanaticism, of insane principles, and we can be sure that some day new wars will spill the blood of our people."[15]

In the debate that followed Múgica's impassioned declaration the liberals sought to stem the tide of radicalism by appealing to reason and to natural rights. They cited facts and statistics to prove that the priests were not a dire threat to the Republic. They pointed to the example of the First Chief, who sat impassively through the session, and to his moderation and rationality. The radicals in turn appealed to emotions, to prejudice, and to the phantasm of the priest as a traducer of the young and a seducer of women, of the priest as a drunkard, a petty thief. In the end, the impassioned oratory changed no minds and did not alter the decision of the Congress. But the debates did bring clearly to light the two philosophies represented at Querétaro. At no time in Mexican history were the principles of liberalism more eloquently championed than in the rostrum of the Constituent Congress and by men such as Rojas, Cravioto, Palavicini, and Macías.

When Rojas stepped down from the presidency to answer Múgica he stood before the delegates as the chief spokesman for Venustiano Carranza. He had served Madero in the Congress and he had labored with Carranza in Veracruz as one of his most important civilian advisers. Rojas agreed with Múgica that this was one of the most significant moments in the revolution. He gestured toward the First Chief for support as he commenced to speak. "We have an opportunity here," he said, "to create a constitution that is truly liberal, truly tolerant, progressive, and modern." But what Múgica and his committee proposed was "jacobin." He asked the committee to retire its proposal and rewrite it to permit more individual freedom in education. Taking note of a telegram to the Congress by Obregón advising the delegates to embrace a radical program, Rojas said: "If I come before you today to support the ideas of the

First Chief, it is because they are perfectly in accord with my own honorable convictions." When he concluded, the delegates rejected his motion by a voice vote.[16]

Dr. Román replied briefly for the committee, stressing the record of the Church in Mexico as an enemy of democratic institutions, and then Alfonso Cravioto came to the rostrum. Like Macías and Rojas, Cravioto was a lawyer and a Renovador deputy in the 26th Legislature under Madero and Huerta. As a newspaper writer during the Díaz regime, he had frequently criticized the dictatorship. His liberalism was deeply rooted, and he was an ardent defender of individual liberties. Freedom of education in Mexico was an integral and necessary part of freedom of belief, he told the delegates, and the State could not interfere with the rights of the individual to seek his own education as he saw fit. The State might rightly insist upon lay education in the public schools, but could not concern itself with the private schools. Cravioto denied that the Catholic schools posed a threat, as the radicals alleged. In 1907, he said, there had been 9,620 public schools in Mexico and only 586 clerical institutions. In any event, he said, "the real focus of religious education is in the home and not in the school. . . . The children do not have their ideas because they are taught them by the priests. The true teacher of the general ideas of children is the father. We all know that. . . ."

"The committee believes that we should prevent distortions and suggests as the means a jacobin attitude. But the committee stops short. If we accept their logic, we would content ourselves with nothing less than taking from the fathers their legitimate right to choose the teachers of their children, and we ought to go into homes smashing statues of saints, breaking up rosaries, tearing down crucifixes, confiscating novenas and other religious gadgets, locking the doors against the priests, prohibiting freedom of association so that no one could enter the churches to come into contact with the clergy, prohibiting freedom of the press because some one might print clerical propaganda, destroying religious liberty, and after all of this, sated with its orgy of intolerance, the commission would have only one article in the constitution: There are guarantees solely for those who think as we do." "I do not know why liberty seems to terrify some revolutionaries. Do not these gentlemen know that liberty is like a hard bread that, at the same time, can make soup or give lumps on the head?" The delegates laughed, appreciating his little sally at the expense of the committee.

"Freedom of education might produce those lumps," he said, "for undoubtedly it permits some abuses. . . . But, gentlemen, to destroy completely one precious guarantee, thinking this petty distinction is only a matter of regulation and not of the constitution itself, would be tantamount to saying that if a man has an earache we should cut off his head!"

"We should not exchange one error for another, one fanaticism for a different fanaticism. Error cannot be fought with error, but with the truth. Fanaticism cannot be defeated with persecution, but with knowledge. The triumph of liberalism over religious education lies not in smashing it with excessive laws, for these can lead only to disastrous consequences. The true liberal triumph over religious education is achieved by fighting it on its own ground, by multiplying our schools. Here is the remedy, the true remedy. Everything else is tyranny."

Cravioto concluded his appeal to the delegates: "Gentlemen: Let us aspire to the august equanimity of the Citizen First Chief. Mark well the great liberal principles destroyed by this projected article, and in the name of the high mission and the high responsibility that the people have given us, reject this jacobin provision of the committee." His peroration was met with thunderous applause from the assembly; there was much handshaking, and several members embraced him as he left the rostrum. The delegates could recognize and appreciate a fine stirring speech, even though most did not agree with Cravioto's sentiments.[17]

Delegates favoring or opposing the article alternated in the rostrum through the rest of the afternoon and evening and into the following day's session, vying with each other in embellishing their oratory. The extreme radicals backed Monzón. The moderate liberals opposed the entire article. As might be expected, Macías and Palavicini stood with the First Chief. Calling the committee's restrictions "subversive," Macías told the delegates: "I am one who loves liberty, one who would grant the broadest freedom to all; for that reason, I think that most of you are jacobins." The revised article was written, he said, "in the language of a dictator."

"Gentlemen, let the clergy be thrown out, but do not allow the freedom of the human conscience to disappear," said Palavicini, pointing out the internal contradiction of the article as presented by the committee. The first sentence read: "There shall be freedom of education"; at the same time, the rest of the article denied that very freedom. "If you eliminate 'There shall be freedom of education,' you will make it consistently restrictive. But if you include the first sentence among the guarantees, then the rest is completely absurd."

Múgica returned to answer the liberals and close the debate: "You accuse us of rudeness to the First Chief because we reject his proposed Article 3," he said. "Well, gentlemen, the committee has been rude. The committee has been impolite. The committee has perhaps shown a great lack of respect for that man who deserves all my respect. Yes, gentlemen, but the committee has not done this with the deliberate intention of appearing before the country to be disrespectful. . . . No, gentlemen, the committee has done it, because it felt that the projected article was not sufficiently radical to safeguard the country . . . , because the committee saw an imminent danger in granting the Rights of Man to the clergy, because it wished to preserve those rights for the masses, and because it wanted to guarantee, gentlemen, something more sacred, something that we could never betray and that we must defend always— the mind of the child. . . ." He agreed, however, to recall the article to rewrite the first phrase, as Palavicini had suggested.[18]

On December 16 the committee presented its revised article to the Congress. The opening sentence now read: "Education is free, but . . . ," and there followed all the restrictions on religious education. It was clear that education would be far from free in Mexico. Many more delegates spoke for or against the measure through the day, and at the end of the discussion the vote was taken. The article of Múgica's committee was approved 99–58, and it became an integral part of Mexico's constitution. Thereafter, the delegates debated each article, often with heat and even anger, but the spirit had gone from the liberals. They knew that the radicals would ultimately have their way on any point whenever they desired. Rampant anticlericalism had won the day at Querétaro. Much of the debate on subsequent articles that concerned religion centered, not on the battle between liberal and radical notions of Church-State relations, but on whether the restrictions on the Church were radical or extreme enough for the delegates.[19]

With the approval of Article 3, Carranza saw that the Congress had gotten out of hand, and he sent Pastor Rouaix, his Minister of Development and Colonization, to Querétaro to attend the sessions and advise the delegates. Rouaix brought Obregón, now Minister of War in Carranza's cabinet, to the Congress hoping to quiet the leftists. But Obregón and the First Chief were at odds over the issue of the successor to Carranza's post, and Obregón placed his great political weight behind the radicals. He sent a telegram to the Congress, after it had approved the article, commending the radicalism shown by the delegates. And the presence of Obregón in Querétaro —he was still the strongest of the Constitutionalist generals— helped strengthen the radicals' resolve to stand up to the First Chief. Nor did Rouaix do his part to damp the fires of radicalism. Though he was an official in Carranza's government, he worked closely with the members of the committees to help rewrite Articles 27 and 123 that dealt with land reform and protection for labor. Advised by Andrés Molina Enríquez, Rouaix and the delegates, in these two articles, placed the keystone of Mexico's social and economic revolution. The articles furnished the means for peasants to obtain lands. They guaranteed urban workers the right to organize unions and to strike, while providing the basis for minimum wages and maximum hours legislation. The delegates were carrying out in one blow what Catholic Social Action had been talking about and working toward for so many years. But the radicals would use the force of the government to expropriate, to coerce, and, if necessary, to destroy in order to win the aims of the Revolution.[20]

It is true that these articles were only part of a blueprint for the future and were subject to hamstringing by whatever government was to direct the Mexican Revolution, especially if civilian liberals remained in power under Carranza. But the tremendous leap forward of the Social Revolution at the Constituent Congress of Querétaro can hardly be overestimated. The constitution now promised an end to the indifference or impartiality upon which liberal rule was predicated. It was a vindication of the Mexican people and of their part in the overthrow of the old regime.

The newspapers subsidized by Carranza's government reacted sharply to the radical attacks upon the Church and upon the liberal system. *El Demócrata* of Rafael Martínez charged that Carranza's constitution, which had been born in an "honestly liberal atmosphere," had now been covered with the "sharp burs of jacobinism" by the Congress. While liberals held no brief for medieval superstitions, the editors said, they felt that the Church was slowly modernizing, was changing its emphasis from the supposedly revealed to the scientifically verifiable truth. Government persecution of reli-

gion had no place in a liberal state. The radicals, said the newspaper, were attempting to clothe Torquemada with the "redingote of
Robespierre."[21] Heriberto Barrón wrote in *El Pueblo* that the Constitutionalist revolution, which had been fought under the banner
of human freedom, could not permit any group to be deprived of
its lawful rights, whether Catholic, Protestant, Jewish, or Mo-
hammedan. Barrón put his finger squarely on the crux of the coming struggle between Catholics and the revolutionary socialists
when he wrote that "ill-intentioned radicalism, which professes the
principle of 'absolute liberty for me and restrictions and slavery for
those who do not think as I do,' is an absurd radicalism that does
nothing but destroy liberty . . . and lower the prestige of the Revolution."[22]

The radical temper of the Congress was nowhere more apparent
than in the articles dealing specifically with the relations between
the Church and the Mexican revolutionary government. Some of
the proposals made at Querétaro would have destroyed the Church
by making impossible the propagation of the faith. Those finally
enacted so severely curtailed the spiritual activities of the clergy,
that no religious body anywhere in the world could have accom-
modated itself to them. The rigid application of the laws could only
lead inevitably to a clash. The traditional intransigence of the
Church toward secular philosophies was matched by the counter-
intransigence of the deputies at Querétaro. The Yucatán representatives, certainly the most radical delegation, proposed that the
government charge rent for the use of its churches, that oral confession be prohibited, that government officials administer Church
funds, that the clergy must be Mexican-born, more than 50 years of
age, and married. Most of the delegates agreed that the confessional
was an unwarranted interference of the clergy into the affairs of the
home. In the debates they took turns painting horror pictures of
wives pouring family secrets into the "crapulous" ears of the priests,
and of the priests using the intimacy of the confessional booth to
seduce innocent wives and daughters. But the majority agreed with
Fernando Lizardi, a delegate from Guanajuato, who pointed out
that there were many evils in the world with which a constitution
could not deal. Certainly oral confession was immoral, but "so was
onanism," said Lizardi, and it would be absurd to ban that practice
in the constitution. As for the proposal to force the clergy to marry,
the only consequence, he contended, would be to "make us procur-

ers of fresh meat for the priests." "The truth is that no one needs to find sweethearts for the priests," he said. The Yucatecan proposal was defeated, but it is significant that nearly 40 percent of the delegates voted in favor of outlawing oral confession and compelling the priests of Mexico to marry.[23]

Some of the restrictions placed upon the Church at Querétaro were nuisances, though they were not crippling. They might cause some annoyance to the clergy, but it was possible for the Church to carry on its main business of saving souls with only minor irritations. Among those provisions were articles banning public worship outside the churches, forbidding the Church to hold real property or make loans, denying ministers the right to take part in politics, to criticize the government, or to be elected to public office, and banning priests not born in Mexico. In contrast, other provisions placed the Church and the priests outside the protection of the law and actually curbed spiritual functions. The constitution declared that religious institutions were subject to civilian and civil procedures; that monastic vows and monastic orders were illegal; that the national government owned the churches and could determine which might be used for services, that state legislatures should have the power to determine the maximum number of clergy "according to the needs of each locality"; and that no trial by jury should "ever be granted for the infraction of any of the preceding provisions." The Constitution of 1857, as amended in 1873 had declared Church and State to be independent. The Carranza document offered the Congress separation of Church and State, to be specified in the constitution. Article 130, as it finally appeared, said: "The federal authorities shall have power to exercise in the matters of religious worship and outward ecclesiastical forms such intervention as by law authorized. . . ." Because there is no reference to a separation of Church and State, the conclusion is inescapable that the delegates at Querétaro did not intend that the Church in Mexico be independent of the civil power.[24]

Article 130, one of the most important and far-reaching in the constitution, was the work of the four men on Heriberto Jara's committee. It was not brought before the Congress until after midnight of January 27 when the delegates were already weary from a long debate on Article 24. They discussed it for less than two hours, and those who spoke against it were not liberals; they did not call for freedom and toleration, but for further restrictions. Múgica and

Recio would put into Article 130 the ban on oral confession that had been rejected in Article 24. Múgica read to the delegates parts of documents taken from episcopal archives by Constitutionalist soldiers, which, he said, proved the charges of immorality against many of Mexico's priests. But the delegates were tired and sleepy. They had labored hard to finish the constitution within the time limit imposed by the First Chief. They were quite willing to go along with Jara's committee and did not want to debate further changes. At 2 A.M. on January 28 the vote was taken. The secretary announced that the results would be made known in the morning. But they were never published either in the newspapers or in the *Diario de los Debates,* so that no true reckoning can be made. It is a safe assumption, however, that the vote was nearly unanimous. Liberal or radical, most of the delegates were anticlerical. They did not care what happened to the priests, and the time for the liberals to uphold principles of freedom and toleration in the assembly had long since past.[25]

And so in the early hours of the morning the delegates finished their task. Mexico had a new constitution. Whether it was a legal document is a moot question. The election of delegates had been fraudulent. Most Mexicans were excluded by the ban against non-Constitutionalist representation. It was a constitution imposed by the logic of military force, by the victory of the men of Carranza over Huerta and over Villa and Zapata. It was never ratified by a popular vote or by the acquiescence of the states. But it was neither more nor less legal than Mexico's other constitutions. They too had been imposed by brute force, by the military defeat of the liberals or conservatives. The new constitution was there to be used or misused, implemented or ignored. As the delegates assembled on the last day of the month to hear Carranza's concluding address, they passed the responsibility of enforcing the constitution on to him as the president of Mexico. Since January 1917 a succession of presidents has governed Mexico, within and without the constitution. It has been amended over a hundred times, but the basic constitution in the 1970s is still that of Querétaro with its freedoms and fetters. Under it Mexico gave land to the landless peasants, reconquered the oil rights granted foreign capitalists, enshrined the principle of labor-management equality, built a modern system of education, and drove the Church into open rebellion against the law. At Querétaro the sword of Mexico's Social Revolution was forged.

As Carranza addressed the final session of the Congress he thanked the delegates for their labors. The constitution might contain defects of "deficiency or excess," he admitted, but it was "a pledge to guarantee the security of the future." "In receiving from this honorable Congress the sacred treasure that you have given me I humbly and respectfully offer you my complete acquiescence, and in a most solemn manner and before the entire nation I give my solemn oath to comply with it, giving thus the proof of my great respect for the Mexican people. . . ." He concluded by taking the oath to the constitution prescribed for all public officials under law. With that the assembly erupted in applause, riotous shouting of "Viva Carranza," and much handshaking and backslapping among the delegates. The delegates dispersed to take up their various revolutionary careers, some with distinction, others in oblivion. None became leaders in the Revolution, though Múgica was to aspire to the presidency in the 1930s and 1940s. The immediate political future in Mexico belonged to Venustiano Carranza and Álvaro Obregón. And in the presidencies of these men can be seen the two extremes of the Revolution, the opposing principles of liberalism and radicalism, both enshrined in the Constitution of 1917.[26]

Carranza promulgated the Constitution on February 5, 1917. The Catholic reaction was predictable, because the restrictions placed upon the Church at Querétaro were completely unacceptable to the hierarchy. It was impossible, however, to organize any effective opposition, for in 1917 there was little cohesion in the Mexican Church. Most of the bishops and many of the priests had been in exile for three years or more. They had lost touch with their people, and the lay organizations were disorganized and weak. During the Congress, as the delegates debated Article 3, they received a letter from "various ladies of Monterrey" protesting the measure as "oppressive of God and our holy religion." The delegates hooted and shouted with laughter when the message was read to the assembly. And on December 25 a group of Catholics in the states of Mexico, Puebla, and Michoacán published a pamphlet deprecating the attacks against freedom of education. More than 80 percent of the signers were women—who could not vote. The Catholic men of

Mexico seemed powerless to act without the presence of their bishops. Meanwhile, those bishops, who whiled away their exile in San Antonio, prepared a collective letter of protest to present to the Mexican people. It was published in Acordada, Texas, in April 1917.[27]

Denying that they were seeking to mix in political matters, the bishops maintained, nevertheless, that they could not accept a constitution so palpably contrary to God's law. They condemned armed rebellion against legally constituted authority, but they affirmed that they would work within the law, using every legal means to change the existing laws governing relations between the Church and the Mexican government. They were especially critical of the constitution's attack on the right of every head of family to educate his children according to his own conscience and his own religion by forcing attendance at lay, hence unreligious, schools. The bishops protested Article 27, which banned Church property or land holding, because without a source of income, they said, the Church would be unable to support its schools, hospitals, asylums, and other charitable works. And in Article 130, the pastoral letter said, the writers of the constitution sought to deprive the clergy of its moral authority over the people. The bishops asked if anyone could read those offending articles and not put the question—what has happened to religious freedom? The Constitution of 1917, they wrote "destroys the most sacred rights of the Catholic Church, of Mexican society, and of Christian individuals. It proclaims principles contrary to the truth taught by Jesus Christ, which are the treasury of the Church and its greatest gift to humanity, and tears out by the roots the few rights that the Constitution of 1857 . . . granted to the Church as a society and to Catholics as individuals."[28]

Archbishop Mora y del Río reinforced the collective protest in a pastoral instruction to his archdiocese. Stressing the immunity of the Church to government regulation, he distinguished between the Church as a sacred institution, subject to God's divine constitution, and secular constitutions, which were human institutions. The latter had no right to tyrannize over the former, he wrote. The Church was "a perfect society, founded by God himself," the archbishop said, and, because of its origins, was "independent of every human power." No man had the authority to oppose himself to the divine constitution of the Church or to attack its personality or its rights.

As the bishops rejected the Querétaro constitution in learned briefs, a group of Catholics in Mexico formed a National Association of Heads of Families to bombard Carranza's government with protests. But the letters were all so similar in phrasing (and almost identical with the bishop's pastoral) that it had the appearance of a clerical campaign, rather than the spontaneous reaction of outraged Catholics. From Rome Benedict XV wrote his condemnation of the constitution and his approval of the actions of the Mexican bishops and laymen. "Some of the articles of the new law," proclaimed the pontiff, "ignore the sacred rights of the Church, while others openly contradict them."[29]

In the United States the Catholic reaction to the constitution was strangely muted. Both Father Kelley and Father Tierney had subsided, and without their strident voices of protest the American Church spoke in words of moderation. Many Catholics had used the Mexican situation to further the Republican campaign against Woodrow Wilson, but without success, for the president had been reelected in the fall of 1916. Now in 1917 an assembly of the American Federation of Catholic Societies in Kansas City adopted a resolution condemning the Mexican Constitution. The American bishops, meeting in Washington drew up a similar letter of protest, though it was not sent to Wilson, for Cardinal Gibbons felt that the president was too preoccupied with the American entrance into the war to concern himself with Mexican affairs. Through 1917 and most of 1918 Americans looked to Europe and to their men in battle, to personal matters of casualties and deaths, and what had once been so important in Mexico no longer seemed to matter. When the State Department and Ambassador Henry P. Fletcher exchanged dispatches on the religious situation in Mexico, they were more likely to touch upon the restrictions of Protestant missionaires than upon the persecution of the Catholic Church. Not until the war was over and the Democrats lost control of the Congress did the issue of Mexico's religious problem erupt once more in the United States. In a partisan effort to discredit Wilson and his administration, Senator Edwin B. Fall of New Mexico led a subcommittee through an investigation of Mexican affairs. A parade of witnesses—diplomats, oilmen, priests and nuns, newspapermen—told and retold, and probably invented, stories of persecution in Mexico. At the conclusion of the investigation the committee recommended that the United States intervene if the Mexican government sought to enforce the constitution against American economic interests.[30]

The furor raised against the constitution in Mexico and in the United States was premature. The fact that Carranza had promulgated the constitution did not mean that it would be enforced. In Mexico, for each article of the constitution, a *ley reglamentaria* (implementing law), to be passed by the Congress, was necessary to fix penalties for offenses against that article. Carranza had not wanted the radical constitution. Yet he had signed it. There was little else he could do when Obregón and other powerful generals had given the radicals their personal support. But if Carranza had to sign it, he was not obliged to enforce it, and those offending articles, offending to Carranza and to the Catholics alike, were allowed to slip into a legal limbo. There were no national *leyes reglamentarias,* hence no crimes and no penalties. It seemed at the end of the 1910s that the radicals at Querétaro had perhaps gained a hollow victory against the supporters of the First Chief.

Carranza was elected president under the new constitution in April 1917 virtually without a contest. Obregón and Pablo González received scattered votes, but there was no real opposition to the First Chief. On May 1 he became the legal president of Mexico, and his long rule as First Chief in the preconstitutional period had ended. Yet the advent of legal government, of restored liberal rule, and the end of the civil wars, brought no real peace and little progress to Mexico. By insisting upon local autonomy the administration of Carranza deliberately weakened the central authority when energetic measures were needed to pull Mexico out of the slough of revolution and destruction. His generals still did what they pleased, making themselves wealthy by confiscating the properties of "enemies of the revolution," running their states like independent satrapies, and in some cases persecuting the Church by the enforcement on the state level of various articles of the federal constitution. When the Spanish novelist Vicente Blasco Ibáñez visited Mexico in 1920 to write a series of articles for American newspapers, he reported that the Revolution had been "of little use." Only a strong man could end the anarchy and restore peace to Mexico, he said. Blasco Ibáñez meant Obregón.[31]

Carranza and his government also ignored the economic and social reforms enacted at Querétaro. When workers' syndicates called for the implementation of Articles 27 and 123, Carranza turned a deaf ear to their pleas. Nor did the land question concern the administration. In 1919 Carranza ordered that any community receiving land would be obliged to pay the nation for that land. This was impossible, for few of the pueblos had the money to reimburse the government or the hacendados for lands granted. In the three years of Carranza's presidency only 190 villages received land from the government and only 180,000 hectares were distributed. The Congress, which met each September, was wracked with factional disputes, and every year it wasted a whole month of sessions with interminable discussions of the credentials of the senators and deputies. Despite the agitation of workers' groups for Congress to implement the reform articles of the constitution, the senators and deputies dallied—talking, wrangling, disputing, completely unaccustomed to parliamentary procedure and the business of getting things done with dispatch. More and more the voices of radicalism in Mexico grew critical of Carranza and looked to the succession of a man such as Obregón, with known radical tendencies.[32]

Carranza, as president, not only ignored the radical articles of the constitution, but in the field of education and religion he tried to overturn the work of the Constituent Congress. He abolished the cabinet post of Minister of Public Education and handed over the controls of the schools to the town governments, thus increasing the atomization of political control in the federal republic. In the fall of 1917 and again a year later the president asked Congress to amend the constitution to bring it more in line with the liberal principles of his government. He asked that Article 3 be revised to read: "Education shall be free, but that in official schools shall be laical. . . . Private schools shall be subject to official programs and inspection." Carranza, through his Minister of Gobernación, sought the repeal of the sections of Article 130 that granted the states the right to limit the number of priests and forbade the presence of foreign priests and ministers in Mexico. But the Congress was too concerned with factional politics and refused to act upon the requests of the president.[33]

Carranza and his cabinet thought that by turning over the schools to the localities the liberals would be creating a free Republic. Instead they hastened the disintegration of Mexico's educational system, for the attempts to institute local autonomy brought disastrous results in the cities and towns. By September 1918 the financial situation of the Mexico City ayuntamiento had become critical.

Because of the lack of funds, municipal services such as education, sanitation, and street cleaning were gravely deficient. *El Pueblo* reported that schoolteachers were "dying of hunger." Tardily made aware of the obvious crisis, Carranza, through Aguirre Berlanga, asked Congress to amend the constitution to give the federal government control over the capital and its finances as in Washington, D. C. Conditions were even more aggravated in the towns outside the capital, for they were poorer still. Mexico City had had a number of schools during the Porfirian era. The rural areas had to start from scratch; they had nothing to work with and no assistance from the federal government.[34]

Without pay for months, the teachers of Mexico City declared a general strike in May 1919. Luis Cabrera, Carranza's Secretary of the Treasury, branded the strike illegal, for the teachers were government employees. If they persisted in striking, he warned, they would give the government an opportunity to reduce the number of teachers on the city's payrolls—which were already too large for the ayuntamiento—by weeding out the undesirables (those who went on strike). In his annual message to the Congress on September 1, 1919, Carranza admitted that the situation was serious. In Mexico City alone 101 schools had been closed for lack of funds, he said. He told Congress that, because of these critical conditions, his government was modifying its policy toward education and intended to found "two superior schools and one kindergarten" in the capital.[35]

Stagnation and decay were widespread in every branch of government and in the Mexican economy. The republic was still not completely pacified. Villa held out in the North. Fighting continued with the Zapatistas, even though their leader was murdered in 1919. Travel was unsafe. Trains were held up or wrecked by rebel or bandit troops. Politicians looted the treasury, and corruption pervaded the national and state governments from the highest to the lowest levels. In some states the Church was virtually outlawed. Though the official restoration of constitutional government in 1917 had permitted the return of the bishops and clergy, some state leaders continued to persecute the Church. Calles refused to allow Bishop Valdespino y Díaz or his clergy to function in Sonora. Various state governors ordered the expulsion of foreign priests. But the harshest persecution of the Church during Carranza's administration took place in the state of Jalisco, one of the most staunchly Catholic areas in Mexico.

Francisco Orozco y Jiménez, the archbishop of Guadalajara, was the scion of a wealthy Jaliscan family and at an early age inherited a large fortune. As bishop of Chiapas he used his family's money for religious and public improvements. He built schools and gave the city of San Cristóbal it's first power and light system. Proud, aristocratic to the marrow, he cut a fine figure in his episcopal robes. Father Kelley, with his middle-class, Irish-American background, was much impressed when he met the patrician Mexican. Orozco y Jiménez lived with Kelley in Chicago for several years while the archbishop was exiled from Mexico. He appeared "born to the purple," wrote the American priest. "One could think of him as a great prelate-politician in the court of a medieval monarch." His social attitudes were those of the colonial, landowning aristocracy of Mexico. Social and economic reforms must fall like largesse from the fingers of the rich and powerful. His attitude toward the lower classes was kindly, but condescending. The poor must respect their bosses, he told his flock in a pastoral letter. A militant archbishop, zealous of his own and the Church's privileges and rights, he towered above the other Mexican churchmen in defense of the Church, and it was natural that he should draw the lightning bolts of the revolutionary leaders. In his personality he summed up the strengths and weaknesses of the Mexican Catholic Church. He was an outstanding archbishop, but his day had passed; he belonged to viceregal Mexico, not to the twentieth century.[36]

The archbishop of Guadalajara left Mexico in 1914 when Obregón's troops occupied Jalisco. For more than two years he stayed in Chicago at DePaul University with Francisco Plancarte, the archbishop of Linares, Leopoldo Ruiz y Flores, the bishop of Michoacán, and Father Francisco Banegas. Both Banegas and Archbishop Plancarte were students of Mexican prehistory, and they passed the time in exile in scholarly research and writing, showing little concern for the religious situation in Mexico. But Orozco y Jiménez preferred action to scholarship. He champed at the bit, eager to return to the fray in his beloved state. He told Kelley: "I have heard that it is being said by some people that the Mexican bishops are not brave, that they deserted their people to save themselves." In late 1916 he decided to go back to Mexico. He kept his mission a secret from his fellow exiles in Chicago and from the group of Mexican prelates and priests around Mora y del Río in San Antonio. In disguise Orozco y Jiménez slipped across the border into Mexico and made his way to Jalisco. For a year and a half he played hare to the revolutionary hounds, keeping on the move throughout his archdiocese. Well-loved by the people of Jalisco, he was protected wherever he went. By means of an elaborate warning system set up to signal the approach of government troops, he was able to avoid capture. From November 1916 until July 1918, he traveled from village to village, sometimes in the guise of a mule driver, often living in caves or hovels, bringing the clergy of his archdiocese together for retreats and administering confirmation to the faithful. At the same time, most of the other bishops of Mexico remained in San Antonio and Chicago, and they made no attempt to return until the Carranza government proclaimed an amnesty.[37]

Orozco y Jiménez could not sign the pastoral protest issued by the prelates in April 1917, because he was not in San Antonio. He wrote and published his own pastoral letter, however, which was read at several churches in Guadalajara on Sunday, July 8. Accusing the constitution makers of seeking to "subject and oppress" the Church in Mexico, he asked how Catholics could "suffer an order of things that obliges them not only to renounce the most sought gift of heaven, but also to ratify this oppression by their acquiescence?" "Now is the time," he wrote, "to revive within ourselves the true Catholic spirit, to eliminate all compromise with modern errors, which are condemned by the Church, and to separate the chaff from the wheat. Then the splendor of high Christian virtue will shine forth; then the enemies of the Church will recognize and glorify God and His Christ!" Three days later the soldiers of Governor Manuel Diéguez arrested the priests of the cathedral for reading the pastoral. Diéguez termed the letter "seditious," and Colonel Fortunato Martínez, military commander in the city, condemned the prelate as "an archtraitor to his country." On July 16 Diéguez closed all those churches in the city in which the pastoral had been read. He pointed out that under the federal constitution the churches belonged to the nation and could be used solely for religious purposes, not for the "dissemination of sedition." At the end of July, with the churches still shut, several committees of Catholic ladies, students, and lawyers went to Mexico City to protest to Carranza. They showed the president a copy of the pastoral letter. While he agreed that it was not seditious, he said that he considered it a local, not a national, problem. He told the Catholics that the matter was in the hands of the state governor and district judges, and that they would settle it in Guadalajara. Meanwhile, the revolutionary troops in Jalisco redoubled their efforts to track down Orozco y Jiménez, but without success. He continued to move about the state as he pleased.[38]

For the next several months the principal churches in Guadalajara remained closed, though there were services in some of the smaller parishes of the city in which the letter had not been read. On October 20, 1917, Diéguez' government permitted the reopening of the cathedral, and on December 12 the Guadalupe church held services. Still, the government maintained its harassment of Catholics in the city. On Ash Wednesday of 1918 Diéguez stationed guards at the doors of the churches in Guadalajara where services were held. Soldiers stopped each person leaving the church with ashes on his forehead and advised him to remove them. If it was not done, they took him to the police station where the spot was wiped off by force and a fine levied. The government announced that it would put an end to this "dirty custom," for the law forbade all "outward signs of religious faith."[39]

General Diéguez, like Calles in Sonora, was a convinced anti-cleric, who believed in strict control of the clergy in his state. Under his direction, the acting governor, Manuel Bouquet, Jr., and the pliant state legislature prepared laws to restrict the number of Catholic priests in the state. Decree 1913 was published by Bouquet on July 3, 1918, to go into effect on August 1 in Guadalajara and a month later in the rest of the state. It stipulated that one priest might officiate in each church that was open, but that only one priest would be permitted for each 5,000 inhabitants of the state. Presumably all churches without priests would be closed by the government. The bishop would designate the priests who could officiate, and each priest would be compelled to register with the public authorities in his town or village, presenting a birth certificate, to prove that he was of Mexican nationality, and three identification photographs. Government lawyers pointed out that the decree was probably unconstitutional, because in permitting the ecclesiastical superiors to designate the registered priest for a church it recognized the juridical personality of the Church, which was forbidden in Article 130 of the federal constitution.[40]

108   THE CONSTITUTION OF 1917

To remedy this defect in the decree the state legislature convened in special session and replaced Decree 1913 with Decree 1927. The principal change was that the priest, not his superior, would make a "solicitation" to the governor to officiate at services or to be in charge of a church. The decree was further modified when Catholics objected to the word "solicitation," and Bouquet published an "aclaración"—without legislative concurrence—substituting the word "aviso" or "notice." Despite the "aclaración" of Bouquet, the decree remained unacceptable to Jaliscan Catholics, for it was based on the government's asserted right to insinuate itself in purely ecclesiastical matters, that is, to determine the number of priests that could serve in the state. Moreover, if the government could force a priest to register, it could presumably refuse to register him and remove the control of the clergy from the bishop to the governor, since an unregistered priest could not use a church. And the decree implied that the churches were the property of the state, to be disposed of as the officials desired. The leaders of the Church were determined to resist. For the first time there would be a real test of the constitutional restrictions imposed by Article 130 on the Mexican Church.[41]

On the day following the promulgation of Decree 1913 Orozco y Jiménez was in Lagos, one of the larger towns in his archdiocese. Now he did not try to hide his presence, and the publicity accorded his coming indicated that the archbishop was no longer running from the government. It seemed as though he was forcing himself upon the attention of the authorities, that he was courting arrest— that by becoming a martyr he might bring about the rising of an aroused people against their oppressors and an unjust constitution. He sang a pontifical High Mass in Lagos' chief parochial church and administered confirmation to the children of the parish. On the evening of July 4 soldiers came to the parish house, where the archbishop was passing the night, with orders from General Diéguez for his arrest. Orozco y Jiménez immediately demanded a writ of *amparo* (similar to an injunction), and a stay of his arrest was ordered by the local civil judge. The soldiers in Lagos refused to recognize the legal decision, however, and Diéguez threatened to "stick the judge, the *amparo,* and the laws into the mouth of a cannon."[42]

When word of the archbishop's arrest became public many Catholics in Mexico and in the United States feared for his life. But

Diéguez had no intention of spilling the blood of a Church leader. He wanted merely to rid his state of a troublesome gadfly, to send the archbishop back into exile with the other Mexican prelates. Orozco y Jiménez was put in a cattle car with some guards—the military commander of the train, General César López de Lara and his staff traveled comfortably in a parlor car—and was shipped off to Aguascalientes, San Luis Potosí, and Tampico. In Tampico he filed a new demand for an *amparo*, but the American consul in the city persuaded him to withdraw it to avoid further trouble with the military. Orozco y Jiménez sent a telegram to Father Kelley in Chicago: "My father is very sick, and I fear for his recovery." It was a code prearranged between the two before the archbishop returned to Mexico to advise Kelley that he had been arrested. Kelley dispatched a telegram to President Wilson, informing him of Orozco y Jiménez' seizure and detention. "I beg of you to do what you can," wrote Kelley. American intervention was unnecessary, however, for the archbishop was already on his way to Laredo by train, and he was put across the border safely to take up once more the life of an exile.[43]

In Jalisco the protests against Decrees 1913 and 1927 merged with those against the arrest and expulsion of the archbishop. The leaders of Damas Católicas, the Catholic Youth Association (ACJM), and other groups met to formulate a plan for united action. Though some asked for a public demonstration later the same day, an inopportune heavy rain shower made this form of protest unattractive, and so the occasion for a serious clash was avoided. In its turn a radical club in Guadalajara circulated propaganda leaflets to support the civil authorities. The Catholics printed posters to be displayed in front windows of homes throughout the city as a means of protest. When the semiofficial periodical *El Occidental* published a story that the government was noting which houses displayed posters and would take appropriate action, most were removed from the windows. By the end of the month the Catholics had decided to seek legal action to stay the execution of Decree 1927. On July 31 Catholic lawyers asked the district judge to issue an *amparo* against the enforcement of the decree on the grounds that it was unconstitutional. The judge refused to grant the request, holding that the decree affected the priests in the state, not the individuals who had brought legal action. In any event, the Catholic priests were unwilling to seek a postponement of the decree, for what they wanted was its repeal. They decided to refuse to accept the decree and to withdraw from all the churches until the government backed down and rescinded its order. On the last day of July the priests were busy as never before, hearing confessions, baptizing infants, marrying Catholic couples in anticipation that services would cease on August 1.[44]

The action of the Catholics in Jalisco was clearly a strike against the state government, though it was not called a strike at the time. There would be no services in the churches until the noxious decree was revoked. On August 2 the vicar-general of the archdiocese (acting in the absence of Orozco y Jiménez) published an instruction to the faithful proclaiming that "one must obey God rather than man." "No one can accuse us of being disobedient or rebellious," he said. It would be a passive resistance, not a resort to armed force. On September 1 the ban against church services was extended throughout Jalisco. A pall of gloom fell over the state as the public religious activity came to a standstill. To bring more pressure on the state government, the Catholics organized an economic boycott. Women stayed at home and bought as little as possible. Theaters were virtually empty. Though the priests and laymen concurred in the boycott, the action against the government was largely in the hands of the upper-class women of Jalisco. They organized flying committees to go about the capital and the state, exhorting other women to stand fast against the decrees. The state legislature met again in November, but refused to heed continued demands for the modification or annulment of the law. In early December there were reports that the vicar-general would celebrate Mass in the cathedral to honor the Virgin of Guadalupe, but the governor refused to permit any priest who had not registered to officiate. The planned service was canceled. There were no Masses in the cathedral on Christmas Day for the first time in Jaliscan history.[45]

The Church strike continued into the first month of 1919, before Diéguez, now in the governor's chair again, decided to give way to the demands of the Catholics. On February 8 he announced that the permanent commission of the state legislature had voted the abolition of decrees 1913 and 1927. In March the legislature met to debate the matter. Those in favor held that the decrees were ineffective, for the "clergy did not observe them." Others attacked the clergy as "rebellious" and opposed changing a law simply because it was disobeyed. But after a heated discussion, the action of the governor was approved overwhelmingly by the legislators, and the offending decrees were offically rescinded. Throughout the state, church services resumed, and the economic boycott came to an end. The Catholics in Jalisco had seemingly won the day. By resolute action against the government, by refusing to accept an unjust law, they had forced the revolutionary authorities to retreat. Seven years later the Mexican Catholics were to try the same tactics on a national scale against the enforcement of the constitution by President Plutarco Elías Calles.[46]

At the end of 1919 the position of the Church in Mexico had improved considerably. The bishops and most of the priests had been allowed to return from exile. Again the leaders of the Church began to take the offensive, composing pastoral letters to warn the faithful against the dangers of socialism, authorizing the publication of books and pamphlets to set forth the Catholic position on education and on the social problems, and promoting the formation and extension of lay societies to implement the program of Leo XIII. The laymen threw themselves once more into the revived Catholic Action movement. A group of Catholics created a new political party to contest the coming election as a successor to Carranza was chosen. Because the constitution prohibited parties that bore religious labels, the founders of the new organization called it the National Republican Party. The leading figures were all closely associated, however, with the old Catholic Party and with the earlier attempt at Catholic Social Action during the Madero era. Heading the executive committee were Rafael Ceniceros y Villarreal (the former governor of Zacatecas), René Capistrán Garza, and Luis M. Flores. The committee worked closely with Emilio Pimentel, once governor of Oaxaca under Díaz, and Carlos B. Zetina, a founder of the Knights of Columbus in Mexico. The party platform promised reform of the constitution to restore religious liberty and freedom of education and to settle labor and agrarian problems, "without prejudice to property rights." Obregón, who planned to enter the campaign also, said mockingly: "The National Republican Party was born dead." There was no chance in 1920 that a Catholic candidate, even wearing a secular disguise, could win against a revolutionary.

Obregón was the logical candidate to succeed the aging Carranza, who was barred under the constitution from seeking reelection. Obregón was still the most powerful general in Mexico and had served in Carranza's cabinet. He had wide support among the revolutionaries who had fought for the First Chief. But Carranza held stubbornly to his notions of civilian control of the government, and he named as the official candidate for the presidency Ignacio Bonillas, who was virtually unknown in Mexico. Bonillas was not a revolutionary; he could not have given Mexico the vigorous leadership it needed. His election seemed to foreordain that the stagnation and corruption inherent in Carranza's laissez-faire attitude toward politics and politicians would continue. The prospect of four more years of Carrancism was too much for Obregón. Certain that the president would manipulate the balloting to secure Bonillas' election, Obregón proclaimed his plan of Agua Prieta on April 23, 1920, launching a revolution against his chief. When Pablo González declared for Obregón's revolution, all support for Carranza melted away. Within two weeks rebel troops entered Mexico City. The president attempted to flee to Veracruz, carrying part of the national treasury with him, but he was overtaken by forces loyal to Obregón and, without the knowledge of Obregón, shot and killed. Carranza died, as Madero before him, because he had unleashed powerful forces that he could not master. Neither could he halt the march of Mexico's Revolution toward the creation of a vigorous national government.

With Carranza's assassination, liberalism ceased to be a force in Mexican politics. The Catholics in Mexico had condemned liberalism, had fought Juárez, Lerdo, Madero, and Carranza, because their political philosophy conflicted with the teachings of Pius IX and Leo XIII. But by the second decade of the twentieth century the hated liberalism was the sole protection of the Mexican Church. However distasteful the Reform Laws had been, the Church had lived with them. In the Congress at Querétaro it had been Macías, Cravioto, Palavicini, and Rojas who had supported Carranza's call for religious toleration. During nearly four years President Carranza ignored the radical features of the constitution. After 1920 the Catholics had no shield but the strength of the Church itself. By 1926 many Catholics in Mexico were regretting their stubbornness toward the liberals. Although they wore no sackcloth and ashes, and there was no beating of breasts—the Catholics never publicly admitted an error—many Churchmen experienced a desire to return to the relationship between Church and State under the liberal governments. But it was much too late, for the nineteenth-century philosophy had died. Carranza was Mexico's last liberal.

5

The Obregonian
Renaissance

ÁLVARO OBREGÓN, who in September 1920 easily defeated the Catholic candidate, Alfredo Robles Domínguez, for the presidency, belonged to the new generation of revolutionaries. The death of Carranza signified the end of the nineteenth-century political views that had guided the Constitutionalists since 1913. Obregón's presidency heralded the new radical phase, the era of social and economic reform. Beginning in 1920 Mexico turned to the fulfillment of promises made three years earlier at Querétaro and included in Articles 3, 27, and 123 of the constitution. But progress was slow, for Obregón was no doctrinaire radical. He favored conciliation and compromise, wherever possible. He replaced the stubbornness of Carranza with a pliability of spirit that encompassed all parties. He decreed an amnesty for the old enemies of the Constitutionalists, and Zapatistas and Villistas joined with Carrancistas to provide a regime of national unity for Mexico. Antonio Díaz Soto y Gama, onetime anarchist and representative of Zapata in the Aguascalientes Convention, became Obregón's close associate and adviser. The president named José Vasconcelos, who had served briefly in the Conventionist cabinet of Eulalio Gutiérrez in 1914 and early 1915, to the newly created post of Secretary of Public Instruction to reform Mexico's educational system. Exiles of all stripes were now free to return to Mexico to resume old careers or to accept new positions with the government. Even Villa, the old personal enemy of Obregón, ended his long struggle against the Constitutionalists, to make his peace with the administration, and took up the life of a wealthy rancher and successful revolutionary.[1]

There were other reasons, besides Obregón's personal desire for conciliation, however, for his failure to implement immediately the decisions of Querétaro. His coming to power coincided with the world-wide recession at the end of World War I, and Mexico's economy, badly damaged by the years of revolution and civil war since 1910, was hard hit by the slump in the silver, copper, and lead markets. Obregón's principal problem as president (and it was a problem he handed on to his successor Plutarco Elías Calles in 1924) was fiscal—to put the government on a firm financial basis. He did not deem this an appropriate time for rapid or costly economic and social reform in Mexico. Moreover, Obregón knew that precipitate action might antagonize the United States.

Because Obregón had come into office by means of a revolution against the legal government of Venustiano Carranza, the American government held that the military coup broke the continuity of recognition that had been granted to the Constitutionalist First Chief in 1915. Recognition for the new regime was a matter to be studied and negotiated, and the administration in Washington was determined to take a hard look at the credentials of Obregón and his revolution. The State Department, no doubt influenced by the oil interests in the Harding administration, was sufficiently exercised by the oil expropriation provision of the Mexican constitution, without Obregón's giving the United States further reason for withholding recognition. Secretary of State Charles Evans Hughes announced the position of the Harding government on the recognition of Obregón: "The fundamental question which confronts the government of the United States in considering its relation with Mexico is the safeguarding of property rights against confiscation.... Whenever Mexico is ready to give assurance that she will perform her fundamental obligation in the protection both of persons and of rights of property validly acquired, there will be no obstacle to the most advantageous relations between the two peoples . . . ." If Mexico agreed not to enforce the restrictions of the constitution against the American interests, the United States would bestow its approbation and recognition upon the pliant regime of Obregón. On the other hand, if the offending articles of the constitution were implemented by the Mexican Congress, and if the government of Obregón moved to nationalize American holdings, particularly the oil properties, Obregón must deal with the United States as an unfriendly power. This was not a prospect to be viewed with complacency by the Mexican government.[2]

Even though the United States might not intervene actively in Mexico, as Wilson had done at Veracruz, the ability of the American government to refuse arms to one faction and to permit them to another meant that, for all intents, the attitude of the administration in Washington was a critical factor in the ability of any Mexican government to sustain itself. This was the blackjack that Harding's government held over Obregón's regime. Washington withheld recognition until August 1923, three years after Obregón came to power. Not until the State Department was satisfied that American interests would receive special consideration in Mexico did it agree to restore normal diplomatic relations between the two countries. In view of the delicate balance of negotiations for recognition, it is not surprising that the Obregón administration took its time applying the constitution.[3]

Obregón's greatest achievement as president was to restore peace and to install in Mexico City a national regime that showed concern for the social and economic well-being of the Mexican people. Gone was the laissez-faire attitude of the Carranza administration. The government in the early 1920s took an active role in promoting labor unions, in preparing the countryside for agrarian reform, in making possible a national renaissance in literature, art, and music, and above all in creating a cohesive national system of education. Under Obregón Mexico's Revolution became frankly nationalistic. Things Mexican, so long despised by the ruling classes, were now exalted. Vasconcelos saw his people as a super race, *la raza cósmica*, the hope for the future of mankind.[4] Mexico began to recover its own heritage. No longer were the Indians considered an inferior race, as they had been by the positivists. The Revolution glorified the native. Ancient ways were revived and emulated. Cuauhtémoc, the last Aztec emperor, became a virtual demigod, the apotheosis of Mexican resistance to foreign conquerors. Mexico rediscovered the merit of its long-neglected indigenous art form. Mexicans recognized the intrinsic worth of the pottery of Oaxaca, Saltillo, and Toluca. In rural schools the ancient arts of weaving and of the rubbed lacquers of Michoacán were revived. The government of Obregón believed that art was a potent force in the attempt to unite all Mexicans under the aegis of the Revolution—and to woo them from their allegiance to the Catholic Church.

During the 1920s Mexico developed a revolutionary art perhaps unequaled in the modern world for its virility and strength of purpose. Nowhere was the religious fervor of the Revolution more apparent than in the secular propagandistic painting of José Clemente Orozco, Diego Rivera, and David Siqueiros. In the colonial era, with the Catholic Church in its ascendance, the native artistic genius found an outlet in the building and decorating of churches. Under the Revolution this genius burst forth again, but now to glorify and explain the new gospel of the secular rival of the Church —the nationalistic government. Mexican artists utilized public buildings to paint imaginative murals on revolutionary themes, bringing the message of the Revolution to the many who could not read.

Much of the messianic fervor in the revolutionary government came through the presence in Obregón's cabinet of José Vasconcelos, the young philosopher-educator. Vasconcelos saw himself as the apostle of the new secular religion, and all his projects, all his public utterances, were imbued with a missionary spirit. His role as Secretary of Public Education, he said, was to "preach the gospel of the mestizo by trying to impress on the minds of the new race a consciousness of their mission as builders of entirely new concepts of life." And Moisés Sáenz, who later served President Plutarco Elías Calles in the Ministry of Education, wrote that his government was seeking "to bring into the fold of the Mexican family the two million Indians, to make them think and feel in Spanish, to incorporate them into that type of civilization which constitutes the Mexican nationality." "In Mexico," he said, "we are consciously striving to bring about national unity by means of the school." It was no easy matter, however, to incorporate the Indians into a national Mexican culture. Many of them spoke no Spanish, and there were over 50 distinct dialects or languages to make communication difficult. Many Indians still lived much as their ancestors had in the days of the Conquest, and because they spoke (to most Mexicans) alien tongues, there could be no meeting of minds or fusion of cultures. Most rural areas lacked a sense of national feeling. Though much adulterated by preconquest paganism, the Catholic religion represented the sole unifying tie in Mexico among the many peoples. Under Vasconcelos and his successor, J. M. Puig Casauranc, the national government, through its rural education program, sought to replace Catholicism with revolutionary nationalism as the force to bind Mexicans together. The antiquated, passively lay school of the liberals gave way to the actively nationalistic school. Education came to be the most potent weapon of the Revolution, and, to the Catholics, a dangerous weapon, for the exclusive nature of revolutionary education, as dictated by Article 3 of the Querétaro constitution, meant the eventual end of all Catholic primary schools. Thus the most important area for potential conflict between the Church and the State in Mexico during the 1920s lay in the field of education. The Obregonian peace allowed the Church freedom to build its social program anew. But it also gave the government the opportunity to construct its own counter way of life, and education provided the bedrock for both programs.[5]

As Vasconcelos prepared in 1921 to take charge of the Ministry of Public Education, he bubbled over with enthusiasm for his new career. He saw his duty as "saving the children, educating the youth, and redeeming the Indians." He would turn over the Department of Indigenous Education, he said, to "teachers who would imitate the actions of the Catholic missionaries of the colonies, sent among the Indians, who did not, as yet, know the Spanish language." Vasconcelos' enthusiasm was contagious, and he communicated his ideas of pedagogical salvation to the employees in his department, from the bureaucrat in Mexico City to the young teacher in the smallest school in the republic. The Secretary of Education sounded a call for intellectuals and teachers to enlist as secular missionaries in the fight to educate the rural population. He asked for "teachers animated with apostolic fervor, who would go into the countryside to teach living, teachers of work and of love." He called for a "holy crusade for civilization." "It is necessary," he said, "that the intellectual cleanse himself of his pride, learning the hard, simple life of the men of the people. . . ." Among those who responded to his challenge was the Chilean poetess, Gabriela Mistral.[6]

Vasconcelos, the philosopher, was also a visionary. Though he brought great quantities of cheap books to the people, often the books, while meat for the intellectual, were a too-rich diet for those who were just beginning to master the difficult art of reading. He issued inexpensive translations of Romain Rolland, Bernard Shaw, Plato, Walter Pater, Upton Sinclair, Dante, Plotinus, Homer, and Euripides. Vasconcelos was the butt of many a jest for his utopian-

ism, and even President Obregón could not resist the temptation to
make sport of his Secretary of Public Education, while the two
toured the Republic together. But the dreamer was not to be despised, for Mexico needed men of vision, who could aspire for what
was perhaps impossible, but who would make the effort to achieve
their dreams. Vasconcelos saw the rural teachers of Mexico in the
roles of Peter of Ghent and Father Motolinía, churchmen of the
sixteenth century, and he inspired the missionary efforts of the
Revolution. If Vasconcelos in his later and more splenetic years
denied his younger revolutionary self and moved to the extreme
right, his important work in the first years of the Social Revolution
cannot be gainsaid.[7]

Yet if Vasconcelos intended his teachers to imitate the Christian
missionaires of the Conquest, the message they carried was of a
different substance, for they brought the Social Revolution to the
people. Vasconcelos told an audience in Washington, D. C., that the
Indian in Mexico would be uplifted through education, through the
labors of Obregón's government, which was replacing soldiers with
teachers, and through the heroic efforts of the educational missionaries. With Vasconcelos the revolutionary byword became "to educate is to redeem"—not from sin, but from ignorance, not to re-
wards in the hereafter, but to sanitation and to a better and more
fruitful earthly life. This was what the new secular religion promised. Its emphasis, despite its religious trappings, was of this world.
It was material; it offered here-and-now happiness.

The missionary teachers marched in the van of the offensive
against "fanaticism" launched by the revolution. Directed by the
Department of Education, the cultural missionary and the rural
teacher came increasingly to take the place of the priest in the
agrarian communities. The school was more than a place to read
and write; it was to be a community institution—the House of the
People. The teacher would help the villagers build chicken coops,
stables, apiaries; he would "awaken the spirit of cooperation and
association." The House of the People would unite all members of
the village and put an end to enmities among its inhabitants. Its
influence would reach into every family, promised the *Bulletin* of the
Secretary of Public Education, establishing a "current of understanding and of cooperation between the home and the school." A
sympathetic American observer wrote: "The teacher had to serve
every office from scribe to medicine man, from agronomist to ar-

chitect. He had to know everything, for no one else had any contact with the modern world." According to the periodical, *Escuela Rural,* the teacher would be not merely a transmitter of knowledge, but a true "leader" of the community. His influence would be felt among children, youths, and adults. He would aid his neighbors to solve the personal problems of daily life; through his sage counsels, he would guide the conscience of the people. The rural teacher was to be a priest without a cassock, carrying the banner of the Revolution, instead of the cross of Christ. And like the earlier Christian missionaries, many cultural missionaries and rural teachers became martyrs to their cause. Many were attacked, some killed, by villagers whose curates preached against the coming of secular education.[8]

The priests conducted a constant campaign against the state schools. Moisés Sáenz said that he knew of but two priests who were not antagonistic to the village public schools. "Experience has taught us," he wrote, "simply to take their hostility for granted." The Church attacked public education chiefly by playing upon the peasants' fears of eternal damnation. The priests and bishops threatened to excommunicate parents who sent their children to the secular schools. Nor did the Catholic clergy scorn the use of underhanded propaganda—they appealed to the passions of the masses by spreading falsehoods and half-truths about public school teachers, garbed in lurid language. While most Mexicans disregarded the clerical threats, the campaign had considerable effect in the western, more Catholic areas of the country. And American Catholics, to turn public opinion in the United States against the Revolution, added fuel to the fire by repeating the tales spread by their Mexican counterparts. The Knights of Columbus charged in a pamphlet that "wholesale prostitution and the ideal of free love" were the objectives of Mexico's revolutionary leaders and their "brothers in viciousness." "The type of instruction now being given in the schools is such that a growing number of young girls are ruined every year." Archbishop Michael J. Curley of Baltimore wrote: "God must be banished. The lights of heaven must be put out. Mexican children must be raised atheistic as far as the red government is concerned."[9]

During the four years of his administration, however, Obregón made no move to resurrect Article 3 or to enforce its restrictions on the Church. Catholic schools, if not encouraged by the government, were nonetheless tolerated. Obregón was not a practicing Catholic, but he was realistic. He told Ernest Gruening, an American writer in Mexico: "Yes, it is illegal, and we are not unaware of the menace of these Catholic schools, whose aim is to inculcate antigovernment and antirevolutionary propaganda. But at the present there is not money enough, nor facilities for the government to teach all Mexican children. It is preferable that they receive any instruction, rather than grow up illiterate." Until 1926 the Church continued to operate and even to expand its own educational system. At the same time that Obregón and Vasconcelos were creating the new nationalistic, revolutionary school, the Catholics promoted the Church school as the basis for the whole Social Action movement. Thus the conflict of ideologies between the Catholic Church and the Mexican Revolution was most sharp in the realm of education.[10]

To determine Mexico's future direction it was essential to control the minds of the youth. Múgica and the radicals recognized this fact at Querétaro and stipulated that all primary education, public or private, be lay and neutral. They reasoned that the child would, in his formative years, be weaned from "fanaticism." That the Revolution did not intend the government to be passively neutral, however, was recognized by the Catholics. State education, they feared, would create the revolutionary child, the child free from religious influences. It was against this threat that Catholic Social Action mobilized its forces in the early 1920s.

Thus Catholic education policies in Mexico had a double goal. The first policy was only temporary. It aimed to educate the Catholic children as well as possible within the revolutionary framework. If necessary, the Catholics would operate their schools according to Mexican law. They would constantly strive to undermine the law, however, ignoring it, if possible, reforming it by legal means, if the government would permit. But the long-range policy, consonant with the Catholic philosophy of education, was more exclusive, demanding nothing less than clerical domination of all education in Mexico. The Catholics, then, under Obregón and later under Calles, blew both hot and cold, demanding religious tolerance and freedom of education for themselves against the exclusive educational activities of the Revolution, and, at the same time, working toward the final goal of Catholicism—an education that would be entirely Christian, entirely controlled by the Church, with no toleration for secular or non-Catholic schools. The second policy represented the true aim of the Church. It would be uncompromising in its attitude toward the Revolution; it was basically antagonistic to the Revolution's aspirations and was entirely incompatible with the revolutionary demands for an actively secular, antireligious educational system. It is at once apparent that there could be no conciliation, no compromise between these two extremes. The revolutionary and Catholic goals were inevitably and eternally exclusive.

The threat to implement Article 3 was a Damocles sword that hung over the head of the Church between 1920 and 1926. When the revolutionary government decided the time was ripe, the constitutional restrictions would be enforced. But even without implementation, the Catholics faced serious problems in finding means to supplant the unreligious state schools with parochial schools of their own. The vaunted wealth of the Church had simply disappeared, swallowed up in the nineteenth-century confiscations under the Reform Laws. The Catholics needed money to build and support their schools, and little was available. The pastoral letters of the 1920s, as in the Porfirian period, were filled with admonitions to the faithful of their duty to tithe. Modern schools cost money, and the Church could never match the means of the Mexican government with its powers of compulsory taxation. But tithing rested on Christian charity and moral suasion, and these were in no sense obligatory. The Mexican Catholics, then, plagued by the lack of money, harried by possible government restrictions on parochial education, had no immediate hope of realizing their dream for Church-controlled education. No hope, that is, without a miraculous reformation of Mexican society. The Mexicans must turn from Mammon to God, from the Revolution to the Church. There must be a mass spiritual conversion of Mexican society. This was the immediate aim of the Catholic Action movement in the early 1920s.

Obregón's firm control of the Mexican government facilitated the rapid development of the two rival ideologies. Social Action grew apace, building on the foundation laid a decade earlier during the era of Maderista democracy. And the government, too, promoted its own system of social reformation. Public education represented the forward salient in the battle of the Revolution against Catholicism in Mexico. Now the government took an active role in solving land problems and in aiding the urban workers. Under Obregón agrarian reforms began in earnest. The vacillation of the liberal Constitutionalists was replaced by the purposeful advance of the Social Revolution. The first steps were small, for Article 27 was not yet implemented in the Congress, but no longer did the government debate whether land should be granted. It was granted. The question was, rather, to whom and how? In the 1920s the emphasis moved from individual holdings to communal or ejidal holdings, from nineteenth-century liberalism to a modern yet ancient native socialism. Contrary to the policies of the Carranza administration, the Obregón government recognized frankly that the villagers would not be able to repay the owner for land expropriated to create ejidos. Government rural banks furnished the money, with the landowner to be repaid over a long period, and at a fraction of the true value of his hacienda.

It was soon apparent that the newly formed ejidos were not capable of self-management, for the peasants had no experience in running complicated fiscal affairs. The national government, therefore, through its Agrarian Commission, came more and more to assume the role of manager, as well as donor, of the communal holdings. And the rural banks, which furnished credit to the ejidatarios, also exercised close control over the management of the land. This process of extended governmental authority over the agrarian classes aided in the centralization process by which the presidency and the national government overrode the restrictions of the constitutional federal system, and it provided the president with a strong loyal force with which to counter revolutionary pronouncements and military rebellions. When Adolfo de la Huerta revolted against the Obregón regime in 1923 because Obregón had imposed the presidential candidacy of Plutarco Elías Calles, he led out a large part of the regular army. Obregón won against de la Huerta in part because of the loyalty of the agrarian and labor groups (and also because of timely aid from the American government, which had only recently extended diplomatic recognition to Obregón's regime).[11]

The Church condemned these revolutionary agrarian reforms, because they did not take into consideration the "just rights of the landowners." Archbishop Leopoldo Ruiz y Flores of Michoacán warned the faithful of his archdiocese that they could accept land only if it belonged to the government or if it had been held illegally. If the authorities forced acceptance at the threat of reprisal for refusing, he said, the peasant could receive the land, but he was under obligation to repay the original owner. The Catholics were partisans of prudent land divisions, wrote Ruiz y Flores, but they also felt that large estates were necessary, for the rich owner was an "example" to his neighbor. Catholics at an agricultural congress in 1921 heard that agrarian reforms, including the creating of small properties, must be achieved slowly, not rudely and illegally under the Constitution of 1917. The solution of the agrarian problem would perhaps be long delayed, but it must come by "intense cultural labor and development through the organization of Catholic Action centers."[12]

The revolutionaries saw in the government program of rural education and agrarian reform an opportunity to establish cooperative groups to aid farm production and the rural consumers. The government organized farm banks, similar to the Catholic Cajas Raiffeisen and invited members of the cooperatives to open savings accounts as a basis for rural credit. Most of the money in these banks came, however, from the national government. In this way the state-sponsored cooperatives held an advantage over the Catholic societies. But even this source of funds was limited, and the cooperative movement made little headway. In the 1920s neither the Mexican people nor the government could support such an ambitious program.[13]

The revolutionary government also took an intense interest in the growth of a strong labor union movement. In 1918 the Confederación Regional Obrera Mexicana was formed to replace the syndicalist union organized in the early days of the Revolution. From its initiation this new labor organization appeared superficially to be Marxist in character, for its constitution was predicated on the existence of class struggle in society. The founders declared that "the exploited class," which constituted the majority of the manual workers, had "the right to start a class war to bring about the economic and moral improvement of their conditions and finally their complete freedom from the tyranny of capitalism." But the evidences of Marxist influences proved to be only illusory, for CROM bore a marked resemblance to the American Federation of Labor in its aims and methods. The organization's official periodical denied that the Mexican workers desired "integral socialism," much less Russian communism. Mexico was in a period of transition, the editors wrote, and it was necessary to make concessions to capitalism. Only through a revolutionary state could the workers achieve control of production. The editors denied that they or the Mexican workers concerned themselves with European ideologies, though they "respected them." The trade union movement, they said, was a Mexican phenomenon brought about to cure conditions that were purely Mexican. Under Obregón CROM was sponsored and protected by the government, and under Calles it became a pillar for the support of the State. Luis Morones, president of the labor organization, became Secretary of Industry in Calles' cabinet.[14]

From its foundation CROM drew the reprobation of the Church. The bishops forbade Catholics to join the secular unions under pain of mortal sin. In turn the unions showed hostility to the Church and to the Catholic labor groups, and many of the leaders and members were frankly antireligious. The unions helped the government against the Catholic groups, trying to end what they called the "hold" of the priests over the Mexican people. By force and by propaganda they prevented the workers from joining the Catholic movement. An editorialist for CROM's periodical wrote that only the secular unions could break the workers' chains, wrought by the capitalists, the latifundists, and the clerics. He termed the National Catholic Farmers' syndicate "a veritable school of abjection, of fanaticism, and of ignominy worthy of the thirteenth century." In this organization the poor farmer would find himself "terrorized by the chastisements of God and the threats of the master."[15]

Alarmed by this rampant radicalism among the working classes, the Catholic Church strengthened its Social Action program. But as in 1913, the underlying current in the movement was fear of the socialists, and this fear turned the emphasis from social amelioration toward a profitless campaign of sniping at the radicals. The antisocialist character of the Catholic movement was apparent from the moment of its revival in late 1919. In a Social Week, held in Puebla, the many priests who addressed the delegates stressed the necessity of scheduling more meetings throughout Mexico to help stem the "rising tide of socialism." Several speakers equated socialism with free love and feminism, both of which the Church had condemned. One priest pointed to the dangers of the socialistic doctrines of class struggle. The Mexican workers, he said, wanted peace, love, and justice, not hate, destruction, and ruin. They wished to extend their arms and "embrace all—rich and poor, bosses and workers."[16] In 1921, Ruiz y Flores warned the faithful of his archdiocese, in a pastoral letter, against the evils of socialism. It was not possible, he insisted, to remain within the Church while following the teachings of the socialists. The archbishop rejected the notion of a classless society as an absurdity, for society could no more exist without classes than could a body live without its members. The classless society, which denied the natural right of some classes to lead others, he wrote, was a state without authority—an impossibility, since all authority was God-given. Archbishop Mora y del Río, the primate of Mexico, also cautioned Mexico's Catholics against joining the socialistic groups. The Church taught, he said, that all classes must live in harmony, not in perpetual strife.[17]

Like his fellow archbishops, Orozco y Jiménez in Jalisco also sounded the alarm against the dangerous encroachments of radicalism. He told members of his archdiocese that the poor could not combat poverty by embracing socialism, for their several masters would be replaced by one master—the socialistic State. He called for a war of ideas against the infiltration of socialism into Catholic Mexico, since ideas could be defeated only with other ideas. He said that principles of strife should be replaced with justice; hate and vengeance should be combatted by the ideal of Christian charity. To aid in this spiritual battle, Orozco y Jiménez called upon "all men of good faith" to enroll in the ranks of Catholic Social Action, though he did not want to see Social Action furthered at the expense of social discipline. Amelioration must not be too precipitate, said the archbishop. Rich and poor alike must give themselves over to Christian charity. To the rich, he said: "Love the poor; take their hands and look upon them as a brother." He admonished the poor to "love your humble position and your labor. Direct your eyes toward heaven—there is where real wealth is." He had only one plea —to the rich, love, to the poor, resignation. "Thus will society be saved," said the aristocratic prelate.[18]

The Mexican Catholics, in their writings and in their public speeches, made no attempt to analyze what socialism meant in their own country, no attempt to understand or appreciate the aspirations of Mexico's radicals. They made no distinction between Marxian communism and gradualist socialism, between the Bolsheviks and the Fabians. Nor did they recognize the phenomenon of Mexican socialism for what it was—a native Mexican answer to an indigenous problem. Instead, they looked to Western Europe, at European problems and European answers. It was enough for the Catholics that the *Syllabus of Errors* had condemned socialism; if the Mexican revolutionaries called themselves socialists, they were already condemned out of their own mouths.

Because the Church rejected all modern secular answers to the

"Social Question," there was no place for Catholic Action to seek
inspiration except in a distorted twentieth-century view of the Middle Ages. Though they did not proclaim it specifically, Mexico's
Catholics strove to reconstruct the medieval polity. They found
their golden age, an era of unity, of love, of orthodoxy, in the
centuries before the Italian Renaissance and the Protestant Reformation. With the guild they hoped to reestablish the system of
labor-management relations that they felt had been so successful in
the Middle Ages. They rejected radical overtures toward a classless
society or toward a society dominated by the proletariat. The
Church held that society was by nature a fellowship of classes,
moreover, that it must be hierarchically ordered. God made some
men to lead, others to follow. Those in the lower classes must know
their place; yet those in the upper classes must remember their
duties toward their inferiors. Christian loving-kindness must guide
the relations among the several classes. All the organizations developed within the framework of Mexico's Social Action movement
were based upon this medieval concept of ruler and ruled. And at
the apex of the social pyramid reigned the churchmen. The prelates
made clear that they would exercise close control over Social Action
and, through the movement, over society itself.

In 1920 Social Action leaders organized a Confederation of Catholic Associations of Mexico to coordinate all activities of the various
groups interested in the social program. From beginning to end the
episcopate maintained firm control of the confederation and of its
affiliated groups. Laymen were permitted to hold titular positions,
but the key offices remained in the hands of the clergy, with most
important posts being filled by episcopal appointments. In the national confederation the governing body consisted of a junta of
three men, designated by the archbishop of Mexico. Other bishops
named local juntas. Each junta would have priests attached as "technical advisers." No group could make changes in the manner of
appointing its members, nor was the confederation (or any group)
permitted to embark upon social works without the approbation of
the archbishop of Mexico. Each junta could formulate its own rules
of procedure, but even these had to be approved by a bishop. In
Jalisco, the junta named by Orozco y Jiménez consisted of eight
members—all priests.[19]

At the same time, Father Méndez Medina organized a Mexican
Social Secretariat, headed by a permanent committee of three of

Mexico's leading prelates, Mora y del Río, Enrique Sánchez Paredes of Puebla, and Manuel Fulcheri y Pietrasanta of Cuernavaca. The secretariat conducted conferences all over Mexico, formed labor unions and women's organization, and spread the teachings of the Church on Social Action. It published *La Paz Social*, a monthly periodical devoted to social questions. And in 1920 the secretariat founded a Union of Catholic Ladies of Mexico with its own publication, *La Dama Católica*. The union would bring women into the movement for Catholic Action, though the editors of *La Dama Católica* protested that they were not "feminists in the exaggerated sense of the word." The place of women was still in the home, they said. But feminine influences—definitely not in political matters—could greatly aid in solving social problems. The clergy dominated the women's organization as well. All the directors of the various union centers were priests.[20]

The back bone of the Social Action movement was the National Catholic Labor Confederation, formed in 1922 of the many workers' circles. The confederation held its first national convention in May of that year in Guadalajara, which remained the organization's headquarters. Secular unions in the Jaliscan capital promised physical violence as the convention opened. They fixed handbills to public walls and buildings threatening to "paint the sacristies with the blood of fanatics." Because of the danger, the delegates were admitted to the meetings only after the most careful scrutiny. Newspaper reporters were admitted or excluded according to the color of their periodicals. The organizing committee of the convention strictly censored the information given newsmen. Despite the threats, there were no overt attacks by the radical unionists. But the convention speeches were marked by antagonism toward the "socialist" groups.[21] The delegates agreed—in line with ecclesiastical admonishments—that no socialists, "partisans of heterodox ideas," or "sectarians" would be admitted as members of their confederation. At the same time, they acquiesced to a "certain amount of confessionality" and agreed that submission to, and inspection by, the ecclesiastical authorities would be necessary. *Revista Eclesiástica*, official publication of the Mexico City archdiocese, saw in the new organization of Catholic workers the "salvation of Mexico," if it could halt the "insidious spread of Bolsheviks in the Republic," which would "convert our unfortunate country into another Russia."[22]

Although most progress was made by the Catholics in the field of labor organization, this was only part of a broad, renewed program of Social Action. The Catholics called for the preservation of family life, minimum wages, regulation of woman and child labor, assistance in housing, social security, workmen's compensation, permanent arbitration committees, participation of labor in capital's profits, protection against the concentration of wealth, and agrarian assistance. It was much more difficult, however, to turn the program into action than to formulate plans. It was easy to form labor unions. But most of the program, as in Madero's time, required legislative assistance, and this was impossible in Mexico. As long as the machinery of government remained in the hands of the enemies of the Church, the Catholics could never enact the necessary laws.[23]

Given the fact that the economy of Mexico was almost completely rural, the heart of Catholic reform should have been directed toward solving the land problem. Here the Catholics continued the modest program of the early 1910s, based on individual initiative and cooperation. They promoted rural cooperatives. They tried to induce the landowner to collaborate voluntarily and (through Christian charity) to help the peasants to secure land. The central committee of the Confederation of Catholic Associations of Mexico issued a proclamation in 1924 calling for "radical" land reforms to bring about class harmony in Mexican society. It was necessary, the Catholics said, that every landowner be prepared to comply with his social responsibilities. But those who lived in an area knew it best. For this reason, it was unwise for outsiders from the capital to dictate the parceling of land. Neighbors should freely bond together to study their problems, trying to harmonize the interests of workers and hacendados. The owners were told not to charge excessive rents, because their avarice would cause them to "lose the confidence and affections of the workers." The landowners must heed the teachings of "Rerum Novarum" and permit their farm laborers to organize. They must allow those who had no land to acquire small properties, but the land must be paid for by the workers, financed by moderate payments guaranteed by a percentage of their crops.[24]

During the four years of Obregón's presidency and the first two of Calles', the antagonism between the two programs of social reform became increasingly apparent. It seemed inevitable—given the extreme demands of both sides to the dispute—that open clashes and violence would occur. The Catholic and radical leaders began the decade in a spirit of amicable enmity, however, with a series of public debates on the relative merits of the two movements. These debates took place on four Sundays in February and March 1921 and were arranged by Father Méndez Medina with the leaders of CROM. If the Jesuit priest hoped to overpower the radicals with the sheer weight of his logic, he was disappointed, for the meetings engendered more fire than light. Méndez Medina opened the debates in an atmosphere of concord, maintaining that he did not come to attack socialism. Most Mexicans, he said, did not know what socialism was. But he insisted that only the Church could reconstruct society on the basis of harmony, while the radicals would bring antagonism and destruction. Rafael Juanco of CROM answered him, charging that the Catholic Church was not sincere in its attempt to unionize the workers. Juanco tried to refute the Catholics out of their own mouths by showing that the *Syllabus of Errors* had called workers' syndicates a "black pestilence." The Church was addicted to lies and was intolerant of new ideas, he said. Juanco added that he would believe in its sincerity when the Catholics repudiated the *Syllabus*.[25]

In succeeding sessions the debates degenerated. A lawyer, Leopoldo Villela, spoke for the Catholics with the intention of demonstrating that there was no contradiction between the *Syllabus* and "Rerum Novarum." His speech was rambling, and in the question period that followed, the audience soon put him on the defensive. A lady asked why, if the Church really favored improving the conditions of workers, the Catholics still paid their schoolteachers but 30 pesos a month. Villela declined to answer. Ezequiel Salcedo spoke for CROM, declaring that it seemed suspicious to him that the Church, which for centuries had labored invariably for the interests of the rich, now suddenly leaped to the side of the poor and the workers. Salcedo, like Villela, failed to reply satisfactorily to the questions put to him. Most concerned the state of the working class in Russia. The tone of the argumentation fell, until in the fourth conference the CROM representative threatened physical violence toward the Catholics, and the contestants found it prudent to cancel further debates.[26]

The conferences had accomplished little toward narrowing the growing breach between the Catholics and the radicals or of increasing understanding of the two antagonistic positions. The speakers were not interested in debating the issues, nor were they prepared to do so. Each side made its own propaganda, but proved unable to defend it rationally against rebuttals by adversaries. The Catholics sniped at the radicals as though they were Russian communists, while the unionists attacked the past of the Church, or what had come to be the revolutionary view of the Church's past. And the Catholics were handicapped, because they could never admit that the Church might have erred before in its social policies. Thus they had no answer at all.

Although no open break between the Church and the government came until 1926, and the Catholics were comparatively free to conduct their own social program, isolated incidents of antireligious activity and even violence against Catholics and Church property occurred. In February 1921 a bomb was planted at the doorstep of the archbishop of Mexico, though it was discovered before it exploded. A Church spokesman blamed a "sovietista." He wrote: "This is the salute of socialism! This is the clarion call of doom! This is the beginning of a terrible era coming to test the mettle of our fatherland!" In June of the same year another bomb exploded near Mora y del Río's palace. Part of the palace wall was destroyed, but the archbishop escaped injury, for he was not at home. This attempt too was laid at the feet of socialists. In July a church in Torreón was "profaned" by "criminals," who, according to *Revista Eclesiástica*, danced in the church, destroyed images, and threw the sacred Host on the floor. The periodical ascribed the attack to a "group of Mexican bolsheviks."[27]

The antagonism between the Catholics and the secular unions manifested in the 1921 debates erupted into violence on May Day a year later, when members of the "red" syndicates clashed with members of the Catholic Youth Association (ACJM), led by René Capistrán Garza. The unionists set fire to the ACJM headquarters, and when the Catholics, shouting "Viva Cristo Rey!" rushed out to protect their building, the attackers fired pistols into the group. Six Catholics were killed in the encounter. After the skirmish, the leaders of CROM wrote to the ACJM explaining that the unionists sought solely the betterment of the workers through the only adequate means—class warfare and direct action.[28]

Catholic periodicals spoke constantly of a systematic government persecution of religion, but the incidents cited were isolated events: A priest was arrested in Chiapas or a church was converted to

secular use; a state legislature limited the number of priests in the
state to 25; radical unionists in Guadalajara attacked a procession
of Catholic workmen; municipal authorities in Guadalajara fined
Orozco y Jiménez 100 pesos for appearing in public in his clerical
garb. But all these attacks were carried out by local officials or by
private individuals and did not form part of the religious policy of
Obregón and his government. The national government was content to leave the matter of implementing the constitutional articles
to another administration.

Yet if Obregón did not intend to enforce the constitution's religious restrictions, he was also determined not to permit the
Church to overreach itself by taking advantage of his preoccupa-
tion with the question of American recognition. In 1923 such an
incident occurred when the Church seemed to the government to
be stepping beyond safe limits, when the mere act of consecrating
a shrine to Christ carried with it such far-reaching implications
that the Secretary of Gobernación (Interior) felt obliged to intervene and order civil proceedings against churchmen. It was the
affair of the Cerro de Cubilete that caused a flaring-up of trouble
and led to the expulsion of the pope's personal representative by
the president. The building of yet another shrine was in itself
unimportant. But the action of the Catholics in consecrating the
Republic to Christ the King was a threat the government felt it
could not ignore.[29]

The affair of Cubilete had its origins as early as 1913 when a
group of Mexican Catholics requested the Vatican's permission to
proclaim the "reign of the Sacred Heart of Jesus in Mexico." They
asked to be allowed to crown the image in the churches as a sign
of their submission and vassalage to Christ the Redeemer. It was the
beginning of a movement in Mexico to supplant the Indian Christ
at Chalma and the dark Virgin of Guadalupe with the more theologi-
cally respectable and thoroughly Europeanized Sacred Heart of
Jesus. Benedict XV granted permission in January 1914 when, with
President Huerta's approbation, the first coronation took place. But
the plan to make an annual event of the ceremony was thwarted by
the civil wars, and further action was postponed until the coming of
the Obregonian peace in 1921. In that year, a movement was
launched to erect a monument to Cristo Rey on the summit of the
Cerro de Cubilete, a mountain near León, supposed to be the geo-
graphic center of Mexico. The monument, wrote Archbishop Mora

y del Río, would "enthrone the Sacred Heart of Jesus all over the Republic."[30]

If this act of honoring the Sacred Heart had been confined to the religious sphere, it would have been of slight importance to the government. From the words and actions of the Catholics, however, it was obvious that the Church meant to crown Christ not only symbolically, but actually to proclaim the temporal acendancy of the Catholic religion in Mexico. It was the same spirit that led the Catholics to assert the primacy of Social Action over the program of revolutionary reform. Mora y del Río's words in a pastoral letter rang out to the Mexicans in 1921 in a clear call for all Catholics to turn to Christ, hence to the Church, as the bearer of Christ's sovereignty on earth. He wrote: "See then, venerable brothers and beloved children, your King, whom God has crowned with glory and honor, and whom God has placed over all His creatures as the great King, because He is the heir of all things. The nations are His portion, and His dominions extend to the confines of the earth and to the heights of heaven . . . , all-powerful King, into whose hands the Lord commanded all things, whom they fearfully obey. . . ."[31]

The prelates chose January 11, 1923, to celebrate the laying of the cornerstone for the proposed monument to Christ the King. As Mora y del Río summoned the faithful to the ceremony, he told them in a new pastoral letter: "Jesus Christ is our King, not only in the figurative sense . . . , but in the real sense that He has true power to rule man and societies. . . . His kingdom is not of this world, but it is in this world, and it is manifested in a human society, visibly perfect, universal, and eternal, which is the Catholic Church, which possesses rights that none can renounce without betraying Jesus Christ and without destroying himself."[32]

The coming event received widespread publicity, and the Mexican Anticlerical Federation sent a strong protest to Obregón, alleging that the proposed open-air ceremony at Cubilete violated the constitution. Plutarco Elías Calles, the Secretary of Gobernación, sent a message to the governor of Guanajuato, ordering that the event be cancelled. The Catholics went ahead with their plans, nevertheless, maintaining that because the ceremony would take place under a tent and on private property, it was not illegal. The apostolic delegate, Msgr. Ernesto Filippi, agreed to officiate at the ritual, though he had some private reservations about a blatant display of clerical power. Thousands of Catholics came from all parts of the Republic to witness the blessing of the first stone, and many slept in the open fields on the night before the ceremony. When Filippi arrived at the railroad station in Silao, he was greeted by a great crowd, who had decorated the platform with flowers and colored lights. Groups of aristocratic horsemen dressed as charros escorted the apostolic delegate through Silao. As Filippi passed along the streets toward the Cerro de Cubilete, the crowds fell on their knees in reverence. Fourteen bishops and archbishops in regal splendor and hundreds of priests in their long black cassocks walked behind the pope's representative. At the ceremony the Mexicans were called upon to "render vassalage" to Christ and to "recognize him as our supreme Sovereign and King, because He is the King of Kings and the Lord of Lords." The multitude of worshippers, many shedding tears of emotion, shouted "Viva Cristo Rey!"—"Long live Christ the King!"[33]

Eleuterio Ferrer, the priest who had initiated the project, told the assembly that "from the moment in which the Sacred Heart is enthroned in Mexico the social regeneration of the Republic will commence." Emeterio Valverde y Téllez, bishop of León, in charge of the ceremony, called it "one of the greatest days of my life," because he had seen the multitudes representing all the states of the Republic coming to render homage to Cristo Rey. And Bishop Miguel M. de la Mora of San Luis Potosí said that on that day "the representatives of 15 million Mexicans were exalting Christ as King of Mexico." The revolutionary government, which considered itself the embodiment of the Mexican people, could not permit the incident to pass without action. Two days later Calles, under the power granted the executive in Article 33 of the constitution, ordered Filippi's expulsion as a "pernicious foreigner."[34]

Calles explained to newspaper reporters in Mexico City: "Mexico in the future intends to take steps to prohibit high foreign dignitaries from practicing their beliefs in Mexico. This privilege belongs to the clergy of Mexico, as is stipulated by the laws. President Obregón is of the opinion that this interference on the part of foreign prelates is degrading to Mexican clergymen, especially as there are sufficient prelates in high standing who can fulfill all obligations to the Church." Filippi expressed surprise at his expulsion: "It was an outdoor ceremony in no sense of the word. I merely blessed the cornerstone, and the entire ceremony took place in less than twenty minutes. I have presided at similar functions numerous times in Mexico, and certainly I had no idea in this instance of setting myself against any federal law." Despite Filippi's expulsion and Calles' elaborate explanations, it is clear that the Mexican government was more exercised with the Mexican prelates than with the apostolic delegate. Filippi, a personal friend of Obregón and his wife, had been entertained many times at the presidential residence on Chapultepec. But the Italian diplomat became the scapegoat, because the government could conveniently expel him under Article 33. It was not legally possible to act against the Mexican bishops, because none of the articles of the constitution dealing with religion had been implemented.[35]

Catholics throughout Mexico protested Filippi's ouster, and many hung black crape ribbons in their windows as a sign of mourning. On January 15 the Mexican prelates sent a strongly worded letter to Obregón, challenging the legality of the government's action. They pointed out that Article 33 had never been implemented, so the president had no power to use its provisions. But Manuel Padilla, president of the Supreme Court, denied the bishops' contentions. He told the press in Mexico City that though it was true that some parts of the constitution had not been implemented, the Reform Laws were still to be enforced by the judiciary. But whatever the merits of the Catholic protest, on practical grounds the bishops had no case. In a country such as Mexico, where precedent has less importance than in Anglo-Saxon countries, and where conflicting decisions can be made in different cases on the same evidence, and where it is frequently possible for a vigorous executive to intervene in the judicial process, the claim of unconstitutionality had no meaning. A strong president such as Obregón could secure the implementation of a constitutional article, or he could ignore it at his pleasure. When the revolutionary government was ready to enforce the constitution, it would do so, regardless of any legal action or outcry of indignation on the part of the Catholics.[36]

In his reply to the bishops' protest, Álvaro Obregón spelled out the true nature of the controversy and at the same time stressed what he felt to be his own reasonableness in the matter. In a condescending little homily he hold the Catholic prelates that they might have avoided the crisis with "a bit more effort on your part." The aims of the Church and his revolutionary government were so similar, he wrote, that there should be no basic disagreement between them. "The present social program of the government emanating from the Revolution is essentially Christian and is a complement to the fundamental program of the Catholic Church." The one "nurtures the spirit of the believers," he said, while the other "nurtures the stomach, the brain, and the spirit." All that was needed for the peaceful development of the Mexican people, said Obregón, was "a small measure of sincerity and good faith" on the part of both groups. "It is certainly clear that the lack of sincerity on the part of some members of the Catholic clergy has continued to foster antagonism between the two doctrines, which should complement each other, provided both act with good intentions. . . ." In conclusion, he "invited and exhorted" the clergy "not to hinder the work of the Revolution."[37]

The bishops refused to see the controversy in the same light as the president and denied that the two movements were in any way compatible. Nothing in Obregón's statement implied that the Revolution's program was either Marxist or socialistic, but in their reply the bishops insisted that the two Mexican solutions, "the socialistic and the Catholic, except for being in accord in recognizing many of the serious evils of the times, are in complete disagreement when it comes to indicating the origin of this bad situation, and in truth antagonistic when it comes to the differences in the principles of applying the remedies." "While the socialists want to find the causes of the evils in private property, in capital, in family relations, and even in the bonds of religion, the Catholics find them in the abuse of property, in capitalism, in the loosening of family ties, in religious ignorance, and in the relaxing of our customs, all causes that directly or indirectly were brought on by the liberal principles themselves, which abolished instead of reforming the old societies." While the Church in its social program taught the "brotherhood of all the classes of society," they said, socialism had done nothing in Mexico but "sow hatred and divisions among the social classes." They denied that the Church opposed unions or even strikes, "with certain conditions," but insisted that they must condemn the "communistic-socialism" that had been propagated by the Revolution.[38]

After Filippi's expulsion the Mexican government ordered a halt to the building of the proposed monument at Cubilete. But Father Rómulo Díaz, writing in *Revista Eclesiástica,* promised that was not the end of the matter. The monument, if not finished in actuality, he said, would be "engraved on the hearts of the public." "And people live longer than their government." Because of these "jacobin" attacks on the Church, *El Obrero,* a Catholic labor periodical in Guadalajara, launched a campaign to adopt the battle cry "Viva Cristo Rey!" against the enemies of Christ. *Acción y Fe* thought the suggestion appropriate and expressed the hope that the slogan would stimulate all Catholics to a campaign against "jacobinisn" that would lead to the establishment of the Kingdom of Christ in Mexico. In the last year of his administration, after dealing with the de la Huerta rebellion, Obregón continued his avowed policy of seeking an accord with the Church, but an accord dictated by the government. The Catholics occupied themselves increasingly with planning a militant defense of their program, while the Revolution went forward with its own dynamic program of radical reform.[39]

Although he had sanctioned the ousting of Msgr. Filippi, Obregón did not intend to use the crisis as an excuse to sever relations with Rome. Nor did the Vatican take an adamant stand on the issue of the expulsion. No statement came from Rome to back up the protest of the Mexican bishops, and Pietro Cardinal Gasparri, the papal Secretary of State, left Filippi's secretary, Tito Crespi, in Mexico City to maintain a liaison with the Mexican Church and government. In the last months of his administration Obregón, through his Secretary of Foreign Relations, Aarón Sáenz, worked out an agreement with Gasparri to permit the Vatican to send a new apostolic delegate, Serafino Cimino. Msgr. Cimino had held several high offices in the papal bureaucracy and until 1921 had been Minister-General of the Franciscan order. Mexico would allow him to correspond with his superiors in code, thus giving him a quasi-diplomatic status. In turn Gasparri assured Sáenz that in the future all new ecclesiastical posts would be filled by priests and bishops who had not participated in politics.

The attitudes of both Obregón and the Vatican seemed conciliatory in late 1924. Not that Rome had any intention of agreeing to the constitutional restrictions on the Church or of harmonizing the program of Social Action with the Revolution. But so long as the Mexican government made no move to enforce the constitution, the pope and Gasparri were content to temporize and leave troubles to the future. The Vatican hoped to avoid an open clash with the Mexican government that might injure the position of the Church. The Holy See recognized that Protestant groups in Mexico were proselytizing energetically, and Gasparri feared that a renewed conflict might cause the government to open to the public the various episcopal archives to show the scandalous lives of some Mexican priests, as several revolutionaries had done a decade earlier. To air these cases, thought Gasparri, could only aid the Protestants and other "enemies" of the Catholic Church. It is clear that by the end of 1924 the Vatican was far from pleased with the state of the Mexican church, especially with the aristocratic and reactionary social attitudes of prelates such as Guadalajara's Orozco y Jiménez, and that reforms would be effected by Rome as soon as possible.[40]

As Obregón and the Vatican moved toward some sort of informal understanding, the Church in Mexico continued its hostile activity against the Mexican government. In October 1924 a Eucharistic Congress was convoked in Mexico City with much ceremony and public display. Though the Vatican thought the moment inopportune for such ostentation, it did not forbid the Mexican clergy to hold the congress. Obregón also took exception to this blatant reminder of the asserted power of the Church, and he asked his Attorney-General to investigate the congress to determine if the clergy had violated the constitution or the Reform Laws. The president also ordered his department chiefs to discharge any government employee who had participated in the religious ceremonies outside the churches. Obregón directed that all statues or other religious adornments be removed from the façades of houses and other buildings in the capital. The Attorney-General announced that he would make a special investigation to see if any of the foreign clergy present, notably the bishop of Camaguey, Cuba, and the archbishop of San Antonio, Texas, had violated the law. Because of these orders, the congress closed without its planned pilgrimage to Guadalupe. But the prelates went ahead with ceremonies in which they consecrated the capital to the Sacred Heart.[41]

If Obregón had continued in office for a second term, the open conflict between the Church and the government might have been avoided, or at least postponed. But the constitution forbade the reelection of any public official, so at the end of 1924 Obregón handed over the presidency to Plutarco Elías Calles, a revolutionary general from Obregón's state of Sonora. The new president was an implacable enemy of the Church. Earlier as governor of his state, he had expelled most of the clergy as enemies of the Revolution. It was he, as Obregón's Secretary of Gobernación, that had initiated the expulsion of Filippi. Where Obregón was conciliatory, Calles was obstinate and inflexible. Though Obregón was as radical as his successor in his social outlook and had supported the radicals at Querétaro, he was willing to compromise for the sake of national harmony. Calles, as a man of principle, was determined to enforce the laws unrelentingly, to limit the powers of the Church and the scope of Social Action. When in December 1924, Pius XI appointed Cimino as apostolic delegate to Mexico, Calles told Obregón that his administration would not be bound by any unconstitutional agreement made with the Vatican. As Calles took office rumors circulated in Mexico City that he would move quickly to implement the religious articles of the constitution.[42]

But Calles, like Obregón before him, had more vital problems than the immediate enforcement of the constitution with an attack on the Church. The revolt of de la Huerta and the long government campaign against the rebels had depleted the treasury and left the new administration a deficit of nearly 60 million pesos. For the first year, then, Calles' main concern as president was the financial security of his government. So successful was Alberto J. Pani, the Secretary of the Treasury, however, that by the end of 1925 he had all but eliminated the deficit.[43]

In the fall of 1925 Calles' government presented Congress a plan for implementing key articles of the constitution. Strong pressure had built up both inside and outside the administration to begin applying Articles 3, 27, 123, and 130. If Calles had been able to command an absolute majority in the Congress, it is certain that Mexico would have seen a sudden acceleration of the revolutionary program. But the absence of true political parties in the country and the lack of unity in the Senate and the Chamber of Deputies made any coherent program impossible. Instead, the senators and deputies frittered away the legislative session without ever coming to grips with proposals presented them by Calles. A great stumbling block to legislative action was the question of a successor to Calles. Though elections were still three years off, the government introduced a constitutional amendment to allow the reelection of a former president—presumably, in this case, Obregón. There was so much opposition to the plan, however, that the sessions were interrupted for weeks on end by the absence of a quorum. Large groups of senators refused to come to Congress in order to prevent action on the amendment. As a result, no other legislation could be considered, and the session ended on December 31 without action on Articles 3, 123, or 130. Only that part of Article 27 pertaining to the oil properties was implemented. The foreign oil companies in Mexico were required to exchange their land titles for fifty-year leases —a device that would insure the eventual reversion of the petroleum properties to Mexican nationals. On the last day of the session the Congress hurriedly, and almost as an afterthought, gave Calles power to issue presidential decrees in certain fields of legislation, notably to reform the penal code.[44]

The law involving the oil companies precipitated a crisis in Mexican-American relations. For some time the Secretary of State, Frank B. Kellogg, had been keeping a weather eye on the Mexican situation. In June 1925 he declared publicly that the Calles government was "on trial before the world." Through most of 1925 the two governments exchanged acrid communications over the supposed confiscatory legislation. Some in the United States called openly for intervention in Mexico to protect the American business interests. At no time was intervention seriously considered, for the Department of State was determined to seek a peaceful solution. At the same time, the public in both countries believed that armed action loomed behind the diplomatic wrangling, and Catholic groups, with the eruption of the Church-State conflict in early 1926, worked actively for such intervention.[45]

The first year of Calles' administration passed without his taking action against the clergy. In his address to the new Congress on September 1, 1925, the president observed the hostile attitude of the clergy toward his government, but he made no specific legislative recommendations to the senators and deputies. Nonetheless, attacks on the Church occurred on the local level, doubtless with Calles' approbation. Indeed, it is likely that state governors and legislatures, well aware of the anticlerical attitudes of Calles, felt emboldened to act against the Catholics. In Tabasco, Governor Tomás Garrido Canabal promulgated a law that forbade unmarried Catholic priests and any priest under 40 and without "good, moral antecedents." In October five Tabascan priests, who refused to marry, were ordered arrested and imprisoned by the state government. By November the bishop of Tabasco, Pascual Díaz, and all of his priests had left the state, and Catholic church services ended in Tabasco. Other states followed the lead of Tabasco with legislation restricting the number of the clergy, though none went as far as Garrido Canabal in their repressions. In Mexico City a group of dissident Catholics took advantage of the known anticlericalism of

Calles' government to start a national schismatic movement against
the Roman Catholic Church.[46]

The so-called Mexican Apostolic Church was not, as Catholics
later charged, a plot of the Calles government to destroy the Roman
Church in Mexico. Rather the movement began almost inadvert-
ently with the defection of two priests and their attempt to seize one
of the Mexico City parishes. But it is true that members of the
government—probably in Morones' office—gave aid to the new
Church, once the schism had started. José Joaquín Pérez was an
octogenarian priest with a long military record in revolutionary
armies spanning the years from Juárez to Calles. In 1925 he left the
army and applied for reinstatement as a Catholic priest. When the
archbishop of Mexico turned him down, he decided to found a
separate Church and enlisted the support of another ex-priest, Manuel Luis Monge, who styled himself "President by Birth of the
order of the Knights of Guadalupe."

During the night of February 22 the two seized the church of La
Soledad in Mexico City, evicting the priests in charge. In the morning the two renegades attempted to hold services, but crowds of
women, stirred up by the ousted priests, pushed into the church in
an attempt to prevent the schismatics from saying Mass. A woman
jumped over the altar rail into the sacristy to strike Pérez in the face.
In the general melee that ensued, benches and chairs were thrown
at the priests, and they were saved from physical injury only by the
timely arrival of a squad of police. Meanwhile, a larger crowd had
gathered outside La Soledad, and the police had to force their way
through the women by firing their pistols. One woman was killed by
the police and several were wounded. Pérez and Monge were sent
home by the police under armed guard. Mora y del Río petitioned
the government to restore the church to its legitimate curate, but
Calles instructed the Inspector of Police in the capital to keep the
schismatics in La Soledad.[47]

For several months through 1925 the dissident priests attempted
to gain followers in the poorer sections of Mexico City by distributing gifts and by proselytizing. They declared their Church independent of the Vatican and modified the Roman ritual by introducing
Spanish translations into the Mass. The new Church gained the
adherence of a Mexican ex-priest who had taken Episcopalian orders and was being subsidized by the Board of Missions of the
American Protestant Episcopal Church. But the Episcopalians

refused to be associated with the schismatic movement, and the mission board cut off the stipend of the young priest. The schismatics then made an attempt to gain apostolic succession through an arrangement with an Eastern-rite Church. Many of the Syrians and Lebanese in Mexico looked with favor on the dissident movement. Quite coincidentally, a Greek Orthodox archimandrite from Boston was visiting Mexico, and the schismatics asked him to consecrate Pérez a bishop in the new Church. Like the Episcopalians, however, the archimandrite would have nothing to do with the group of Mexicans. In March 1925 Calles settled the conflict over La Soledad by ordering the church closed to both factions. He said that the schismatics had taken it "without fulfilling the requirements of the law," while, on the other hand, the Roman Catholic clergy had declared themselves in open rebellion against the constitution, "despising the authorities through their most prominent spokesman." He did direct, however, that the dissidents be given another church in the capital, Corpus Christi, fronting on the Alameda in the center of the city. The Mexican National Church struggled on in a few parishes in various parts of Mexico, but despite the alarms raised by the prelates, it made few inroads into the basic Roman Catholicity of the country.[48]

Because the dangers from the schismatics seemed more real in early 1925 than they proved to be later, a group of lay Catholic leaders met on March 9 in Mexico City to organize a National League for the Defense of Religious Liberty. They proposed the Liga Nacional as a "civic army, duly trained and disciplined," whose principal weapons would be propaganda, the electoral process, and legal petitions. The founders named an executive committee made up of the most active laymen in the country: Miguel Palomar y Vizcarra, long a leader in the Social Action movement; Luis G. Bustos, head of Mexico's Knights of Columbus; and René Capistrán Garza, president of ACJM. Rafael Ceniceros y Villarreal, once governor of Zacatecas in the Huerta era, became the League's president. Some of the prelates regarded the new organization with suspicion, because it had been formed without prior episcopal approval and, unlike the Social Action movement, was not subject to hierarchical control. The bishops wanted no independent laymen speaking for the Catholic Church. But Ceniceros y Villarreal made a hurried trip to Morelia to talk with Ruiz y Flores, and after their conference the archbishop agreed not to oppose the league, although he was launching a similar lay organization (firmly under ecclesiastical supervision), a secret group to be known as the Association of the Holy Ghost.[49]

As the Catholic laymen met and planned the defense of their religious liberties, and the Calles government denounced their activities as seditious, Msgr. Serafino Cimino, the new apostolic delegate, arrived in Mexico. Though newspapers in the capital reported his arrival, the Secretary of Foreign Relations announced that the administration would take no official notice of his presence in the country. Cimino brought a message from the pope counseling moderation, and he promised that he would work only for the spiritual welfare of the Mexican Catholics and remain aloof from politics. He was an easygoing cleric, who displeased the Mexicans by his seeming irresolution, and he soon found himself at odds with the more militant bishops, who wanted him to take an inflexible stand against the government. After several unproductive weeks in Mexico City, Cimino went to the United States, ostensibly because of ill health. When he tried to return, however, the Mexican government refused him a reentry permit. Once again relations between the Mexican Church and the Vatican were left to Tito Crespi, who had no authority and could act only as a messenger for the papal Secretary of State.[50]

Political changes, too, boded ill for the possibility of peace between the government and the Catholics. Until the summer of 1925 Gilberto Valenzuela occupied the post of Secretary of Gobernación in Calles' cabinet. While he was not a moderate and indicated to Cimino that the government would watch his actions carefully, he did restrain Calles' intemperance toward the Church. But in August, Valenzuela resigned in a disagreement with Calles over the imposition of a gubernatorial candidate in the state of México. He was replaced by Adalberto Tejeda, a man of little ability, a politician who would do whatever Calles required of him.[51]

Hoping to win the support of the Vatican for a militant course against the government, the Mexican prelates sent José María González Valencia, archbishop of Durango, and Miguel M. de la Mora, bishop of San Luis Potosí, to Rome in late 1925. Cardinal Gasparri, still fearful of an open conflict with the government, refused to sanction a more forceful attitude on the part of the Church in Mexico. And Pius XI, in a secret consistory on December 14, while lamenting the persecutions in Mexico, saw as the resolution of the country's problems "divine intervention," rather than a political campaign. He prepared an apostolic letter for the Mexican Church, "Paterna Sane Solicitudo," in which he cautioned the bishops to hold themselves "entirely aloof from every kind of political party or function."[52]

As the year 1925 came to a close the prelates in Mexico chafed at the Vatican restraints and the admonitions of the pope, while Calles seemed preoccupied with political problems, both internal and external. The contentious factions in the Congress made impossible any coherent legislative program. Members of Calles' cabinet came under heavy public criticism for immorality and corruption. There were spots of local rebellion in various parts of the country to be dealt with by the army. The government of the United States continued to insist upon the sanctity of American properties in Mexico. As the new year began, and with the many troubles brewing for Calles, there was as yet no indication of an imminent conflict between the Church and the government. The Congress would not meet until the following September, and the administration looked forward to a nine-months hiatus in its legislative program. Meanwhile, Calles would issue decrees as they were needed, under the broad powers conceded him at the end of the 1925 congressional session.

Yet if the religious conflict seemed more chronic than critical in the first days of 1926, it was evident that only a single spark was necessary to ignite passions in both camps. By 1926 the battle lines had been drawn between the Catholic Church and the Mexican revolutionary government—in agrarian reforms, in the formation of labor organizations, and in education. Against the Church were arrayed the legions of the Revolution. They were radical and saw the Catholics as fanatics and archreactionaries. Above all, the attitudes of the politicians who ran the revolutionary State matched the authoritarianism of the Church hierarchy. Both showed an equal lack of toleration for the ideas of others. It was impossible to reconcile the extreme claims made for the rival ideologies. Neither side to the dispute cared or tried to. Given the intransigence of the Church and the Mexican State, the clash—which came in early 1926 —was perhaps unavoidable. The conflict occurred, not because the Church wished to mix in politics or because the revolutionaries were bolsheviks, but because both the Church and the State desired to control the Mexican people, and neither was willing to share that control. It was a battle between incompatible and mutually exclusive ideologies, not a struggle among politicians. And in 1926 the greater power, despite the impressive theological arguments of the churchmen, lay with the government. During the bitter conflict the ambitious Social Action movement disappeared once more, swallowed up in the maelstrom of civil strife.

The Church Strike

"THE ARCHBISHOP AND PRIMATE of Mexico is a decrepit old man, an opportunist without will-power, a believer in political intrigue, who for a long while has not had any real voice in the conduct of Church affairs." The French chargé d'affaires in Mexico City, Ernest Lagarde, made this harsh assessment of José Mora y del Río in a lengthy report to his superiors at the Quai d'Orsay. Lagarde exaggerated, for "decrepit" was not the word to describe the Mexican prelate. But it was true that Mora y del Río had lost the vigor that had characterized his actions first as bishop of Tulancingo and then in his early years as archbishop of Mexico. He was 76 years of age in 1926, and his powers had begun to fail. He was crotchety and given to strange and often inexplicable behavior. In early 1926 a report circulated in the Mexican capital that the archbishop, during a pontifical High Mass at the basilica of Guadalupe, had been displeased with the taste of the communion wine. He turned to the curates to ask where the wine had come from. And when he was told, he interrupted the service to send one of the priests out to obtain another wine, more to his liking.[1]

Mora y del Río's appearance and attitudes bespoke his aristocratic lineage. From his face it was apparent that he had little or no Indian blood in his veins. His hair was white, his eyes mild with no sign of physical energy behind them. His face was lean and angular, and his brow was seamed with age; pressed tightly together, his mouth and thin lips gave him an air of constant petulance. His gaunt and corded neck protruded from a too-large Roman collar. The almost ascetic slightness of his figure contrasted with the corpulence of most of Mexico's prelates. Mora y del Río's colleagues gave the impression of living well, of enjoying the higher clergy's prerogatives of an ample supply of good food and wine.

Because Mora y del Río could no longer give the Mexican Catholics strong leadership, no single voice in the country spoke with authority for the Church. Indeed, there were almost as many opinions as there were prelates. On matters such as the principles of Social Action the hierarchy united, for the papacy had laid down the guidelines to be followed throughout the world. But when it came to the means of implementing the program, to questions touching on political affairs, or to relations with the government, for example, each bishop or archbishop felt free to follow his own counsels. The problem of ecclesiastical unity was complicated by the age and physical and mental condition of Mora y del Río and the imminent need to choose his successor. His associates played at ecclesiastical politics, seeking to maneuver themselves into a favorable position so as to gain papal favor when the archbishop of Mexico should die. None had more ambition than Pascual Díaz, the fifty-one-year-old bishop of Tabasco.

Díaz was an Indian and a Jesuit. Unlike most of his colleagues and predecessors, he had been born into a poor family, and his selection as a prelate, at an early age, evidenced a new Vatican policy of giving preferment to vigorous, but plebeian, Mexican priests. There was nothing ascetic in the features of Pascual Díaz. His Indian eyes, like carved pieces of obsidian, seemed to glow with the primordial energy of the volcanic fire behind them. His face, the color of polished mahogany, was heavyset and jowly, his neck thickset on burly shoulders, his body like a barrel. When he wore a business suit (to comply with Mexico's constitutional ban on clerical garb in public) and a stickpin in his cravat, he might have been a highly successful petit entrepreneur in any small Indian town. Díaz achieved success in his episcopal career by embracing the methods of the marketplace. To Ernest Lagarde he was "intriguing and intolerant." He burned with an intense desire to rise to clerical eminence, and he did not mind stepping on a few jeweled fingers as he mounted the ecclesiastical ladder. If the Vatican preferred resistance in Mexico, Díaz could be the most obdurate. If compromise with the government became the order of the day, he was the most compliant. Díaz moved to Mexico City in late 1925 when Governor Tomás Garrido Canabal outlawed the Catholic Church in Tabasco. From that moment on his rise to eminence was sure and swift.

In early 1926, however, other prelates seemed likelier choices to succeed Mora y del Río. Francisco Orozco y Jiménez matched the young bishop of Tabasco in vigor and ambition, and he was more militant in defense of the faith. From his earliest days as bishop of Chiapas, through the 1910s and 1920s in the archdiocese of Guadalajara, Orozco y Jiménez had aggressively pushed the Church's interests, had undergone privations and risked death to remain with his people when most Mexican prelates went into exile in the United States. But his zeal, his intolerance, his contempt for the civil authorities in Mexico had more than once brought upon his head the censure of the Holy See. In the days of Pope Boniface VIII the haughtily aristocratic prelate would no doubt have carved out for himself a highly successful career. But in the Mexican Church of the twentieth century his attitudes, his prejudices, his methods belonged to the dead past. Though he could not know it in 1926, he had no chance whatsoever of succeeding to the position of Mora y del Río.

Of the other prelates in Mexico, three demonstrated outstanding ability as ecclesiastical administrators. Leopoldo Ruiz y Flores, archbishop of Morelia (formerly Michoacán), belonged to the same social class as Orozco y Jiménez, but his mentality was of the modern age. Lagarde called him "a remarkable theologian, an energetic man of very high morals." During the crisis of 1926 he set the pattern in Mexico for his staunch insistence upon the rights of the Church, while showing, at the same time, an ability to deal realistically with actual political conditions. In early 1926 he seemed the most likely heir to the archiepiscopal throne in Mexico City. Miguel María de la Mora, now bishop of of San Luis Potosí, at 52 was also a courageous fighter for the Church, as well as a practiced administrator, whose diocese was perhaps the best run in the Republic. And the young archbishop of Durango, José María González Valencia— he was only 42 in 1926—was already marked for success as an ecclesiastic diplomat. But he was too young and without sufficient experience to be considered as Mora y del Río's immediate successor. González Valencia and de la Mora were named to a delegation in 1925 to report to the Vatican on the state of religion in Mexico under the Calles administration. And González Valencia went again to Rome in the following year as a spokesman for the Mexican hierarchy.

Of the remaining prelates, some were fanatically jealous of the Church's position; some were moderate, and would accept a measure of compromise with the persecuting government, trimming their sails to the prevailing winds; while a few were ineffectual, wishy-washy, or downright incompetent. Of the first, the bishops of Huejutla and Tulancingo were representatives. José de Jesús Manríquez y Zárate, bishop of Huejutla, was a contentious gamecock who challenged the powers of Caesar with a stridency and a pugnacity unmatched in the Mexican Church. Seeming to court martyrdom, he defied the government of Calles again and again at a time when the president was determined to bring the Mexican clergy to heel. Manríquez y Zárate was daring and bold and irresponsibly tactless. His courageous statements of religious principles in his controversial pastoral letters were in the best tradition of Catholic theological writings. He spent nearly twenty years in exile because he refused to come to terms with what he considered the Godless tyranny of Calles and his successors. Vicente Castellanos y Núñez, bishop of Tulancingo, too, brought the wrath of Calles' administration upon his head by his intemperate pastorals. Both bishops were haled before civil tribunals in 1926 for their public attacks on the government.

The other prelates of Mexico had little positive influence on Church policy. Francisco Banegas, bishop of Querétaro, took more interest in his historical research than in the worldly problems of administration. Rafael Guízar Valencia (bishop of Veracruz), Pedro Vera y Zuria (archbishop of Puebla), Francisco Uranga y Sáenz (bishop of Cuernavaca), and Manuel Fulcheri y Pietrasanta (bishop of Zamora) favored a temporizing policy. And because they took no definite stand, they suffered least from the government.

The Church in Mexico was far from ready for a showdown with the government in 1926. As an integral part of the Church Universal, it sought to give the appearance of unalterable and irrefutable truth and the strength of an unassailable fortress. In their joint pastorals and other public statements the bishops thundered Jovian anathemas on the heads of the Mexican revolutionaries. They proclaimed the program of Social Action the sole remedy for Mexico's social and economic ills. But behind the façade of unity lay grave weaknesses. The greater number of the Mexican Catholics, the rural

Indians and urban proletariat, were uneducated and superstitious and had no sense of belonging to the Universal Church. The much-vaunted program of Social Action was in the hands of laymen with no national stature and little or no experience in public matters. The great popular heroes of the day were revolutionaries, not Catholics. Widespread corruption prevailed among the lower clergy; the foreign clergy were mistrusted because they were not Mexican. The prelates were divided in their counsels, and unsure of the correct course to follow in the event of trouble.

The government, on the other hand, had the backing of the army, the agrarian groups, and the labor unions. The president and the members of his cabinet could boast long revolutionary careers and much experience in civil administration. That corruption was rife in the Calles government could not be denied. But it was a shortcoming that the administration, as well as the Mexican public, looked upon with almost callous complacency. A corrupt priest was an offense to God and man. A corrupt bureaucrat—well, what could you expect from politicians? The government was not the weaker because it was also depraved. The successful revolutionary hierarchy from Calles down had all profited materially from their revolutionary careers. Palatial homes, fine estates, prosperous ranches, flourishing businesses—these were the fruits of revolution. Calles was wealthy, powerful, cynical, and capable of great cruelty toward his enemies. If the Revolution had taught men one thing it was the value of swift, decisive, and ruthless action. A government in Mexico did not stay in power by vacillation and leniency. The conflict between the Catholic Church and the revolutionary government that began in the second month of 1926 found the government strong where the Church was weakest—the State had the advantage of sheer physical power.

At the end of 1925 and during the month of January 1926 it had become evident that the Catholics were moving toward a showdown with the government because of the implementation of Article 130 by various state legislatures. In December the bishop of Huejutla published a pastoral letter protesting a new state law that limited the number of priests in Hidalgo to 60. Manríquez y Zárate wrote that his priests "were not disposed to submit to the decree and would defend their rights." When his letter was brought to a district judge for possible civil action, Manríquez y Zárate refused an order to appear in his own defense. A civil judge had no authority over a bishop, he said. On January 11, a collective statement of the Mexican episcopate was given to the press in Mexico City indicating that a public protest would soon be made against the religious situation in Chiapas, Tabasco, Hidalgo, Jalisco, and Colima. In Chiapas a recently enacted state law forbade baptisms without a certificate of civil registration and a religious marriage ceremony without a previous civil marriage. In Tabasco but two or three priests remained, while in Jalisco and Colima the state governments had closed a number of seminaries and parochial schools. The bishops wrote that it was "necessary to declare collectively that such measures and any others that are contrary to religious liberty cannot be obeyed by the prelates and the clergy."[2]

The bishops awaited the return of González Valencia and de la Mora from Rome with instructions from the pope, however, before taking any definite step against the restrictions. They planned an assembly of the national episcopate at the end of February to discuss means to defend their religious liberties "in conformity with the Vatican's instructions." They proposed to initiate a campaign "within the law" against various constitutional restrictions—on education, on monastic orders, on outdoor ceremonies, on the holding of properties by the Church—as well as the failure to grant legal recognition to the Church. On January 28 Mora y del Río, in answer to a reporter's questions, confirmed that the prelates would soon meet to plan their program. "The campaign against this unjust legislation is not new," he said. "In 1917 the Mexican prelates published a declaration refusing to recognize the principles of the constitution that are contrary to natural law."[3]

González Valencia and de la Mora were on their way back from Rome with a message from the Holy See advising continued moderation. The pontiff sent a secret letter to the bishops of Mexico (not made public until April 29), directing them to refrain from all political action and to devote themselves to their spiritual task in the Social Action movement. The admonition of the pope came too late. By the time the two prelates had returned to Mexico the simmering storm had broken, and total and irreconcilable conflict was a reality. And the government of Calles, in order to appear in the best possible light in the controversy, placed the responsibility on the Church and especially on the frail shoulders of Mora y del Río. In his annual New Year's Day message the president made no mention of the Church question. He seemed content to leave the implementation of the constitution to the state governors and legislators.[4]

After the appearance of articles in various Mexico City newspapers concerning the planned assembly of prelates, Ignacio Monroy, an enterprising reporter for *El Universal*, sought out the archbishop to obtain an exclusive and official statement of the Church's position. On February 4 his newspaper printed Mora y del Río's statement on the first page, though not conspicuously. (It appeared in a small box at the top of column 2 without any explanation or comment.) According to Monroy, the archbishop told him that "the doctrine of the Church is invariable because it is divinely revealed truth. The protest that we Mexican prelates made against the Constitution of 1917 and the articles that are contrary to liberty and religious dogma is maintained firmly. It has not been modified, but strengthened, because it is derived from the doctrine of the Church. The information that *El Universal* published on January 27 to the effect that a campaign would be undertaken against the laws that are unjust and contrary to Natural Law is correct. The episcopate, clergy, and Catholics do not recognize and will combat Articles 3, 5, 27, and 130 of the present constitution. We cannot modify this position for any reason without committing treason against our faith and our religion."[5]

The national government seized upon this policy statement by Mora y del Río as an opportunity to launch a swift and massive assault against the position of the Church in Mexico. On the same day, Adalberto Tejeda, Calles' Minister of Gobernación, announced to the press that his office had been "observing with the interest the affair merits the public declarations of the archbishop." His government could not and would not permit the Church to "deny and combat" constitutional laws. "As a consequence," Tejeda said, "I have turned over the facts in the case, which are well documented, to the Attorney General. . . ." If the evidence warranted, he added, Mora y del Río would be brought to trial for civil disobedience. The chief newspapers of the capital, especially *Excélsior* and *El Universal*, rallied to the defense of the archbishop. *El Universal*'s editors wrote on February 6: "To criticize or oppose the supreme law of the Republic by word of mouth, in books, or in the daily press is not an act of rebellion, but the exercise of a free right." Various Catholic groups, such as Damas Católicas and ACJM, proclaimed their solidarity with the archbishop. René Capistrán Garza told reporters that Tejeda had "confused the meanings of the words "rebellious" and "opposition." "We Catholics are not rebels, but clearly opponents" of the government actions.[6]

The government initiated its campaign against the Church on two fronts. The Attorney General would bring the archbishop of Mexico to trial for his seditious statements, and the president would implement Articles 3 and 130. On February 8 Romeo Ortega, Calles' Attorney General, announced that he had studied Mora y del Río's statement and that he had sent his report to the district judge for legal action against the archbishop. Three days later Ortega declared that all Church properties would be taken over by the government. Orders went out to the state governors to expel every foreign priest immediately. In the capital Calles' police descended on the parish churches, arresting all priests not of Mexican nationality. Those arrested had no time to prepare themselves for travel or to pack their belongings, but were brutally thrust aboard trains for Veracruz and ousted from the country. Some had been living and working in Mexico for many years.[7]

Mora y del Río's ringing public declaration of the Church's rights was not matched by his demeanor in this moment of adversity. In alarm he began to back away from the extreme statements attributed to him by Monroy, asserting that he had been misquoted in the press. On February 11 he denied that the prelates planned a meeting to formulate a campaign against the laws, and his statement to Monroy, he said, consisted of "impressions contained in a document published by the Mexican Episcopate in 1917." "Our most vehement desires have always been, and are now, to cooperate for the prosperity of the country, with mutual respect for our obligations and rights." The district judge ordered the archbishop to appear in court on February 13 for a preliminary hearing. When Mora y del Río pleaded that he was too ill, the judge agreed to take his declaration in the archiepiscopal residence. The archbishop confronted Monroy and again denied that he had made the statement about a meeting of the prelates that was printed in *El Universal*. He said fervently that the Church had never conspired, nor did it intend to conspire, against the Mexican constitution. At the end of the hearing, however, the archbishop protested against the "intervention of a civil court into questions that are purely ecclesiastical. I, as an archbishop, am not obliged to answer for my acts to anyone but God in heaven after my death and to the Pope here on earth."

With Mora y del Río in retreat there was nothing for the judge to do but throw out the indictment. He announced that he had found no cause for legal action against the prelate.[8]

The legal exoneration of Mora y del Río failed to satisfy Calles' government. The crux of the question was not whether the prelates would meet to plan a program, but the clergy's continued opposition to the constitution. The archbishop did not and could not disavow the protest made in 1917. The Church still found the offending articles totally unacceptable. Though the Attorney General did not bind Mora y del Río over for trial, therefore, the federal government used the incident as a pretext for an all-out campaign against the Catholics throughout the republic. The president gave orders that Articles 3, 27, and 130, where they applied to the Church, would be rigidly enforced. All foreign priests and nuns, including some Americans, were expelled from the country. Schools that were operated by foreign religious orders were summarily closed. On February 22 J. M. Puig Casauranc, the Secretary of Education, announced that Article 3 would be implemented. He ordered a nationwide investigation of Catholic schools "to guarantee that those institutions do not violate the law." And Adalberto Tejeda, on February 17, ordered the priests in charge of those churches that had opened since the promulgation of the Constitution of 1917 to register with the local government. The ayuntamiento would then grant them permission to remain at that church. Among the new churches was the Sagrada Familia in Mexico City.[9]

Civil registration of the clergy presented a thorny problem for the hierarchy because for priests to come before public authorities seeking permission to keep a church open was tantamount to recognizing the State's authority over religion. And it meant too that the priests had acquiesced in the seizure of the ecclesiastical properties by the government under the Reform Laws and the Constitution of 1917. Thus this came to be the chief bone of contention between the Church and the Mexican government in 1926. As in Jalisco, eight years earlier, the prelates would not permit the priests to register with the government, and Calles would not allow the clergy to continue in charge of the churches unless they did. On the afternoon of February 23, agents of the Ministry of Gobernación came to the Sagrada Familia, ostensibly to inventory the goods in the church (under the constitution the building and all religious objects in it belonged to the government). Actually, the agents were there to take the priests into custody for violating Tejeda's order.

The news that the church had been closed and the priests arrested spread quickly through the parish, which was in the Roma and Juárez districts. Within fifteen minutes a crowd of 2,000 women had gathered before the church to demand the curates' release. When the police tried to break up the demonstration and disperse the crowd, the women set upon them with stones and brickbats. The police then called for aid from the fire department. The firemen turned their hoses upon the angry, shouting mob, and though it was one of the coldest days of the year and the women were thoroughly soaked, they refused to leave. Only when the police fired pistols over their heads did the crowd break up to escape the shots. But the parishioners regrouped and marched to the office of the Secretary of Gobernación on nearby Bucareli Avenue and made another demonstration. Again the firemen brought out their hoses, and the police used pistols to drive the women away. Two of the women were killed and 16 wounded by gunfire before they were dispersed. Tejeda was unmoved by the demonstration. He announced to the press that the churches affected by his order would remain closed until the priests agreed to register with the government.[10]

As a result of the clash at the Sagrada Familia, the leaders of the ACJM in Mexico City issued a public protest against "attacks on the freedom of conscience" and against the closing of churches and schools and the expulsion from Mexico of priests and nuns. They protested, they said, "in the name of the rights of Christ, the King of the world, and especially of Mexico, as proclaimed in the last Eucharistic Congress." The young Catholics insisted that they could not accept the "interferences of the civil power in the affairs of the Church. . . . As Mexicans, we demand the reform of the constitution that destroys our religious liberty. We swear before the entire nation that we shall employ our energies, by all legal means, to obtain its reform." Leaders of Damas Católicas in various Mexican cities telegraphed protests to Calles and petitioned the president and the Congress to amend the constitution. *El Universal*, in an editorial on February 25, deprecated the closing of the churches: "Mexico is and will remain Catholic for a thousand years, whatever may be the laws, as one cannot change the souls of the people by decrees."[11]

Calles ignored the pleas and demands of the Catholics and seemed unmoved by the bloodshed at the Sagrada Familia. He told a CROM convention that these protests did not represent the opinion of the nation. His government would continue to fulfill its program, point by point, he promised, "without regard to the sacristans' grimaces or the farts of the monks." To reporters the president stressed the dangers inherent in the attitude of the clergy: "Now what is a government of any country to do when a social group, religious or otherwise, publicly rejects the fundamental laws of the country and announces its purpose to fight them, inciting the people to repudiate the constitution? What could my government do but devote its attention to those constitutional clauses . . . and demand a strict obedience to the law?"[12]

Responding to the president's call, the various state legislatures passed laws to curb further the local activities of the Church. On February 24, Colima, with 62,000 inhabitants, fixed the number of priests in the state at 26. Two days later the legislature of Nayarit limited the number of priests to 40. Restrictions followed rapidly in other states throughout the Republic: San Luis Potosí, ten priests for the capital city, and a lesser number in smaller towns and villages; Nuevo León, one priest for each 2,500 persons in the state; Tamaulipas, 13 priests for 350,000 inhabitants; Aguascalientes, one priest for each 50,000 inhabitants; Yucatán, one for each 10,000; Puebla, one for each 4,000; Hidalgo, one for each municipality and two for the capital (Pachuca); Tlaxcala, 36 for the state (and forbidding more than six priests to assemble in one place at any one time); Sinaloa, 45 for the state; México, 140 for a million inhabitants; Jalisco, 250 for 1,250,000 persons; Chihuahua, one priest for each 9,000 inhabitants; Campeche, three for the entire state; Guanajuato, one for each 5,000; and Zacatecas, 30 for the capital and no more than one for each other municipality.[13]

To pass laws in Mexico was one thing; it was quite another to carry them out. The enforcement of this legislation varied widely from state to state, and even within states, according to the temperament and mentality of the state officials and the vigor of the bishops and the clergy. In the state of Veracruz the governor, Heriberto Jara, reached an agreement with the bishops. On March 13 the mild-mannered Guízar Valencia denied publicly that the Church was being persecuted in his diocese. It was his desire, he said, "to establish a new era of harmony between the civil government and the Church, each complying with its duties and obligations." The bishop of Huajuapan in Oaxaca, Luis Altamirano y Bulnes, also denied that his priests were being attacked. He would run his diocese in strict accordance with the law, he said. In Colima, on the other hand, the governor dealt with the clergy in the most brutal way. Bishop José Amador Velasco said that he could not obey the laws, that he preferred suspending public services to giving in to the government. By the end of March, the Church had virtually ceased to function in that state. The bishop of Tamaulipas accepted the persecutions in his state, but made it clear that he was bowing to superior physical force. In the states of Puebla, Querétaro, and Michoacán, where the Church had a strong hold on the population, energetic defense of religious liberties by the prelates brought some moderation of the excessive legislation. The bishop of San Luis Potosí, de la Mora, and 38 of his priests went to court to obtain an *amparo* against the enforcement of the legislation in their state. When another judge suspended the *amparo*, de la Mora ordered the closing of churches in San Luis Potosí. But after three days of negotiations, the bishop and Abel Cano, the state governor, reached an accord, and the churches reopened.

In Michoacán, Archbishop Ruiz y Flores, and the bishop of Tacámbaro, Leopoldo Lara y Torres, took forceful stands against the state law. Lara y Torres directed a lengthy memorial to Calles and the Congress, asking them to reform the Constitution. He suggested that the national government hold a plebiscite on the religious issue, insisting that the majority of the Mexicans would support his position. In a pastoral letter the bishop directed the priests of his diocese to celebrate Masses and to hear confessions in places other than the churches, so long as the government insisted upon restricting the clergy. He cautioned the faithful to respect legitimate authority, but advised them to vote for parties that favored the interests of the Church. Calles' Attorney General, Ortega, ordered the local authorities to take action against Lara y Torres, and the bishop was arrested and given a jail sentence. He was freed on bail, however, and never actually served his sentence. Ruiz y Flores, in his archdiocese, was able to work out an arrangement with the state authorities to avoid strict application of the law.[14]

The most vigorous defender of the Church was the fiery bishop of Huejutla, Manríquez y Zárate. On March 10 in his famous Sixth Pastoral Letter, "Viva Cristo Rey," he condemned and anathematized the entire constitution, not simply those articles that restricted religious liberty. He wrote: "It means nothing to me if the laws be fundamental, or organic, or of any other nature, present, past, or future, if they violate in any way the rights of the Church. . . . The president of the Republic recently declared to a North American newspaper that the religious persecution in Mexico was the result of the intervention of the Catholic clergy in the political affairs of the country. . . . The president of the Republic lies if he says such a thing. If the clergy of Mexico have committed any crime it is precisely that of not having taken part in dirty politics, and, as a result, the people have had representatives foisted upon them whom they neither know nor respect." Manríquez y Zárate called upon all Catholics in Mexico to unite in defense of their faith. They should not yield to violence, he said, but must suffer martyrdom, if necessary, before they submitted to the orders or laws of the "jaco-bin" government. At the same time, the bishop wrote to the state legislature that he was "not disposed to accept the implementation of the law" that restricted the number of priests in Hidalgo.[15]

For his forthright defense of religious liberty, Manríquez y Zárate brought upon himself the full might of the Mexican government. On April 13, Tejeda announced that the bishop would be brought for legal action before the district judge in Pachuca, the Hidalgo state capital. Three days later Romeo Ortega ordered his indict-ment. The bishop, wrote the Attorney General, "has denigrated our institutions, has provoked the public to anarchy and disobedience of the laws, has attempted to disturb the peace of the Republic, and has attacked and insulted the highest officials of the government. . . ." On April 17 the district judge ordered the bishop to come to Pa-chuca to stand trial. Manríquez y Zárate ignored the order on the ground that, under canon law, a bishop cannot be compelled to submit to civil procedures. While the civil court awaited the arrival of the bishop, he launched a new offensive upon the laws in a telegram to Álvaro Torre Díaz, governor of Yucatán, who had put into effect legislation limiting the number of clergy in his state. The bishop wrote: "The intervention of the civil government in ec-clesiastical affairs is an affront to the morality of our civilization. Your law implementing Article 130 is offensive and ridiculous."[16]

When Manríquez y Zárate ignored a second summons by the district judge, troops were dispatched to his residence, and he was placed under arrest. From Huejutla he was forced to walk to Tulan-cingo—a distance of 50 miles—while his armed escort rode horses. In Tulancingo the bishop complained of illness, and the soldiers permitted him to ride the rest of the way to Pachuca in an auto. In court he refused to name or to accept a defense attorney. To do so, he said, would be to admit the legality of this civil proceeding. The judge ordered him to remove his episcopal robes in the court, for the constitution prohibited ecclesiastical vestments in public places. Again the bishop refused, calling the laws "offensive." When the judge asked him how many primary religious schools he maintained in the diocese of Huejutla, Manríquez y Zárate replied six. Asked why he refused to close them in obedience to the laws of Mexico, the bishop answered that he recognized only the higher authority of "Natural Law." At the end of the brief hearing, in which the bishop refused to retreat from his strong stand against the constitution, the judge ordered his indefinite imprisonment for "seditious activity." Though Manríquez y Zárate was not sent to a prison, he was kept under armed guard in his residence for several months.[17]

The arrest and confinement of the bishop of Huejutla brought a strenuous protest from the Mexican episcopate. On May 28 the bishops wrote to Calles asking his intervention to obtain Manríquez y Zárate's freedom. On June 2 Calles responded, accusing the prelates of seeking to arouse public opinion against the government. Scorning the niceties of ecclesiastical or official salutations, Calles addressed his letter to "Señor José Mora y del Río." "I hope that you understand once and for all that neither the agitation you are seeking to provoke at home, nor that which you have been provoking in an unpatriotic way abroad, nor any other step that you may take in this way will be able to change the firm purpose of the federal government," he said. He cautioned the bishops to "submit yourselves to the mandate of the laws," for the government would remain inflexible. "All acts of rebellion will be punished," Calles promised. "The situation in which the bishop of Huejutla finds himself is the result of his own acts and of his haughty attitude and lack of respect for the authorities and for the law."[18]

In the weeks that followed the publication of Mora y del Río's statement of February 4, the Calles government maneuvered its forces on a broad front against the Church in Mexico. But the enforcement of the legislation continued to be spotty. In vain, Calles attempted to secure the strict application of the laws. Official circulars and directives flowed to the states from Mexico City. Police commissions and troops of soldiers were sent into the countryside to enforce the restrictions. But the federal troops could not be everywhere, and until the nationwide closing of the churches at the end of July there was never any uniform treatment of the priests or their parishioners. Here justice (or injustice) was swift and sure; there it was pliable and accommodating. Ernest Lagarde described the religious situation in the spring of 1926: "The local authorities, obliged to take into consideration the action of intermediaries, resistance, and their own interests, adopted a policy, not of principle, but of circumstance. Many a convent or college was closed and then after collusion reopened and authorized. But this situation engendered everywhere a perpetual nervousness, which alarming rumors, constantly circulated, increased and by which a group of *agents provocateurs* and adventurers endeavored to profit, proposing, for money, to settle difficulties encountered." "The only common quality in the enforcement," reported the American consul general in Mexico City, was the "innate loutishness and callousness" of the government officials toward priests and practicing Catholics.[19]

On March 4, 1926, George J. Caruana, an American citizen and the titular archbishop of Sebaste, crossed the border from Laredo, Texas, into Mexico. He was also the pope's new apostolic delegate to Mexico, although there was no public announcement of his appointment. Nor did he disclose his real mission to the customs officials in Nuevo Laredo. He was dressed in civilian clothes, and his passport, which identified him as a "religious teacher," failed to indicate that he was a priest, much less the official representative of the pope. Subsequently the Mexican government accused Caruana of illegal entry, charging that he had passed himself off as a Protestant. This was certainly not true. But it is true that his coming was most irregular and secretive, almost furtive. Concerning his casual attire, a British diplomat commented that "not even the shrewdest observer could divine his priestly calling." Later Caruana explained to the American Secretary of State, Frank B. Kellogg, that he did not mention that he was a bishop, "since I was not going to exercise my clerical function." And he told a reporter for the New York *Times* that when the immigration inspector inquired about his profession, "I stated the profession I really have, of teaching, without, however, any intention of hiding any other titles that I have." Not until March 12—after Caruana had been in Mexico City for nearly a week—did the Vatican publish notice of his appointment. In the meantime, Caruana conferred with the leading prelates in Mexico on ways to deal with the worsening religious crisis in that country.[20]

The choice of Caruana, Maltese by birth and a naturalized American citizen, was an attempt by the Vatican to avoid the trouble brought on by the appointment and expulsion of Monsignor Cimino. Evidently Pietro Gasparri, the papal Secretary of State, believed that Mexico would not dare to expel an American citizen when the two countries were engaged in crucial negotiations over the oil properties. If this was Cardinal Gasparri's intent, he erred, for the Mexicans saw the appointment as a deliberate affront to their nationalism. When the Mexico City newspapers published accounts of his mission, the Secretary of Foreign Relations, Aarón Sáenz, ordered Caruana to turn in his passport while the department investigated the means by which he had entered the country. The Spanish minister to Mexico, José Delgado y Olazábal, Marquis of Berna, added fuel to the flames by pointedly asking Sáenz why Mexico permitted Caruana to remain in the country while Spanish clergymen were being expelled. As the Secretary of Foreign Relations deliberated on what action to take against the apostolic delegate, Caruana continued to meet in Mexico with members of the episcopate and—secretly—with representatives of Calles' government.[21]

Through the month of April Caruana conferred with the bishops to plan a course of common action. Some, such as Archbishop Vera y Zuria of Puebla, cautioned against any precipitate action. Pascual Díaz favored a more militant stand. Impressed by the evident abilities of the bishop of Tabasco, Caruana arranged to bypass the older and more senior prelates and give Díaz a leading role in directing the policies of the Mexican Church. He organized an Episcopal Committee that would "guide the conduct of the Mexican Catholics." Though Mora y del Río became president, the designation of the aged prelate was merely honorary, for real power rested in Pascual Díaz, the committee's secretary. Thereafter, all public statements from the Mexican hierarchy came through Díaz' office, and his stiff attitude toward the government became the official policy of the Church.[22]

In an attempt to moderate the government's campaign against the clergy, Caruana sought to meet Luis Morones, Calles' Secretary of Commerce and the most influential member of the cabinet. Through the personal intervention of the American historian, Frank Tannenbaum, the apostolic delegate conferred with Morones "at 12 o'clock midnight after Morones had sent everybody in his office home, including his private secretary." From the tenor of their conversation, which took place with Calles' permission, if not approval, Tannenbaum felt that a way had been opened to a peaceful solution. He wrote later: "I was under the impression then that with a little more firmness on the part of the papal delegate, some working agreement could have been reached, but the insistence of both Mexican and American advisers that the Calles government should not be placated under any circumstances proved too strong." Caruana faced an impossible task. The Episcopal Committee, backed by the Mexican Knights of Columbus, the ACJM, and the Liga Nacional, wished to take an even stronger stand against the laws. Nor was Calles willing to make an agreement that would allow the Church to ignore the constitution.[23]

On May 15 the Mexican government ordered Caruana's deportation on the ground that he had entered Mexico illegally, and his expulsion served only to increase the tension between the government and the Church. The Episcopal Committee published a new letter of protest to Calles, insisting that the apostolic delegate had been expelled "without sufficient cause." They saw the action as "yet another affront to the Holy See by the Mexican government." They told Calles: "We make before you and the world a most solemn protest and declare our irrevocable adherence to the Pontiff." When the American ambassador to Mexico, Henry Sheffield, remonstrated with the Mexican government over the incident, Sáenz told him that under canon law the mere fact that Caruana was apostolic delegate demonstrated that he was carrying out religious functions in Mexico, and therefore his actions were illegal.[24]

Though Catholics in the United States complained bitterly in public statements, the American government took no official action on Caruana's expulsion. Michael J. Curley, archbishop of Baltimore, said: "We protest to President Coolidge and Secretary Kellogg against the action of Mexico's bolsheviks. . . . But what's the use?" "If it were a case of this injustice being inflicted upon the little handful of Methodists in Mexico, I have no doubt about our seeing this administration extremely active to prevent the contrivance of such a persecution." Francis C. Kelley, now bishop of Oklahoma, telegraphed Coolidge, calling upon him to break diplomatic relations with the Calles government.[25]

As earlier during the Wilson administration, Bishop Kelley continued to take a keen interest in Mexican affairs, and he raised his voice (though not so stridently as in the Democratic years) against the policy of maintaining relations with the Calles government. In 1926 the principal Catholic critic of the Coolidge administration was the peppery, often intemperate, Irish archbishop of Baltimore. In the Congress two representatives from New York, John J. Boylan and Benjamin L. Fairchild, took up the cause of the Mexican Catholics. As the Calles government moved in early February 1926 to expel the foreign priests and nuns, Democrat Boylan offered a resolution in the House of Representatives, directing the Secretary of State to make available information on the expulsion of American citizens. He had discussed the matter with Archbishop Curley, he told the press. He said of the Mexican action: "The drive against the priests and ministers violates the deepest instincts of humanity. Even savages have permitted holy men to come among them and live unmolested while preaching the word of God." A week later, as the expulsions continued, Boylan took a stronger stand, demanding that the United States government "take prompt steps to protect its citizens in Mexico." "We are one of the greatest countries in the world. It is our duty to enforce respect for our citizens in any country in which they may domicile." Fairchild, who was a Republican, joined Boylan in demands that the United States take stern measures to protect American citizens in Mexico. Mexico, he said, was "like a sore fist thrust up into the very bowels of the United States." He told reporters that the current crisis could focus American attention on Mexico and "arouse our public . . . to the need of effective measures for a permanent cure."[26]

While Boylan and Fairchild stressed the necessity of protecting American interests, the prelates and the lay Catholic organizations in the United States showed more concern for the broader issue of the persecution of all Catholics in Mexico. On February 18 Curley attacked the State Department again for neglecting the Mexican Catholics. As priests were "chased from the country like mad dogs," he said, the government of the United States had "taken Mexico into our national arms." The leading American Catholics harped on the theme of the Communist threat in Mexico, alleging that the attack of the government on the Church—and on the oil properties as well—was part of a worldwide bolshevik plot. Bishop Kelley told a meeting of the Knights of Columbus in Brooklyn that "the tirade on the Church is to cover up something else, and this time the something else is the theft of the capital of Americans in Mexico." Kelley hoped that by tying the religious persecution to the oil question the American government might be led to intervene against Calles. Though the avowed purpose of the intervention would be to aid the oil companies, the result would be the overthrow of Calles and the salvation of the Church in Mexico. As the Mexican crisis heightened during the spring and summer of 1926, the voices of outraged Catholicism in the United States grew even shriller. The American Knights of Columbus played a leading role in a campaign to bring about the overthrow of Calles.[27]

On March 8 Boylan told a mass meeting in Washington, sponsored by the Knights, that the Calles government would collapse immediately if American recognition were withdrawn. The Catholics should demand that the United States withdraw recognition from the "bolshevik and robber government of Mexico," he said. As a result of Fairchild's and Boylan's charges, the House Foreign Affairs committee agreed to hold hearings on the withdrawal of recognition. The witnesses came almost exclusively from the vociferous group of Catholics, and almost nothing was said about the oil properties. Mother Margaret Semple, one of the American nuns expelled from Mexico, told the committee of her harsh treatment at the hands of the Calles police. She urged the committee to recommend a break in diplomatic relations between the United States and Mexico "until such time as the conduct of that government in respect to education and religious institutions justifies resumption of such relations." Archbishop Curley did not appear personally, but he was represented by Charles W. Darr, a Washington lawyer. Darr told the committee; "Mexico has evidenced through its constitution a strong desire to eventually become as red as the bolsheviks."[28]

Another Catholic layman, Judge Alfred J. Talley of New York, testified that Mexican soldiers had taken a group of Carmelite nuns from their cloister and attempted to sell them to houses of prostitution. He did not reveal the source of his information or say when the event had occurred. Talley reiterated the cries of other Catholics, maintaining that it was unwise for the United States to support a government in Mexico that was "honeycombed with soviet ideas." After Boylan read into the record a letter from the Catholic Press Association (representing 100 Catholic newspapers in the United States) that echoed his proposal, the committee members agreed to take no action at that time. The witnesses had presented insufficient evidence, they felt, to warrant recommending a break in diplomatic relations.[29]

Unable to secure action in the Congress, the Catholic spokesmen took their campaign to the president and the Department of State. Curley complained bitterly that while the Catholics of Mexico were being tyrannized by their government, President Coolidge entertained high Mexican officials at a White House dinner. Coolidge gave the impression, said the archbishop, of approving the "bitter anti-Catholicism of the gunmen now ruling and ruining Mexico." "If Washington would only leave Mexico alone," he wrote, "and cease its unfair support of the present bolshevist government, Calles and his band would not last a month." On April 15, Curley and other American prelates directed a letter to Coolidge that urged the breaking of relations with Mexico. They charged that under the original agreement granting recognition to the Carranza regime, the Mexicans had bound themselves to respect religious liberties. It was the duty of the United States, they said, to insist that the Mexicans comply with that agreement. And even more important for the American government than guarding the rights of foreigners, they felt, was the "protection of religious, civil, and human rights" in Mexico. For the bishops it was not simply a question of diplomacy, but of actual intervention in internal Mexican affairs.[30]

The president passed on the protest to the Secretary of State, and on April 21 Kellogg conferred with Father John J. Burke of the National Catholic Welfare Conference, pointing out that the bishops' letter contained many inaccuracies. If the prelates published their letter, he said, he would need to make a formal reply defending the department's policy. Because the religious legislation of Mexico was a domestic matter, he told Burke, the United States had no right to protest formally unless the laws injured the vested rights of Americans. In specific instances that involved American churchmen in Mexico, he said, Ambassador Sheffield had used his good offices to secure a satisfactory settlement. Father Burke agreed that he would get in touch with the prelates and would report to them the attitude of the State Department. Three weeks later Father Burke met Franklin M. Gunther, Chief of the Division of Mexican Affairs, to press the bishops' case. Gunther reported later to Kellogg: "I think his attitude so far has been governed by the feeling that the Catholics in the United States were so important politically that more action should be taken on their behalf than in behalf of others." Subsequently, the bishops agreed to make the changes in their letter suggested by Kellogg, but when it was released in May it still made a strong plea for American action against the Calles government.[31]

The propaganda and political pressure exerted by the Catholics failed to modify America's foreign policy. The expulsion of foreign clergy affected only a handful of American citizens, and the Mexican government punctiliously observed correct diplomatic procedures in ousting the Americans, giving them ample notice and more time to obtain adequate transportation than the Spaniards. If the petroleum issue could be settled satisfactorily, the State Department saw no reason for taking action in Mexico to protect Mexican citizens from their own government. From time to time the State Department through Sheffield made observations and suggestions concerning the effect of Mexico's religious policy on world opinion. But at no time did the United States consider forcing out Calles by withdrawing recognition from his government. Moreover, the American Catholics erred in believing that they had sufficient political power to force a change in the Mexican policy of the government. In an era of strong anti-Catholicism, when the Ku Klux Klan waxed strong, not only in the South, but in northern states as well, many Protestants were pleased to see the Catholic Church in Mexico get its comeuppance. As often as an American Catholic leader raised alarums against a bolshevik Mexico, a Protestant minister stressed the democratic qualities in Calles' administration and insisted upon a policy of friendship between the two countries. As for the American Protestant ministers in Mexico, they were only too glad to obey the law and to cooperate with the government. Of the few Protestant missionaries forced to leave the country, most were Mormons whose polygamous practices and energetic proselytizing had long irritated the Mexicans.[32]

In the face of the many attacks on Catholics, the Mexican prelates, under the leadership of the Episcopal Committee, closed ranks and prepared to defend their principles. On April 21 they published a lengthy pastoral letter setting forth in clear and unmistakable terms the position of the Church in the modern society. The words of the bishops gave no hint of retreat, condemning in forthright terms, not only the revolutionary government of Mexico, but the entire religious, political, and economic structure of the non-Catholic world. The letter asserted the ultimate supremacy of the Church over the secular authority. If the principles laid down in the pastoral letter were followed to their logical conclusion, Protestantism would have disappeared in Mexico, and Catholicism would have become the sole legal religion of the country. Toleration of other political philosophies would have ended, as the Church took control of the educational system and political and social action as well.

Of the existing political conditions in Mexico, the prelates said flatly: "We cannot tolerate them." Bishops had been molested and persecuted, priests violently expelled, schools closed, "virgins" thrown into the streets by the police of Calles. "It is our duty and our right to see that the constitution be reformed without delay and by all legal means in order to satisfy the legitimate aspirations of the people for complete freedom. This conduct is not rebellion, for the constitution itself establishes its amendability and opens the way for its reform. . . ." The Church, they insisted, "does not seek conflict, but if it is compelled to renounce its liberty and to disappear, or to defend itself legally, but vigorously, it will never betray its cause, which is that of God and of country."[33]

Tejeda sent the pastoral letter to the office of the Attorney General for possible prosecution of its signers under Article 130. "The Catholic clergy is seeking to create an ecclesiastic government," he said, "invading the sovereignty of the government of the Republic." The president asked only that the clergy obey the laws, Tejeda said. To suggestions of some peacemakers that Mexico confer with the Vatican as a means to end the crisis, he replied: "The only modus vivendi acceptable to the government is respect for our laws and the punishment of those violating them."[34]

Despite the truculence of Tejada and the seeming resoluteness of the Catholic leaders, the crisis subsided during May and most of June. The Liga Nacional busied itself collecting 500,000 signatures for a petition asking the Congress to modify the religious laws. At the same time, the Catholic leaders traveled throughout Mexico establishing centers of action in the event the conflict intensified. The government, aware of the failure of many local officials to enforce the constitution, worked out means to insure uniformity of action against the Church. As June began the attention of Mexico's Catholics shifted to Chicago and the great Eucharistic Congress held in that city. In January, before the crisis had erupted, clerics and laymen had been making elaborate plans to send a large delegation to Chicago. But now the government made clear that bishops attending the Congress might not be permitted to return to Mexico. The always dauntless Orozco y Jiménez ignored the warning and journeyed to Chicago. Subsequently, he slipped back across the border unnoticed. Publicly and officially the Eucharistic Congress had little to do with the Mexican situation. But many secret meetings took place in Chicago between Mexican priests and Catholic leaders from other countries, in which the Mexicans asked for aid in their struggle. Calles' government seized upon the occasion of the Eucharistic Congress and the presence of Mexican priests in Chicago to justify new penal legislation, putting teeth into Article 130 and the sections of Article 27 that referred to the clergy.[35]

In reality, however, government lawyers had worked for weeks on the enabling legislation to enforce the constitution's antireligious provisions. Calles' anticlerical campaign was hindered by the lack of any means to punish offenders against the two articles. Article 33, because it stated the means of punishment, could be easily enforced. The foreign priests were in Mexico illegally and could be deported by presidential order. The president could also order the closing of monasteries and nunneries, though the monks and nuns might assemble in secular houses. But Articles 3 and 130 could not legally be enforced. On June 14, therefore, Calles decreed the necessary *leyes reglamentarias,* though they were not published in the *Diario Oficial* until July 2. (It is important to note that the laws were not enacted by the Congress, which was not in session at the time and would not meet again until September.) Calles based his action on the broad and undefined powers granted him by the Congress in the previous session to reform the civil and penal codes of Mexico. But the original grant of authority had made no mention of specific areas of legislation, and at the time no one anticipated the implementation of the religious articles. Further, the Congress had given the president the extraordinary authority only until the following legislative session, when the two chambers would review his use of the powers. Calles' decree of June 14 applied only to the Federal District and the territories of Mexico, not to the individual states. Additional legislation by the Congress would be required before the penal code reforms could be legally effective in the greater part of the Republic. Nonetheless, both the government and the Church subsequently treated the decree as though it applied throughout Mexico.[36]

The decree made a massive assault on the position of the Church in Mexico. In many ways it was more drastic than the constitution itself, going beyond the restrictions imposed at Querétaro in 1917.

It specifically forbade any religious function by foreigners, religious education in primary schools, and the control of schools by a religious body; it outlawed monastic orders and nunneries. If an "excloistered" person should return to community life after his order had dissolved, he was liable to imprisonment for from one to two years. Calles said: "The state cannot permit any contract, pact, or agreement that may have as an object the deterioration, loss, or irrevocable sacrifice of the liberty of man, whether it may be for the reason of work, education, or religious vows." Persons who induced or led a minor to renounce his liberty by taking a religious vow would be fined, even though there might be "bonds of relationship between them."

Severe penalties were provided for political activity by the members of the clergy. Priests were forbidden "to associate themselves for political purposes," and no meetings of a political character could take place in the churches. The decree banned political parties with names "relating to any religious creed." No religious acts would be permitted outside the churches, and the churches and all buildings associated with them—the episcopal residences, parish houses, seminaries, asylums, colleges, and convents—were declared to be the property of the nation. Calles' decree required the priest in charge of each church, within one month after the law became effective, to register with the public authorities. Failure to do so would lead to his imprisonment for 15 days or a fine of 500 pesos.[37]

The Catholic laymen of Mexico responded with vehemence to the publication of the decree. Mora y del Río would make no comment to the press, but the leaders of ACJM and the Knights of Columbus were unanimous in condemning Calles. ACJM announced: "We are studying a plan of action that we shall soon put into practice, for we cannot remain silent in the face of the latest decree, which we believe is religious persecution." The central committee of the Liga Nacional, after studying various means of combating the decree, decided on an economic boycott. Because this method had succeeded in 1919 in forcing the Jaliscan government to end its restriction on the number of clergy in the state, the Catholic laymen believed this to be the most effective method of dealing with Calles. Hoping for ecclesiastical support, the lay leaders met with the Episcopal Committee in Mexico City. The principal directors of the League, ACJM, Damas Católicas, and the Knights of Columbus attended, in addition to the chief prelates of Mexico. The League's

president, Ceniceros y Villarreal, informed the Episcopal Committee of the proposed boycott. Mora y del Río asked him to make his
proposal in writing. This was done, and a week later the League
received a letter from the prelates giving their official sanction to the
boycott. Ceniceros y Villarreal, as head of the organization, and
Capistrán Garza and Luis G. Bustos, the League's vice-presidents,
began to prepare circulars explaining the boycott to the public.[38]

If the laymen were united and militant, the prelates seemed disorganized by the government's show of force. Most members of the
Episcopal Committee, in contrast to their uncompromising stand in
the pastoral letter of April 21, now in the first week of July favored
a cautious course of action. Some believed that the requirement for
the registration of the clergy was not contrary to canon law, and that
some means could be found to circumvent the other provisions of
the decrees. They feared that a protracted struggle with the government could have only dire consequences for the Church in Mexico.
Msgr. Tito Crespi, in charge of the apostolic delegation once more
after Caruana's expulsion, proposed that the bishops seek to conciliate Calles, rather than oppose him openly. Crespi saw that the
suspension of services in Tabasco and Colima had harmed the faithful without having any visible effect on the government. Pascual
Díaz was now among those who favored temporizing, but he kept
a weather eye out for changes in the episcopal sentiment.

During the evening of July 11 the Episcopal Committee assembled in the residence of Mora y del Río to make a final decision on
the course to be followed by the prelates. Orozco y Jiménez and
González Valencia spoke strongly and passionately for militant action, and their arguments carried the day. The bishops decided that
the moment for a showdown with the government had arrived. The
committee determined to combat the decrees by refusing to permit
the priests to register and by suspending all services in the churches
until the obnoxious decree was rescinded. Bishop Díaz, as secretary
of the committee, prepared a letter to Caruana (still the apostolic
delegate to Mexico, though he resided in Havana), informing him
of the prelates' action. He told Caruana that if the Mexican bishops
received no reply from the Holy See, they would assume that the
Vatican approved their decision. Because he hesitated to communicate with Caruana through the official telegraph system, Díaz sent
Manual de la Peza, of the Knights of Columbus, to Havana with the
note.[39]

Tito Crespi feared that the bishops' decision was suicidal, and he cabled to Gasparri his apprehension concerning the suspension of services. The papal Secretary of State also favored a policy of conciliation, but he told Crespi that he would accede to the wishes of the Mexican bishops, if their decision was unanimous. On his own initiative, however, Crespi decided to make a personal appeal to the government for conciliation. He asked Ernest Lagarde to secure an interview with Tejeda, the Secretary of Gobernación. When Tejeda agreed, Crespi begged the French chargé d'affaires to accompany him to the interview, for he had misgivings about Tejeda's well-known violent anticlericalism. Crespi sought in every way to make a favorable impression upon Tejeda. He pointed out that the Holy Father had long recognized the shortcomings of the Mexican clergy, and that he was determined to see a reform. The pope, said Crespi, had insisted that the priests and bishops keep out of politics. And to demonstrate this new outlook of the Vatican, he pointed out that the traditional practice of private worship by rich Mexicans in their own chapels would be ended. Finally, getting to the point of this interview, Crespi asked the Mexican government to suspend the applications of the decree until a satisfactory solution could be worked out.

Tejeda was unmoved by Crespi's pleas for moderation. He insisted that his government did not oppose the principle of religious freedom, but wanted simply to squelch the political ambitions of the clergy. The priests were in open rebellion against the constitution, he said, and his government was determined to enforce the law in its entirety, whatever the cost. The president would neither modify the law nor suspend its operation. Tejeda told Crespi that the Church had legal means to secure the reform of the laws, and that he hoped that Rome would ask Mexican Catholics to stop their agitation and work within the constitution. Crespi saw that it was useless to talk further with Tejeda, and the interview ended.[40]

It was, indeed, too late for conciliation; Gasparri had already agreed to the course proposed by the Episcopal Committee. He telegraphed Caruana: "The Holy See condemns the law and, as a consequence, every act that might signify or be interpreted by the faithful as an acceptance or recognition of that law."[41]

As the lay and ecclesiastical leaders perfected plans for their campaign to force the government to end its persecution of the Church, representatives of both sides worked through the last two weeks of

July to seek some new means of keeping the Catholic schools open. Mixed committees negotiated on the government demands that all primary education conform to the constitutional restrictions on religious teaching in the schools. The government required the removal of all religious objects from the schools. On instructions from the Vatican, however, the Catholics insisted, as a minimum requirement, that they keep the figure of Jesus Christ on the classroom walls. The government negotiators remained adamant, refusing to concede even this point to the Catholics. On July 23 Calles published his decree implementing Article 3, thus effectively putting an end to the negotiations. Following the constitutional ban on religious education, the decree stipulated that all primary schools would be lay and would not "teach, defend, or attack any religion." The schools could have no chapel or oratory and religious decorations or objects of any sort. No minister could teach in or direct a primary school, and the curriculum of all the schools would be supervised by the Ministry of Education. With the expulsion of great numbers of foreign priests and nuns, who had formed the backbone of Mexico's Catholic educational system, and the implementation and enforcement of Article 3, the Catholics had little choice but to close their schools. The Catholic leaders hoped that the lack of educational facilities, as well as the pressure of Catholic parents whose children were denied schooling, would force the government to change its course.[42]

More and more, as the bishops and priests prepared to shut down the schools and churches, the effective leadership of the Catholic movement passed to the laymen. With great energy the leaders of Liga Nacional pushed their program of economic boycott to cripple the government. On July 17 the League published details of the plan "to paralyze in every way possible the social and economic life of the country." The League called upon all Catholics to cooperate in refusing to buy any goods except "absolute necessities for the day's subsistence." They would not purchase clothing, fruits, candy, ice cream, refreshing drinks, or lottery tickets. They would abstain from using all vehicles, "except the plainest and least costly." They would not attend theaters, movies, dance halls, or parties. They would limit their consumption of electric energy. And the League asked the faithful to withdraw their children from the public schools.[43]

The reaction of the government to the threatened boycott was immediate and decisive. Romeo Ortega denounced the plan as "seditious," and he ordered the arrest of those responsible for printing and distributing the boycott circulars. On July 21 two young Catholics, Humberto Pro Juárez and José del Rincón Leguelichi, were taken into custody by the police while distributing broadsides in front of a church. On the following day the police raided the League headquarters in Mexico City, arresting everyone they found in the office, including René Capistrán Garza. Other agents captured Ceniceros y Villarreal and Bustos at their homes. None of the prisoners sought *amparos* to obtain his release, and all were taken to the military prison of Santiago Tlatelolco. The arrest and confinement of the League's leaders did not stop the campaign, however, for ACJM members vied with one another for the dangerous task of distributing the circulars. They devised ingenious means of propagandizing the League's program, including the launching of small balloons carrying their literature. The Attorney General ordered Pascual Díaz to come to his office to explain the Church's position on the boycott. The bishop of Tabasco disclaimed ecclesiastical responsibility for the circulars, affirming that the campaign was the work of lay groups only. Ortega permitted Díaz to return to the archiepiscopal palace, but the arrest of young Catholics went on. By the end of the month the effects of the boycott were noticeable in the capital and other principal cities in the Republic. To signify their adherence to the boycott women wore black clothes and large black rebozos.[44]

Calles was unmoved by the determination of the Catholics to resist his decree. Each new act of the laymen and bishops only confirmed his prejudices and made him more resolute. On a speaking tour of northern Mexico, Calles referred again and again in bitter and at times coarse language to the rebellious attitude of the clergy. The American ambassador reported that Calles, "while sane on other matters, completely loses control of himself when the matter of religion comes up, becomes livid in the face, and pounds the table to express his hatred and profound antagonism to the practice of religion." In Monterrey the president told a cheering crowd: "No domestic or foreign influence, including the farts of the pope, will be able to change the attitude of my government." The president ridiculed the lay Catholic leaders as "ladies who leave their husbands at home while they organize processions of female servants, and lawyers whose object is to become trustees of camouflaged religious institutions and obtain social and therefore business connections with men of fortune." Nor was Tejeda, who was responsible for enforcing Calles' decree, more temperate. He told the French chargé d'affaires: "Whatever happens, we will not yield, and we have the force to exact obedience. We have the clergy by the throat, and we shall do everything to strangle them." The leaders of CROM backed the government's stand, charging that the Church had leagued itself with the capitalists to oppress the Mexican workers. They promised to oppose the boycott in every way possible, declaring that a rally would be held in the capital on August 1 to support Calles.[45]

On July 24 the bishops and archbishops of Mexico published a collective pastoral letter to announce their plans for resisting the government. They emphasized that since 1917 "our conduct has been one of prudent silence, because the antireligious articles were not applied up to the point of making impossible the life of the Church." But the decree of July 2 was "so contrary to natural law" that "it would be a crime for us to tolerate such a situation." It was clear, they wrote, that the decree, instead of promoting the common welfare and freedom of religion, would de-Catholicize Mexico. "For this reason, following the example of the pope, before God, before civilized humanity, before the country, and before history, we protest against this decree." "Counting upon the favor of God and your help," they told the Mexican Catholics, "we shall not rest until we have attained our purpose." The bishops were determined not to register the priests, lest Calles' government subsequently refuse to recognize some and take into its own hands the power to decide who could function as a priest in Mexico. Because of the "impossibility of practicing our sacred ministry under this decree," they wrote, "and after having consulted the most Holy Father, His Holiness the pope, and with his ratification, we order that after July 31 until we order otherwise all religious services requiring the intervention of priests shall be suspended in all the churches of the country." The bishops directed that the faithful withdraw their children from the public schools and support the economic boycott proclaimed by the Liga Nacional. And they threatened excommunication against those in the government who attacked the rights of the Church, the priests, and the bishops.[46]

The last week of July witnessed an orgy of religiosity unparalleled in the nation's history. As though they feared the millennium, thousands of Catholics flocked to churches to make amends for the years of neglecting their religious duties. From July 24—the day the pastoral letter was read in all the churches of the Republic—until the end of the month the churches were crowded from early dawn until late at night with countless numbers of Mexicans, receiving communion or bringing their children for baptism or confirmation. The Sagrario Metropolitán, adjacent to Mexico City's cathedral, had long been a favorite baptismal place. Now thousands of parents, carrying their babies, made their way to the capital. Long lines formed in the church and outside completely around the Zócalo. In one day over 2,000 children were baptized in the one church. Inside, though the Church was comparatively cool, the priests sweated profusely over their labors. So great was the press of massed bodies that two children reportedly suffocated in their parents' arms. Outside in the Zócalo vendors set up stands to sell tortillas, candy, ice cream, and cold drinks, doing a thriving business throughout the day. The government of the Federal District took advantage of the occasion to station sanitation officers outside the doors of the cathedral, forcibly vaccinating everyone who left the church—many thousands with the same needle.[47]

In the cathedral, next door, three bishops confirmed the older children almost on a production-line basis, while several priests administered First Communion. The children of the more affluent wore the white dresses and the fussy, almost effeminate white uniforms affected by the boys for the singular occasion. In the crowded church their elegance contrasted starkly with the tattered garb of the poor. For 14 straight hours children and their parents moved in long lines through the cathedral. On July 28 the aged archbishop of Mexico collapsed from his exertions, and his doctors ordered him to stop administering confirmation. On the same day, Pascual Díaz confirmed more than 5,000 children. Marriages too, were performed at an unprecedented rate, more than 600 in one day in Mexico City alone, as many participants sought to regularize free unions or to gain religious sanction for civil marriages. (There was the further undoubted advantage that these wedding ceremonies were performed free of charge on this occasion.) On July 25 a panic occurred in the cathedral when a photographer exploded a magnesium flash to take a picture of the crowded church. More than 3,000 persons were in the cathedral, and the flash caused some one to shout that a bomb had exploded. The crowd rushed to the exits in great terror, the stronger pushing over the weaker, heedless of their welfare. Many were injured before the crowd could be quieted, though fortunately no one was killed.[48]

Similar displays of piety took place at the basilica of Guadalupe, as thousands of other Mexicans trudged the dusty miles from their villages or their homes in Mexico City to the Virgin's shrine at Tepeyac. In the basilica a lone priest said Mass at a side altar, assisted by a single acolyte, but the pilgrms, in the main, ignored the service. They had come to pay their respects to the dark Mother of God in their own Indian way. All of the cities, towns, and villages of the Republic experienced the same abnormal demonstrations of Catholicity. Throughout the week the newspapers of Mexico and the United States reported in detail these religious manifestations. The good, grey New York *Times* offered its readers minute descriptions of the crowds and of the churches, often in flights of poetic fancy rare to its news pages. On July 29 the *Times* reporter wrote: "From the wretched hovels and the sumptuous residences of grandees, from the burning tropics to the frigid mountain places, from sea to sea, from lonely ranches and all but forgotten villages to the very plaza of the president's palace itself, on which also faces Mexico City's great cathedral, the faithful of the Catholic Church swept in countless multitudes to their places of worship, beseeching the divine authority to come to the relief of the faith they hold dear, and which they believe is endangered."[49]

The government took a jaundiced view of the religious demonstrations. Police agents continued to arrest members of the Liga Nacional and the ACJM. The editor of *El Faro,* a Catholic newspaper, was jailed for publishing allegedly seditious material. In an effort to still the anxieties of the faithful, Mora y del Río announced on July 28 that the priests' leaving the churches did not mean a complete cessation of religious services. Masses could be celebrated and baptisms and marriages performed in homes of the priests. The bishops issued instructions, also, to permit lay baptisms in emergencies. And the Catholics were told that in lieu of a formal confession before a priest a simple act of contrition could be considered satisfactory for administering extreme unction or the marriage rite. Further, the churches would be kept open by the laymen of the parishes, who could read together from the missal as though the priest were actually saying Mass.[50]

To avoid trouble with the government, Mora y del Río ordered the suspension of services advanced one day, from the original date of July 31. Late in the night of July 30—all of the churches remained open until midnight that week—the age-old continuity of Catholic religious services was broken. For the first time in the history of the Republic no Masses, no confessions, no ceremony requiring the presence of a priest took place in the churches. Armed federal troops patrolled the streets to insure the peace. The transformation came with a minimum of trouble, though isolated acts of violence occurred. In Mexico City, the police fired into a crowd of women in the Church of San Rafael when they refused to leave the building. In Guadalajara and in Torreón there were local riots. But as July ended the government seemed calm and confident. Calles announced that most of the churches would be kept open and that his government would enforce the constitutional provision of lay control over the buildings.[51]

The Church leaders, too, entertained hopes of success. And the weapons available to the prelates and laymen must have seemed impressive. To the Church the spiritual armament was most potent of all. Though the Vatican and the bishops had toyed briefly with the idea of imposing an interdict, they rejected this device as archaic. But the cessation of services was intended to achieve the same purpose. The overwhelming number of Mexicans, being members of the Catholic Church, would feel keenly the lack of public religious services and would force the government to accept the bishops' conditions. From the Church's viewpoint the logic was impeccable —man's greatest fear is of eternal punishment, not of temporal inconveniences; therefore, the Mexicans would respond by insisting upon the restoration of services on terms laid down by the prelates. But the argument that may have seemed overwhelming in the day of Thomas Aquinas, no longer applied to modern man. And especially it did not apply to most Mexicans, who had demonstrated for generations that they did not consider the ministrations of a priest essential to their religious life. They could still make pilgrimages to Guadalupe or Chalma. They could still pray to and scold their favorite saint. The cessation of services did not measurably change their wonted devotions. Moreover, the Church did not intend to deprive the Mexicans of the services completely. They were still provided, though on an irregular basis, in homes and other private buildings. Priests carried the sacraments to the old; they performed weddings and baptisms; they administered extreme unction. Thus the priests' withdrawal from the churches had almost no effect on the traditional religious practices of Mexico.

If spiritual weapons did not suffice, the Church had other arms in its ecclesiastical arsenal. These were temporal and material— armed revolution and economic boycott. The Catholics might deal with the government in terms that the government could understand and appreciate. Church leaders were handicapped, however, by the theological ban on revolution against a legally constituted government. It was a fine theological distinction, for the question of whether Mexico's revolutionary government was legally constituted was difficult to decide. It had come to power through military force. It maintained itself by authoritarian means, without free elections. The constitution had been imposed by a small minority of revolutionaries and had never been submitted to a vote for popular approval or rejection. The Catholics could have made a good case, therefore, for the contention that Calles' regime was illegal. Yet the bishops did not push the point. For whatever, reason, with only two or three exceptions, the prelates never gave official approval to armed revolt against the government. If Catholic laymen turned to revolution to overthrow the tyrannical government (and many soon did so), the bishops maintained an aloofness from the dirty business of life-taking that came to vex the Catholic rebels. Despite the charges of the government and of the Catholics' enemies in the United States, the hierarchy in Mexico did not sanction the Catholic revolt. The bishops took care, however, not to condemn the revolts. They saw that the rebels' cause was just. They sympathized with the aims of the religious revolution. Nor did the Vatican restrict the freedom of the Mexican Catholics to take up arms in defense of their religion. If the rebels had succeeded in toppling Calles and installing a new regime, it is certain that their government would have been highly acceptable to the bishops. They would be glad to proclaim that this government was legally constituted and would take advantage of the change of regimes to bring about the constitutional reforms they demanded.

As the Church strike began, the economic boycott proclaimed by the Liga Nacional seemed the most important arm of the Catholics. Its effect was immediately apparent. Store business slacked off. Merchants, particularly in Jalisco, were hard hit by the campaign. But the success of the boycott proved illusory and short-lived. The summer of 1926 saw a general economic stagnation in Mexico. Many states experienced poor harvests, caused by bad weather and the dislocations of the government's modest agrarian reform program. Oil production had fallen off, and the sisal industry of Yucatán was hard hit by the loss of foreign markets. As a result, all the boycott campaign could do was to make a bad situation worse. Soon after the closing of churches, the American consul-general in Mexico, Alexander Weddell, asked each consular agent to assess economic conditions in his area. Only Dudley Dwyre in Guadalajara (and his report was corroborated by the British vice-consul) could see that the boycott had any effect whatsoever, and even in that most Catholic city the campaign had begun to peter out by the end of August.[52]

The ebullient plans of the young Catholics to overthrow Calles through the boycott were dashed on the hard rocks of economic realities. Too much depended on the lower classes, who were to bear the brunt of the privation. The poor of Mexico rarely bought luxuries. For the Liga Nacional and the ACJM to say that Mexicans should buy no more than they actually needed, that they should not travel first-class in trains, that they should not go to dances or theaters was tantamount to saying that they should live precisely as they had always done. For this reason, the boycott failed. After August the only avenues open to the Church were a sudden turn of heart by Calles and his government (and Pope Pius asked all Catholics throughout the world to pray on August 1, the Feast day of St. Peter in Chains, for the Mexican Catholics), a military victory by the Catholic rebels, or the withdrawal of diplomatic representation by the American government.

Calles made it abundantly clear that he would never change his attitude toward the Church. On August 1—it was a Sunday—he celebrated the closing of the churches by picnicking with friends at a presidentail hideout near Xochimilco. It was not a family affair. A friend of Calles described it as a "love nest," and noted the presence of four American women, "high class adventuresses," who could not speak Spanish. Calles fairly glowed with satisfaction, and exulted that it was "one of the greatest days in Mexican history." To a reporter the president looked like a "well-trained athlete." His friends told an American diplomatic agent that they had never seen the president "so expansive and so cordial."[53]

Earlier the same morning Calles had reviewed a parade in the capital organized by CROM, to show the "solidarity of the labor class" and the workers' approval of Calles' religious policy. Though union leaders had billed the parade as a massive demonstration of popular support and had predicted that more than 150,000 persons would participate, it proved to be a relatively small and peaceful affair. Mora y del Río requested all Catholics to keep off the streets to avoid trouble. The heads of the various government departments in the capital ordered their workers to take part under pain of dismissal, but Alberto J. Pani, Calles' Minister of the Treasury, refused to put pressure on his employees and left them free to attend or stay away as they pleased. Probably no more than 10,000 workers actually took part in the demonstration. The marchers included hundreds of "emancipated" women with bobbed hair— flouting Mora y del Río's edict that any woman who cut her hair in his archdiocese would be refused admittance to the churches.[54]

Many expected Obregón, who still commanded a wide political influence, to break with Calles, or at least to abstain from taking part in the controversy. But Obregón was already laying the ground for a deal with Calles, whereby the constitution would be amended so that the former president could return to office. When a reporter interviewed Obregón in Nogales, he placed the responsibility for the crisis solely on the bishops. "It is evident," he said, "That the high dignitaries of the Catholic Church have provoked this conflict, since through the mouthpiece of their highest representative, Archbishop Mora y del Río, they issued their first declaration in a spirit of manifest rebellion against the fundamental laws that govern us." For Obregón, the chief issue remained obedience to the laws by the Catholic clergy.[55]

In an effort to bring a quick settlement, several Latin American governments tendered their good offices to Calles and the Mexican Church. President Augusto B. Leguía of Peru cabled Calles that all the Latin American countries were "watching with pain" the religious strife in Mexico. Calles rejected Leguía's offer sarcastically: "I am quite convinced that your Excellency is expressing a purely personal opinion that will not and cannot influence in any way this question, which is purely a Mexican one." Calles turned down all proposals for a truce with the Church, insisting that he would enforce the law. In turn, *Osservatore Romano* made clear the Vatican's position that so long as Mexico's "persecuting religious laws" remained in effect, negotiations were impossible between the civil and ecclesiastical authorities. In Mexico City the prelates took an equally firm stand. Though Mora y del Río refused to make a statement to the press, on the ground that the government "misinterpreted" everything he said, Pascual Díaz, now almost the sole public spokesman for the Mexican Catholics insisted that the Church would not back away from its stand. But he disclaimed any intention to support armed rebellion. The Church, he said, could approve only "peaceful and orderly action," such as the Liga Nacional's boycott.[56]

On August 16 the prelates made what the newspapers called a "definite peace offer" to Calles. But the terms were those of the Church, and it did not represent a retreat from the position they had previously taken. The Episcopal Committee sent a memorial to the president asking him to use his influence to bring about a reform of the constitution. The prelates pointed out that Carranza had voiced his disapproval of the religious restrictions in the constitution, and that the articles had not been enforced during the two previous administrations. They asked as "Christians, as citizens of a civilized nation, and as men" for the rights of freedom of conscience, thought, belief, education, association, and the press. They petitioned also for the recognition of the juridical personality of the Church. Because it would take time for the government to reform the constitution—the Congress would not meet until September 1 —the bishops requested Calles to suspend the application of his decree and of the offending articles of the constitution.[57]

In his reply Calles assured the bishops that they had every right to appeal to the Congress to change the constitution or take their case to the courts. "But I should tell you, in all sincerity, that I am the least likely person to do what you ask. For the articles of the constitution, which you are attacking, are in perfect accord with my philosophic and political convictions." He refused to suspend the laws and insisted that under the constitution the Church could never be recognized as a juridical personality. Pascual Díaz expressed satisfaction to newspaper reporters with "the frankness of Calles' answer," and promised that the Episcopal Committee would accept the president's invitation to submit the matter to the Congress.[58]

Hoping to head off a protracted struggle, however, Eduardo Mestre Ghiliazzi and Agustín Legoretta, prominent lay Catholics who were friends of Calles, sought to bring about a negotiated peace by means of a personal interview between the president and representatives of the Episcopal Committee. Business interests feared the economic consequences of a long boycott, which in the first two weeks of August seemed more effective than it actually was. Mestre proposed to Archbishop Vera y Zuria of Puebla that the bishops request an interview with Calles, and the president readily assented —"whichever ones you like," he said. In the evening of August 21 Archbishop Ruiz y Flores and Pascual Díaz came to the presidential palace to ask Calles personally for an end to the conflict. Díaz and Ruiz y Flores found the president in "good humor," though somewhat nervous and ill at ease to be dealing, face to face, with high church dignitaries. The interview proceeded smoothly, however, with some apparent meeting of minds. At the end of their first meeting, the president and the prelates agreed to meet again the following night. After the second session Díaz emerged from the president's office "beaming with smiles." He told reporters that the conference was "truly satisfactory." He said that Calles had given them assurances that the requirement for the registration of the priests was only for administrative purposes and did not signify the right of the government to interfere in ecclesiastical matters. There would be no obstacle to the resumption of services, he said, as soon as the procedures demanded by the bishops were fulfilled. He felt confident that the Congress would accept the petition of the Church because most of the Mexicans were Catholics. But Ruiz y Flores was less optimistic. When a reporter asked him if he thought Congress would reform the laws, he replied with a rueful smile: "Not for a moment."[59]

Calles was enraged when he read the published statements of Bishop Díaz. He had made clear to the prelates that he would not agree to suspend the laws while the Congress considered the Catholic petition. All the newspaper reports implied that the government had made concessions, which was not the case. On August 26 he talked with Ernest Lagarde and told the French chargé d'affaires that he had been "trifled with." He complained that the Catholics had begun a "campaign of vilification" against him and his policies. Though his measures were "humane, firm, and reasonable," his enemies had pictured him as "a butcher of women and priests." Calles seemed obsessed, Lagarde wrote later, that this was not merely a local conflict between the Church and the State but a "battle without quarter between religious and lay ideas, between reaction and progress, between light and shade, a battle in which he was supported, not only by the majority of the Mexican people, but, in addition, by all liberals abroad." The president launched into a bitter diatribe against the bishops and the clergy. Bishop Guízar, he said was "a man without morals," and "an intimate friend of all of the procuresses" of Mexico City. Pascual Díaz was an "intriguer, who blindly obeyed the suggestions of his Jesuit advisers." Calles told Lagarde that he looked forward to the "progressive de-Christianization" of Mexico. Each week without services, the president said, would cause the Catholic religion to lose about two percent of its adherents.[60]

When the reports in the Mexican and American newspapers of the meetings between the two bishops and Calles reached Rome, the Vatican was alarmed by the possibility that the Mexican bishops were negotiating an unacceptable settlement with the government. Cardinal Gasparri cabled Mora y del Río, asking for an explanation. The archbishop replied immediately, scotching the newspaper reports. "In no way, with the help of God, will we depart from the instructions given by the Holy See," he said. The Mexican bishops continued in their plans to present to the Congress their petition signed by more than a half-million Mexican Catholics.[61]

Despite the public optimism of Pascual Díaz, the Catholic petition gave little real hope of success. Yet the bishops were determined to exhaust every legal means of obtaining their end. Already many of the younger laymen chafed under the restraint imposed by the bishops. They wanted to take matters into their own hands, to turn to armed revolt. On September 1 Calles addressed the opening session of the Congress and reported with satisfaction the closing of churches and monasteries and the expulsion of foreign priests by his government. At the conclusion of Calles' speech, Deputy Gonzalo N. Santos responded for the Congress, congratulating the president on the "firm and patriotic manner that you have taken during the so-called religious conflict." On September 6 Mora y del Río and Díaz brought their petition to the Congress. They asked for freedom of religion, education, and association, and they requested the Congress to revise Article 130 to include the phrase: "The state and the religious associations and groups known as churches, are independent." In this way they hoped that the institution of the Church would gain legal recognition. They did not stipulate the means of reform, but they asked that all the offending articles be rewritten.[62]

At the same time, the Mexican prelates addressed another collective pastoral letter to the faithful, exhorting them to continue resisting the tyrannous laws. "Do not lose faith," they wrote. "Do not permit your strength to fail. Do not unfold to the world and to Heaven the sad spectacle of the soldier who is a traitor to his flag and surrender to the enemy. Do not imitate the unnatural son who abandons his mother in the moment of danger. On the contrary, imitate the true lovers of liberty, who have known how to stand in the breech until they died or won." The bishops were concerned by reports from priests throughout Mexico that the Catholics were not as staunch as the clergy had expected or hoped, and they intended the pastoral letter as a reminder to Catholics of their duties during the hard months to come.[63]

The Congress gave the bishops' requests short shrift. On September 22 the Committee on Petitions of the Chamber of Deputies reported that although Article 8 of the constitution granted citizens the right to petition Congress, Article 37 provided that any Mexican who compromised himself before a minister to disobey the law would lose his citizenship. Since Díaz and Mora y del Río had done so, the committee said, they had lost their citizenship and hence could not legally make a petition. In the long discussion that followed the presentation of the committee's report, the church found only one defender, Ernesto Hidalgo, once an editor of *Universal Gráfico*. Other deputies attacked the clergy as "egoists" and "fanatics" or charged that the priests had leagued themselves with American capitalists to restore the reactionaries to power. They attacked the Knights of Columbus in the United States and in Mexico. Antonio Díaz Soto y Gama, who had demonstrated his anticlericalism a decade earlier in the Convention of Aguascalientes, now inveighed at length against the intriguing priests. "If the Mexican Church had today representatives such as Fray Bartolomé de las Casas, or Bishop Zumárraga, or Vasco de Quiroga, or such as the first Franciscans who came to Mexico, I would support the Church. But when the Mexican Church only helps the rich and excommunicates the Indians who ask for land and denies baptism to the children of the workers, it does not merit our respect." On the following day the Chamber rejected the petition by a vote of 171 to 1. Only Ernesto Hidalgo stood firm for the rights of the Church.[64]

In the United States the more clamorous spokesmen for the Catholic Church seized upon the Church strike as additional evidence of the influence of Russian communism in Mexico. On August 5 the Supreme Council of the Knights of Columbus, meeting in Philadelphia, adopted a resolution calling on the American government to put an end to the "ignominous contempt" shown by Calles toward American citizens. The Catholics of the United States, they proclaimed, could not endure the "Russianizing" of Mexico. "Liberty, justice, and right have been assassinated by the Red rulers of Mexico," the Council charged. The Council authorized the Knights' Board of Directors to assess the membership one million dollars "for a campaign of education to the end that the politics of Soviet Russia shall be eliminated . . . , and the ideals of liberty of conscience and democratic freedom may extend to our afflicted fellow human beings beyond the Rio Grande." The Council placed the responsibility for the persecution at the door of the American government and especially the State Department. "All of this system in Mexico has been created under American auspices, sustained by the American executive authority," they wrote. The Knights' campaign, the Council promised, would eradicate "these evils at our own doorstep, fomented and approved by the official action of our State Department."[65]

The Knights of Columbus published and distributed a number of pamphlets to implement their campaign against the Calles government. One proclaimed: "The people are awakening to the peril that is brewing in Mexico. They are beginning to see through the smoke screen of Red propaganda. They realize now that Calles and his associates are engaged in a project more potent for evil, more destructive of liberty and justice and human happiness than any mere religious persecution could possibly be. . . . The millions of men and women who love true liberty have heard the warning. They are determined that Red Russia shall not, through the mouths of traitors, rule Mexico and the American continent." Again and again the Catholic laymen called upon the American government to intervene in Mexico and to force Calles out.[66]

James A. Flaherty, a Supreme Knight of the organization, sent a copy of the resolution to Calvin Coolidge and asked the president to see a delegation from the Knights to hear their case in person. But Coolidge was determined to follow a hands-off policy in the religious controversy and refused to meet the Catholic leaders. Instead they talked with Kellogg, who pointed out with some heat the gross inaccuracies of the charge that the American government was responsible for the persecution. Privately Kellogg concurred with the Catholics' opinions about the Mexican government. But he told them that his government had "no right to impose its form of constitution and guarantee of liberty upon the people of other nations, however much we may believe it would be to their benefit to have them." Flaherty agreed that the charges against the State Department were "unjust and without foundation," and he promised that the impression left by the resolution would be corrected. He accepted Kellogg's declaration that the United States could not protest to a foreign government unless personal or property rights of American citizens were involved. The State Department released a statement to the press demonstrating that no American citizen had been "subjected to indignities" or had "suffered in person or property" in the Mexican conflict. Therefore, the American government had no grounds for official action against the Calles regime.[67]

The American hierarchy was more moderate in its proclamations than the laymen of the Knights of Columbus. In a collective pastoral letter the bishops stressed the virtues of the American system of religious toleration. God's law, they said, was consonant with the Constitution of the United States and the Declaration of Independence. "We agree that 'all men,' Mexicans included, 'are endowed by their creator with certain inalienable [sic] rights, that among these are Life, Liberty, and the Pursuit of Happiness.'" They implied that to settle Mexico's religious problem, it was only necessary to introduce the American constitutional guarantees into that country. The call of the Americans for religious toleration in Mexico was not echoed, however, by the Mexican bishops, who continued to uphold the primacy of the Catholic religion in their own country.[68]

American Protestants countered Catholic propaganda by opposing intervention of any kind. A group of ministers toured Mexico and returned to report that they had found no religious persecution there. On August 12 the editors of the *Congregationalist* wrote that however much the American Catholics might sympathize with their Church's difficulties in Mexico it was "not the business of the United States to intervene in that country." And the Ku Klux Klan offered a resolution of sympathy with the Mexican government in its attempt to "free the Mexican people from stultifying foreign [that is, Roman Catholic] influences."[69]

If the American government would not intervene or withdraw recognition from Calles, if it would not lift the embargo against the

shipment of arms to Mexican revolutionaries, the only solution to
the religious problem, or so it seemed in late 1926, must come from
within Mexico. When the Congress rejected the bishops' petition,
the Catholics prepared a second petition, to be presented by laymen, which would bear the signatures of over a million Mexicans.
The Catholics were not sanguine about its success. They simply
went through the motions of exhausting every legal recourse to
amend the constitution. Calles pressed ahead with his program to
subject the Church to government control. On October 15 he sent
the Congress a proposal to restrict the number of clergy of each
faith in the Federal District to 90—for a population of nearly one
million. And in the first week of November the president submitted
Article 130 to the legislators, so that the two houses could ratify his
executive decree of June 14. The Congress was still wracked by
factional quarrels, however, and though the Chamber of Deputies
pliantly voted Calles' request, the Senate became fouled in its own
political maneuvering and the session passed without final action on
the bill. The enforcement of Article 130 continued, therefore, to
rest on the original presidential decree of July 2, 1926.[70]

With the apparent failure of the economic boycott and the refusal
of the Congress to heed the Catholics' demands, only two courses
remained for the Church—abject surrender or armed revolt. And
the latter seemed the only feasible means as 1926 ended. The bishops could not advocate rebellion; they could not participate in the
military plans or even give advice to the Catholic military leaders.
The fate of Mexican Catholicism then passed into the hands of the
laymen and especially of the Liga Nacional. Young Catholics such
as René Capistrán Garza, Luis Segura Vilchis, and Luis G. Busto
threw themselves wholeheartedly into a campaign of armed resistance. There was no talk of temporizing or conciliation in the lay
circles. The young men fought—and many died—for their religious
principles. They were zealous in their faith, uncompromising in
their opposition to the Calles persecution. The bishops issued public statements; they corresponded with the Vatican about possible
plans of action; but the laymen acted. And when Calles exiled several of the bishops in early 1927, only the Liga Nacional gave any
semblance of national Catholic leadership in Mexico.[71]

Though it was a great responsibility for the laymen, they did not
shrink from the task. They organized campaigns, plotted battles,
planned for sources of supplies, and debated the type of govern-

ment Mexico should have when their revolution succeeded. The laymen had the help of many priests, who did not follow the bishops in their determination to remain aloof from the military action. Priests and laymen labored side by side to create a united national revolutionary force capable of toppling the regime of Plutarco Elías Calles. They embraced the banner of Christ and battle cry, "Viva Cristo Rey." Their enemies dubbed them "Cristeros" or "Christers," and it is by this name that the Catholic revolutionaries came to be known. At the end of 1926 it remained to be seen whether armed revolt, however just the cause, could succeed where spiritual weapons, legal action, economic boycott, and external agitation had failed.

¡Viva Cristo Rey!

IF THE PRELATES of Mexico, and the Church as a divine institution, could not advocate or support armed rebellion, no theological inhibition stayed the hand of the secular leaders. Within a few days after the priests withdrew from the churches at the end of July 1926 Catholics began to take up arms to defend their religion from government persecution. In the towns and mountain villages of Zacatecas and Jalisco, of Michoacán and Nayarit, and of Puebla and Oaxaca groups of armed men declared themselves in rebellion against the tyranny of Calles. The movement was spontaneous and disorganized with no semblance of national cohesion, and only a small minority of Catholics participated. Here a local leader would recruit one or two hundred horsemen as a fighting force. There a similar number of peasants would band together as an infantry unit. Few of the Catholic fighters could claim any military experience. And although the rebels had sufficient rifles to equip their small forces, most lacked the more potent weapons with which to wage modern warfare—machine guns, mortars, and artillery pieces. But to a man they possessed the one quality lacking in the federal troops—they fought, and were willing to die, for a cause greater than themselves, their sacred religion. And many Catholics believed that, because their cause was just, they would ultimately prevail.

The state of Jalisco had long been a center of intense religious loyalty, and here in 1926 the Catholic revolution took a deeper hold on the population than anywhere else in the republic. The archbishop, Orozco y Jiménez, made no pretense of hiding his sympathies with the faithful in his state who chose to defend their religion by turning to armed rebellion. He refused to associate himself with the other prelates of Mexico who abjectly obeyed the orders of the national government to come to Mexico City and place themselves under the surveillance of the Minister of Gobernación. In public statements—many of which were never printed by the muzzled press of the capital—the bishops and archbishops denied again and again that the Church or the members of the hierarchy were responsible for the revolutionary bands now springing up in the western and southern states. In Jalisco, however, Orozco y Jiménez remained with his people, as he had nearly a decade earlier, always in danger of capture and possible execution by the government troops, but serene and secure in the knowledge that he could trust the villagers and townspeople of his archdiocese to shield his comings and goings. And in Jalisco priests took an active role in the rebellion, helping to recruit and organize troops, planning their campaigns, marching or riding with their men into battle. Many a priest in the West of Mexico was to lose his life in combat or before a firing squad as a prisoner of the federal army.[1]

The ritual of the Catholic Church permeated the revolutionary movement from the moment an individual entered a rebel unit until the conclusion of battles with the enemy. To each man, the priests —ostensibly as chaplains for the rebel troops—gave a specially blessed scapular. They anointed the standards carried into battle. Before every encounter with the federal troops the rebels heard Mass and received the Holy Eucharist. Rifles in hand, their full equipment on their backs, the rebel troops in prayer or at Mass made a bizarre appearance. At the most sacred and awesome moment of the Mass, the elevation of the Host, the soldiers presented arms as though to a military commander. And closing with the enemy they shouted their battle cry to Christ the King: "¡Viva Cristo Rey!" If by chance the rebels succeeded against the government troops and took prisoners, the hapless federal soldiers were promptly shot—though they were first permitted to make their last confession before a priest, if they desired.[2]

The last six months of 1926 saw a gradual increase in the revolutionary activity and a broadening of the opposition against the government. In the northwestern state of Sonora, Yaqui Indian tribes, egged on by the inflammatory statements of Juan Navarrete y Guerrero, the exiled bishop of Sonora, and by seditious rumblings from the camp of Adolfo de la Huerta in the United States, declared war against Calles. One of the most militant of the Mexican prelates, Navarrete y Guerrero had been ousted by the governor, Leandro Gaxiola, in September 1926 under direct orders from President Calles. The bishop remained at Nogales, Arizona, just across the border, to keep his hand in the ecclesiastical affairs of his diocese. By the first month of 1927 the government found itself dealing with a hydra-headed enemy throughout the republic. One center of resistance was wiped out, only to have several others spring up elsewhere. The mountainous terrain made it particularly difficult for the federal troops to deal effectively with the rebels. Catholic or Yaqui forces would descend on a town or garrison and escape before the army could retaliate.

The military situation within Mexico was complicated by the presence of many exiles in the United States, who bided their time on the frontier, waiting for the opportune moment to raise the standard of rebellion once more against the Mexican government. Some were reactionaries who had left Mexico with the defeat of Huerta in 1914. Others were revolutionaries who had made the mistake of choosing the wrong side in one of the many attempted coups of the 1910s or 1920s. They unfolded elaborate schemes, hatched countless plots. Couriers made their way back and forth between the two countries carrying secret messages about new blows against the government. In the breasts of exiled leaders burned the flame of high ambition—ambition to topple the regime of Calles and become the president of Mexico in his stead. The American government gave no encouragement to these plotters, but at the same time, so long as the oil question remained unsettled, rarely bothered to suppress the rebel activity. In Texas and in California Adolfo de la Huerta, Enrique Estrada, Pablo González, José Ortiz Monasterio, Félix Díaz, and many other exiled Mexican soldiers nursed dreams of a successful revolution. Pablo González and Estrada (Obregón's Minister of War) had supported de la Huerta in 1923. Ortiz Monasterio, like Féliz Díaz, had favored the military dictatorship of Victoriano Huerta.[3]

Though the opposition against Calles was widespread, and the Catholic rebels fought fiercely against the federal troops, the government was never in serious danger of defeat. Indeed, the division of Manuel Ávila Camacho, which was chiefly responsible for dealing with the rebels in the West, showed no inclination to give the movement a crushing blow. Instead Ávila Camacho and his officers toyed with enemy bands as with a mouse. The corruption that pervaded the higher levels of Calles' administration penetrated into the general and officer ranks of the army as well. General Ávila Camacho, to avoid the exertion of waging a strenuous military campaign, offered bribes to the rebel leaders to give up their opposition to the government. None accepted. Other federal officers carelessly allowed weapons and supplies to reach the enemy. In some engagements the Catholics possessed newer and better equipment than the government troops. For many months the federal forces made occasional sorties against the elusive rebels, who took full advantage of their superior knowledge of the terrain in the western mountains. Like the Catholic soldiers, the government forces ruthlessly shot or hanged anyone captured bearing arms. In 1927, as the government campaign intensified, the troops took hostages, made retaliatory raids on villages suspected of sheltering the rebels, and looted the countryside systematically and without mercy. Calles' government furnished money regularly to the officers to pay their men, but the federal soldiers were sufficiently equipped and provisioned by the goods taken from the civil population. The payroll money went instead to the higher officers, such as Ávila Camacho, who were building substantial personal fortunes on their military careers.[4]

On both sides the campaigning was amorphous and unsystematic. The rebels gained small successes against trains, blowing up bridges or crippling the engines and then stealing the mail. At the same time, the government hit here and there at the Catholics. This aimless sparring brought neither side closer to victory. The rebel bands fought on their own, showing little cohesion even with other Catholic groups in their own state. Most of the commanders came from the ranks of the ACJM or from the semi-secret organization of Catholic laymen known as the "U." They were courageous, inspired, and daring. But they did not know how to fight a battle. One of these young rebels, Jesús Degollado Guízar, wrote later in his memoirs that in his first encounter with the enemy he did not anticipate a flanking attack, and as a result his men were completely dispersed and forced to flee for their lives. In late 1926 the Liga Nacional took two steps to give the Cristero movement cohesion and to make it more effective against the regular army of Calles. The national Catholic lay leaders decided to accept full responsibility for the rebellion, and in December they named René Capistrán Garza as head of the movement. In the same month Enrique Gorostieta, the son of a Huertista general, assumed supreme command of all the Catholic forces in the West.[5]

Capistrán Garza was 29 years old in 1926. Like the other Cristero leaders he had no military experience. Long active in lay Catholic affairs, as president of the ACJM and as a founding member and an officer of the Liga Nacional, Capistrán Garza was by profession a journalist. His avocation was the cause of Catholicism in Mexico, and he took on the enemies of the Church in passionate and intemperate debate, both on the public platform and in the press. One of the first Catholics arrested in July 1926, as the Liga Nacional planned its economic boycott, Capistrán Garza was taken into police custody three times within a fortnight, and each time he was released on bond. But as the strike began, and the first evidence of revolt appeared, Capistrán Garza decided to leave Mexico. He feared that if he were arrested again he would be shot for inciting armed rebellion. As yet the Liga Nacional was not prepared for military action, and Ceniceros y Villarreal and the other officers hoped to link the fortunes of the Catholics with those of the exiled Enrique Estrada. Reports persisted in Mexico that the former War Minister would soon cross the border to lead a nationwide revolt against the Calles regime. On August 14, Capistrán Garza left Mexico City with a proposal from the League—the Catholics would give Estrada popular support, while he would provide the military forces.

Capistrán Garza's departure from the capital was highly dramatic in a penny-dreadful, cloak-and-dagger atmosphere. He disguised himself with a false mustache and boarded the train for Laredo with elaborate precautions and secrecy. Undetected by the police (who were not actually looking for him, as it turned out), he made his way to the border where he crossed into Texas with the aid of Roberto Zúñiga, the head of a customs brokerage agency. The young Catholic leader entered the United States at 3 P.M. on August 16. Four hours later he read in an American newspaper that General Estrada had been arrested by agents of the United States government. His revolutionary plotting had become too flagrant, and he was taken into custody, charged with organizing a rebellion against a friendly country on American soil. The great hopes of Capistrán Garza and the Liga Nacional for a quick victory were snuffed out with the abortion of Estrada's revolution.[6]

Capistrán Garza hesitated to return to Mexico, and he asked the

Liga Nacional in Mexico City for further instructions. The officers
told him to remain in the United States and launch a campaign to
secure the aid of American Catholics for the economic boycott. To
assist him the League sent two other young Catholics, the brothers,
Ramón and Luis Ruiz y Rueda, to the United States. They met
Capistrán Garza in San Antonio, which had become a refuge for
Mexican exiles and a hotbed of revolutionary planning. Capistrán
Garza sent Luis Ruiz y Rueda back to Mexico City to get credentials
from the League and from the Catholic hierarchy, if possible, to
present to the American church leaders during a tour through the
United States. Naively the young Mexicans talked of floods of
money pouring into their movement. They bought a touring-model
Studebaker for their trip, without considering the rigors of the
approaching winter season in the midwestern and eastern parts of
the country.[7]

As they awaited their credentials, Capistrán Garza and Ramón
Ruiz y Rueda went to Brownsville to ask César López de Lara,
another exiled revolutionary, about the possibility of joining forces
with the Catholics. There they found that López de Lara was interested only in his own personal fortunes and not the success of the
Catholic movement in Mexico. Back in San Antonio they were
joined once more by Luis Ruiz y Rueda with letters from the League
officers and from Archbishop Mora y del Río. Ceniceros y Villarreal
wrote that Capistrán Garza was "fully accredited by the Executive
Committee to represent it in the United States." The archbishop of
Mexico sent a letter to the hierarchy in the United States, assuring
the American bishops that Capistrán Garza was an agent of the
Mexican prelates, as well as the Liga Nacional. And to James A.
Flaherty, of the Knights of Columbus, Mora y del Río wrote a second letter stressing that Capistrán Garza was, "among the seculars,
our sole representative and the representative of the interests of the
Mexican Catholics in your country." The instructions of the League
officers and of the archbishop of Mexico seemed explicit and clear
enough. There is no doubt that the three young Mexicans felt, as
they started their mission through the United States, that they had
official sanction from the primate of the Mexican Church.[8]

Setting out on their tour with great expectations and in high
spirits, the Mexicans soon found disappointment mounting upon
disappointment. From Brownsville they drove to Corpus Christi, to
Galveston, to Houston and Dallas, to Little Rock and St. Louis, and

then through the Middle West to the East Coast of the United States. The American bishops listened to their pleas and then gave the trio an episcopal blessing and a few dollars from their own pockets. In all Capistrán Garza collected two thousand dollars, much of which they used for the expenses of their trip. The trio arrived in Boston in the middle of a bitter cold snap, and with little money, to see William Cardinal O'Connell. The prelate received them affably, and, after examining their credentials and hearing their case, he exhorted them to "suffer with patience the trials that God has sent you." By now it was abundantly apparent that the American Church did not intend to give material aid to support the cause of the Liga Nacional.[9]

As Capistrán Garza crossed the United States, the Mexican government and the Church took up ever more divergent positions, making reconciliation increasingly difficult. Álvaro Obregón, with an eye to the presidential elections more than a year away, took pains to support the Calles government in its conflict with the Church. He called upon the priests to cease their opposition to the social program of the Revolution. On November 6, 1926, he told a reporter for *El Universal* that "the latest friction between the clergy and the government, provoked by the declarations of Archbishop Mora y del Río, . . . constitutes one of the many errors committed by the Catholic clergy in opposing systematically our social revolution." He said that the program of the Church required the subjection of the workers to the rich and payments for sacraments by the poor who could not afford them, and he accused the Mexican priests of conspiring with North American Catholics to bring about foreign intervention. Three days later, Pascual Díaz gave the press a long statement in the name of the Episcopal Committee as an answer to Obregón's charges. He made no attempt to conciliate the revolutionary government. "If the Church is to exist in Mexico," he said, "it must exist as it was founded by Christ, and not as the government wishes to have it." Referring to Obregón's observation that Catholic opposition to the government's "socialistic" program underlay the religious conflict, the bishop of Tabasco insisted that the incompatibility between Catholicism and socialism was "fundamental and eternal." He added that if Obregón wished to become the savior of Mexico he should give the people a constitution that was not "bolshevistic."[10]

The Vatican, too, refused to sanction any compromise with the

Mexican government. *Osservatore Romano,* the semiofficial voice of
the Holy See, announced that there could be "no accommodation
whatever" with the "unjust" Mexican laws. Gasparri told the British
minister to the Vatican that the struggle would be long, but that the
"staunch passive resistance" of the hierarchy and the clergy would
eventually compel the Mexican government to modify the laws. He
even saw some advantage to the persecution in "strengthening" and
"invigorating" both the clergy and the people of Mexico. On
November 18 Pope Pius XI issued an encyclical "Iniquis Afflictisque," painting in somber colors the state of the Church of Mexico. His Holiness synthesized the revolutionary persecution of the
Church since 1914 and condemned the government's actions as the
work of men "still under the influence of barbarism." The pope
praised the staunch peaceful resistance of the Mexican clergy and
lay groups such as the Knights of Columbus, ACJM, and Damas
Católicas. "All members of these institutions, instead of fleeing
from danger," he wrote, "seek it and are glad when they are made
to suffer." He expressed complete confidence in the final victory of
the Church. The Mexican prelates heralded the pope's encyclical as
a defense of the Catholic faith "against bolshevism and communistic
principles." With the diplomatic crisis between the United States
and Mexico in mind, the Episcopal Committee insisted that there
were "two factions in the fight, Christianity and bolshevism." "The
defense of Christian civilization," the bishops said, "is based upon
religion, the sanctity of matrimony, private property, and sane liberty, as against the communistic utopias of socialism, free love, and
the subjection of religion to the state."[11]

Nor did the Calles government budge from the position it had
taken in July. After rejecting the petitions of the Catholic clergy and
the laymen, the Chamber of Deputies ratified Calles' presidential
decree by voting on November 25 to implement Article 130. As a
concession to the various foreign colonies in Mexico, the measure
stipulated that each nationality—except the Spanish—might have its
own clergymen to conduct services in its own language. But after six
years (during this time Mexican ministers would presumably be
trained by each cult) the foreign clergy must be withdrawn in
compliance with Article 130. Still hopelessly deadlocked over
Obregón's candidacy, however, the senators took no action on any
of the legislation presented by Calles. For several weeks the Senate
could not meet, as recalcitrant members again absented themselves

to prevent a quorum, thus avoiding a vote on an amendment to the constitution that would permit Obregón's reelection and lengthen the presidential term to six years. During the entire session no piece of legislation cleared the Senate, even the national government's budget for the following year. As a result, Calles continued to govern the country in 1927 by decree.[12]

On January 18 *Diario Oficial* announced Calles' proclamation of Article 130 as the law for all of Mexico. Since only the Chamber of Deputies had acted on the measure, it was still of dubious legality. Nonetheless, the government continued to enforce the "law" with all its rigors and severity. In his annual message to the nation on January 1, 1927, the president called attention to the "seditious and rebellious" attitude of the clergy and promised renewed vigilance on the part of his government.[13]

In the last two months of 1926 the military activity of the Catholic rebels continued to spread to new areas. And in Mexico City the Liga Nacional shifted the focus of its attention from the economic boycott, which had patently failed to deal the government a body blow, to the revolutionary opposition of the Cristeros. Many requests reached the capital from rebels and from local representatives of the League, asking the national group to unify the movement and give the Mexican people a program of government. Heretofore, the League had insisted that its functions were purely defensive and peaceful. Before taking this crucial step, the officers of the League preferred to consult the bishops on the lawfulness of armed revolt.

On November 26, at the residence of Bishop Pascual Díaz in Mexico City, the lay leaders and the bishops met to consider the case for Catholic rebellion. Virtually the entire hierarchy of Mexico attended. A notable exception was the militant archbishop of Guadalajara. Representing the League were its president, Ceniceros y Villarreal, and other national leaders—Luis G. Bustos, Palomar y Vizcarra, Carlos F. de Landero, Manuel de la Peza, and Juan Lainé, as well as their ecclesiastical adviser, the Jesuit Alfredo Méndez Medina. Ceniceros y Villarreal showed the petitions that the League had received and asked the bishops' approval of their plan for a national revolution. The prelates told the laymen that they would need a few days to reach a decision. A second meeting took place four days later. Now the League was also represented by its other clerical adviser, Rafael Martínez del Campo, like Méndez

Medina, a Jesuit. Bishop Díaz announced that the prelates had studied the League's memorial. He could not give blanket approval to their proposed course of action, he said, but he did not forbid the League to join the Cristero rebels. The bishops would grant permission, he said, for priests to serve the rebel troops as chaplains. Though the bishops' support was not explicit, the League officers believed that their plan had been given official sanction, and they turned to the herculean task of organizing the Catholic military campaign.[14]

Though full of enthusiasm and energy, the men of the League made woeful mistakes. Most were lawyers or priests, and their enthusiasm did not compensate for their ignorance in matters of command, supply, organization, and tactics. They committed their initial error when they chose René Capistrán Garza as chief of the rebel movement, for the journalist was not even in Mexico and had no intention of returning. In early December 1926 pamphlets appeared in Mexico City outlining the political program of the Cristeros. The Liga Nacional promised Mexico freedom of religion, education, the press, and association and advocated separation of Church and State. For foreign and national capital it offered guarantees of the sanctity of private property against government expropriation. The officers indicated that the new regime—if the rebels succeeded—would be based on laws drawn from the Constitutions of 1857 and 1917. A League officer brought a copy of the plan to the American embassy and requested Ambassador Sheffield to secure his government's support for the revolutionary movement.[15]

René Capistrán Garza had reached New York when he received word of his appointment to head the Catholic revolution. He was completely surprised and nonplussed by the League's decision. Twice he had been interviewed by American reporters, and each time he indicated that the campaign of the Mexican Catholics would be peaceful and economic. When one reporter asked if he intended to return to Mexico, he drew his forefinger across his throat and said: "When I desire to commit suicide." Capistrán Garza refused to assume a responsibility for which he knew he was incompetent. He sent a message to Ceniceros y Villarreal rejecting the position. But the League officers in Mexico City insisted that he accept, even though he was by now thoroughly disillusioned by the lack of support from American Catholics.[16]

Despite his appointment as military commander, Capistrán Garza did not come back to Mexico. Nor did he concern himself with the military plans of the rebels. He continued to move about the United States seeking to drum up support for a lost cause. In Washington he found official doors closed. The American government, though exercised with Mexico over the oil question, had no interest in a Catholic revolution. And would-be revolutionaries, both inside and outside the League, worked at cross-purposes, each pushing his own plans and interests. One of these was José Gandara, a Mexican resident of El Paso, Texas, whose father was a lawyer for the American Smelting Corporation, which owned mining properties in northern Mexico. The young Gandara came to Mexico City to tell the League officers that he represented a revolutionary junta in El Paso that would soon invade Mexico. He said that the junta had chosen January 1, 1927, as the date for capturing Ciudad Juárez, and he asked their help in obtaining finances by designating certain national properties as security for a loan of "several millions of dollars." He needed only the approval "of a certain person living in Europe," he said, to get the loan. The League officers agreed to his plan, for they had not completely abandoned hope of linking their movement with one or many of the revolutionaries on the border, and they sent him to Europe. But Gandara's fanciful scheme came to naught, for the "certain person" would not consider giving money for a revolution. And January 1 passed without any sign of an invasion of Ciudad Juárez.[17]

Though he had failed in Europe, Gandara, on his return to Mexico, asked the League to designate him the supreme chief of their revolution. He was told that Capistrán Garza had already been named to that position, and the League advised him to subordinate himself to the young lawyer if he desired to aid the Catholic cause. Knowing nothing of Gandara or his background, Capistrán Garza readily consented to name him chief of military control of the revolution, while he kept the overall direction in his own hands. Instead of cooperating with his chief, however, Gandara used his position in the movement to undermine Capistrán Garza's leadership.[18]

The Cristero commander found himself hemmed in by the criticisms of many detractors. To Dr. Luz Franco de Perches, an agent of Féliz Díaz, he was a "nice boy," but totally unfit for military leadership. A Jesuit priest, Ricardo Álvarez, wrote that he was "disgusted" with Capistrán Garza as a military leader. And Juan Lainé, of the Liga Nacional, and Leopoldo Escobar, of Mexico's Knights of Columbus, worked openly for Félix Díaz.[19]

Meanwhile, Capistrán Garza had stumbled upon a plan that he believed would bring a large sum of money to the Catholics and pave the way for their ultimate success. While in San Antonio he met William F. Buckley, an American Catholic with oil interests in Mexico, who proposed to offer the Mexican rebels 500,000 dollars to aid their revolution. Buckley had long been active in the Mexican petroleum industry, first as a legal adviser to American companies and later as a director of the Pantépec Oil Company. In the Huerta era he had been close to the Mexican government, and he came to Niagara Falls, Canada, in July 1914 as an unofficial representative of Huerta in the mediation conference that followed the American seizure of Veracruz. In the early 1920s, Buckley lost many of his properties, when they were taken over by the government of Obregón. He now saw an opportunity to recoup his fortunes in Mexico by financing the Catholics in their attempt to overthrow the Calles regime.

Buckley did not intend to furnish the money himself. Instead, he offered to introduce Capistrán Garza to Nicholas Brady, who, Buckley said, would give the League representative the half-million dollars. Brady was a highly successful American capitalist, in 1927 president of the New York Edison Company and the United Electric Light and Power Company, as well as the trustee or director for more than fifty other corporations. He was also the most prominent lay Catholic in the United States. The first American layman to receive the title of Papal Chamberlain, Brady was a close personal friend of Pius XI and the papal Secretary of State, Cardinal Gasparri, and American newspapers reported in 1926 that he had given the pope his personal check for one million dollars. Capistrán Garza was delighted by the possibility that he might be able to revive his faltering campaign, and he set off for New York immediately, buoyed up by the prospect of his meeting with Nicholas Brady. Once again he was foredoomed to failure and disappointment, however, for he never saw the American financier. Pascual Díaz was now in New York, and he interposed himself between Brady and the League's representative. Thereafter, there was no chance that the Mexican rebels would receive aid in the United States, either from the American government or from the bishops or any Catholic laymen.[20]

Pascual Díaz had been expelled from Mexico by Calles' government for his alleged complicity in the military activity of the Cristeros. As the year 1927 began, the Catholic rebels stepped up their campaign against the government. There were still no large-scale engagements, but the Cristeros' harassing tactics proved vexatious enough to move Calles to new action against the Church leaders. On January 10 Pascual Díaz and five other prelates were arrested in Mexico City, charged with directing the Cristeros' campaign. Subsequently, the police released all but Díaz, for General José Álvarez, Calles' Chief of Staff, decided to make an example of the contentious bishop of Tabasco as the principal spokesman for the Church in Mexico. Álvarez announced that Díaz would be deported.[21]

The Episcopal Committee protested the arrests, denying that the bishops had played any part in the Cristero rebellion, which, they insisted was the work of laymen. "In matters of dogma and morals, if one is a Catholic," they said, "one must submit to the teachings of the Church." But in everything else, they stressed, laymen were free to act on their own responsibility. The bishops did not condemn the rebellion, however, or reprove the Catholics who had exercised their right to resist the destruction of their religious rights. "There are circumstances in the life of the people," they said, "when it is licit for citizens to defend with arms the legitimate rights that they have been unable to save by pacific means."[22]

General Álvarez scouted the contention that the Church bore no responsibility for the revolution. The committee's own statement proved, he said, that the rebels were led by the priests and bishops. Only the "children of the ACJM" could believe in the bishops' innocence, Álvarez said. "The rest of the country knows perfectly well . . . [the Liga Nacional] was created and is directed by the episcopate." So that the government could keep track of their activities, Álvarez ordered all the priests of Mexico, like the bishops, to come to Mexico City. Many of the clergy complied with this new restrictive order. But in Jalisco the priests feared that Álvarez' order was a ruse to secure their arrest, and rather than fall into the hands of the vengeful government, they chose either to remain in hiding or to leave the country. The American consul in Guadalajara asked permission of the State Department to take their visa applications in the seclusion of private homes instead of at the consulate, in order to protect the priests. At the same time, Attorney General Romeo Ortega tightened the restrictions on religious ceremonies outside the churches. On February 2 he announced that henceforth Catholic priests would be permitted to say Masses in private homes only if they complied with the order of his government to register with local authorities.[23]

Pascual Díaz left Mexico City on January 11 on a train bound for Veracruz. A large group of Catholics gathered at the railroad terminal near the dock to demonstrate their support for the bishop and to give him food and clothing for his trip into exile. But Díaz got off the train at Córdoba instead and went to Suchiate on the Guatemalan border. He preferred to remain in Central America, he said, where he would be closer to events in Mexico City. At first, the Guatemalan government refused him entrance, for an anticlerical law barred foreign clergy and Jesuits. He was finally permitted to pass through Guatemala, if he would leave the country immediately for the United States. In Guatemala City he released a statement to the press denying complicity in the Cristero revolution. "There is no doubt that a state of rebellion exists among the Mexican people in defense of their freedom of conscience," he said. "But as a bishop and a citizen I reprove revolution, whatever its cause." From Central America Díaz came to New York by way of Cuba. Instead of going on to Texas to join the other exiled Mexican clergy, however, he elected to stay in the East, in Washington or New York, where he could have greater influence with the American government and the American Church.[24]

Díaz' choice marked a turning point in the conflict between the Church and the government in Mexico. He realized that the key to the solution of the conflict now lay outside his country. The positions of Calles and of the Mexican prelates had hardened to such an extent that there seemed no way out except the surrender of one or the other of the parties to the dispute. Since it was obvious that Calles' government was little harmed either by the economic boycott or the Cristero revolts, the issue must now be resolved by foreign influences. Díaz now began to associate himself with the Catholic clergy in the United States, especially his fellow Jesuits, and with the apostolic delegate in Washington, Monsignor Pietro Fumasoni-Biondi, who favored a negotiated settlement. Once an obdurate opponent of compromise, Díaz became more pliable in the United States, and he took steps to undermine the influence of the Mexican laymen and the militant Liga Nacional in their attempts to get American support for their movement. Outwardly cordial to Capistrán Garza and the other representatives of the League, Bishop Díaz told Father John J. Burke, general secretary of the National Catholic Welfare Conference, that the American Church should "have nothing to do with any of his countrymen who might come here seeking aid for a revolution against the Calles government."[25]

While Pascual Díaz was in Mexico City, though he spoke for the Episcopal Committee, he always stood in the shadow of his senior colleagues. They, not he, looked down from the eminence of archiepiscopal thrones. To be merely bishop of Tabasco was certainly not the choice of an ambitious and highly intelligent prelate such as Díaz. Tabasco was isolated and provincial. Of all the dioceses of Mexico it was probably the least Christian. There was little that even Díaz could do to build a strong Church there. But in the United States, away from his colleagues, Díaz assumed a new luster, particularly to the American churchmen and the representative of the Vatican. He had the very qualities of aggressiveness that had pushed the Irish clergy to the front of the American Catholic Church. To the Americans the bishops who remained in Mexico or who came later to San Antonio seemed quarrelsome, antiquarian, the essence of fustiness. They had in part, the Americans believed, brought on the quarrel themselves with their out-of-date, reactionary policies. From the moment he came to the United States, Díaz' star was in the ascendant. In a sense, then, it was to his own good fortune, and the making of his subsequent ecclesiastical career, that he had been chosen by the Calles government as the one prelate to expel in January 1927.

Bishop Díaz arrived in New York on February 6 aboard a United Fruit Company freighter. Dressed in a business suit (because of the requirements of the Mexican law), he looked more like an itinerant peddler than a cleric. Only the heavy episcopal ring on his pudgy right hand betrayed his ecclesiastical rank. To reporters he was moderate in his criticism of Calles' government. He insisted that the Catholics of Mexico did not wish a conflict between the United States and his country "for oil or any other reason." He expressed optimism about the chance for a future solution of the crisis, assuring the reporters that "the Church always does win in the long run."[26]

When Capistrán Garza in San Antonio learned that Díaz had begun to oppose his campaign in the United States, he sent Manuel de la Peza to New York to remonstrate with the bishop and then, a few days later, came himself to tell Díaz of Buckley's proposal. De la Peza's meeting with Díaz was stormy, as the League's representative threatened to denounce the bishop in Mexico if he continued to hinder the work of the lay Catholics. In turn, Díaz warned de la Peza that he would publicly disown the League, if the laymen persisted in their "wayward path." Díaz promised Capistrán Garza that he would talk with Buckley about the plan to obtain money for the Mexican Catholics. But when Díaz met the American oilman, he said that Capistrán Garza did not represent the Mexican Church and was in no sense the emissary of the prelates. And when Nicholas Brady inquired about Capistrán Garza, Díaz told him that under no circumstances should he give money to further the armed conflict. The bishop of Tabasco was by now committed to a peaceful settlement of the religious conflict. As a result of Díaz' opposition to the League, the tentative proposal made by Buckley in San Antonio was withdrawn.[27]

If Díaz now saw no hope for the Church in an armed clash with the Mexican government, there were still priests and even prelates in Mexico who disagreed. Orozco y Jiménez remained in hiding in Jalisco, giving his tacit support to the rebels. If Manríquez y Zárate of Huejutla no longer called openly for revolt, it was only because he was under house confinement and dared not speak in public. And in Rome the archbishop of Durango, José María González Valencia, represented those Mexican prelates who wished to pursue a course of hostility to Calles' government, even if civil war resulted. González Valencia came to Rome in the fall of 1926 with Emeterio Valverde Téllez, bishop of León, and Genaro Méndez del Río, bishop of Tehuantepec, to present personally to the Vatican the case of the Mexican episcopate. On October 29 His Holiness received the three prelates in a private audience. It was largely on the basis of information brought by González Valencia that Pius wrote the encyclical "Iniquis Afflictisque" the following month, in which he expressed his approbation for the activities of the Liga Nacional. And the three prelates remained in Rome to promote a policy of militancy.[28]

The pope insisted that the resistance must be by peaceful means, but the archbishop of Durango gained the impression during his stay in Rome that the Vatican had not ruled out armed conflict. On February 11, 1927, he issued in Rome his famous First Pastoral Letter urging the faithful of his archdiocese to further effort against the Calles tyranny. "God well knows, venerable brothers and beloved sons," he wrote, "with what sentiments of veneration we address ourselves on this occasion to you who find yourselves on the field of battle, front to front with the enemies of Christ." "In our archdiocese many Catholics have resorted to arms and ask a word of their prelate. . . . We believe it to be our pastoral duty to face the issue squarely and, assuming with a clear conscience the responsibility before God and before history, we dedicate to them these words: We never provoked this armed conflict. But once all pacific means had been exhausted and this movement began, you, our Catholic sons, rose in arms to defend your social and religious rights. After having consulted with the sagest theologians of the city of Rome, we say to you: Be tranquil in your conscience and receive our benedictions." Of his meeting with the pope, González Valencia wrote: "We have seen him moved on hearing the story of your struggles. We have seen him bless your resistance, approve all your acts, and admire all your heroisms."[29]

Having effectively stopped the cannons of the Liga Nacional in the United States, Pascual Díaz decided to go to Rome to present his own arguments for a peaceful solution to the Holy Father. De la Peza, too, went to Rome, but for the opposite purpose. He wanted to ask the pope for money to carry out the "armed defense" of the rights of the Church and of the Catholics in Mexico and to oppose Díaz. De la Peza was received by Pius, and he conferred twice with Gasparri, but the Vatican turned a deaf ear to his pleas. The Vatican had no money, said Pius, to give the Liga Nacional. As a result of his visit to Rome, however, de la Peza did persuade several Catholic laymen of Europe to form a "Pro-Mexico Committee" to collect funds from private sources.[30]

On April 11, a week after the coming of de la Peza, Pascual Díaz arrived in Rome. With his colleagues, the archbishop of Durango and the bishops of León and Tehuantepec, he was most reserved, for he wished to separate himself from the extreme views of González Valencia. In conferences with Cardinal Gasparri he depreciated the work of Capistrán Garza and the leaders of the Liga Nacional. He denied that the Mexican journalist had the capabilities to lead a movement of Catholic resistance. He proposed, instead, that if compromise was impossible, the Church might throw its support to someone of proved leadership, such as Félix Díaz or the Huertista, Nemesio García Naranjo. But Díaz insisted that there was no hope in Mexico for the Cristero movement.[31]

In Mexico City, too, things went poorly for Capistrán Garza. Alarmed by reports from Juan Lainé and others that the young journalist was totally incompetent and was destroying the work of the League, the Executive Committee sent three agents to San Antonio to investigate the charges. Luis G. Bustos, a vice-president of the organization, came in April 1927, and José Mesa y Gutiérrez and Father Martínez del Campo the following month. After listening to the many dissident voices in San Antonio, the three recommended that Capistrán Garza be asked to resign his position. Bustos was appointed in his stead to represent the League in the United States.[32]

The replacement of Capistrán Garza did nothing to improve the situation for the Liga Nacional or the Cristero rebels. Instead, it widened the schism between Capistrán Garza and the more militant laymen on one side and Pascual Díaz and various Mexican Jesuits on the other, a schism that soon became public knowledge. Capistrán Garza complained bitterly to newspaper reporters in the United States that the bishop of Tabasco had plotted to destroy him and the League by sabotaging their efforts to get money from Nicholas Brady and other American Catholics. And Díaz, who had returned from Rome, denied that Capistrán Garza had come to the United States as an emissary of the Mexican Church. Under no conditions, he said, could laymen speak for the hierarchy.[33]

In Mexico representatives of the Church began to look for a peaceful solution to the religious crisis. As it became evident in the first months of 1927 that Álvaro Obregón would succeed Calles, Archbishop Mora y del Río asked Eduardo Mestre, as a friend of both Obregón and of the prelates, to take the lead in bringing together the presidential candidate and members of the hierarchy. In early March Mestre went to Sonora to confer with Obregón. Obregón told Mestre that he preferred to have the religious issue settled before he became president. If Mestre would use his influence with the bishops to achieve a compromise, Obregón said, he would get Calles to accept it. On his return to Mexico City Mestre met Archbishops Ruiz y Flores and Valdespino y Díaz and advised them that services could begin immediately if the episcopate would notify the Secretary of Gobernación that the clergy would end their strike. The prelates told Mestre that nothing could be done in Mexico, however, without the approval of the Holy See, and to propose a solution to the Vatican it would be necessary to have concrete guarantees from the government. As a result of Mestre's intercession, Obregón met Bishop Fulcheri on March 23 on the terrace of the presidential palace at Chapultepec. Though Obregón denied that he spoke as an agent of the government, it was clear— since the interview took place at Calles' official residence—that the conference had his approval. Obregón told Fulcheri that the bishops should order the renewal of services, trusting the good faith of the government. But to the Church this was an admission of surrender, not a compromise. Fulcheri responded that when the clergy and the Catholic laymen in the previous autumn had obtained two million signatures on their petition to reform the religious laws, the president had ignored it. He saw no sign of good faith, he said, in Calles' unchanging attitude toward the Church problem.[34]

When newspapers in the United States and Mexico reported Mestre's attempts at conciliation, a spokesman for the Mexican bishops told the press that the Catholics could accept no solution that did not ensure the complete restoration of the rights and liberties enjoyed by the Church before the Calles regime. "The bishops of Mexico cannot enter into any agreement that does not guarantee the Church all her rights," he said. He added that all proposals would require the approval of Rome.[35]

Whether an agreement could have been reached in the spring of 1927 was problematical, for the constant reference to Rome irritated Calles and his government. The Mexicans wanted the bishops to settle the matter themselves without bringing the Vatican into the negotiations, while the prelates feared to take any steps on their own initiative. In any event, the situation soon worsened with a widely publicized Cristero attack on a crowded passenger train, and in the atmosphere of ill-feeling that resulted, no one gave immediate thought to another try at reconciliation. The government expelled more bishops in reprisal, and there was no one left in Mexico of sufficient authority to speak for the Church. Of necessity, any attempt at concord must come from outside the country— from the exiled Mexican prelates, from agents of Obregón or Calles meeting with exiled Catholics, or from other interested parties in the United States.

In March and April the rebels continued their practice of attacking trains and railroad bridges in order to disrupt the government's military campaign. One such attack in Jalisco brought swift retaliation from the government against the rebels and against the Church leaders, and in the end the Catholics lost much more than the Cristeros gained in momentary satisfaction and in the money stolen from the train.[36] On the night of April 19 the regular passenger train from Guadalajara to Mexico City had passed through the station of Ocotlán—about 95 miles out of Guadalajara. Because of the danger of a rebel attack, the train carried an armed guard of fifty soldiers and two officers. Shortly after eight P.M. the train suddenly left the track, and all the lights in the coaches went out. From both sides of the track rifle bullets poured into the train. The government soldiers quickly took up positions in the passenger coaches and began to fire indiscriminately in the dark. Outside there were between four and five hundred rebels. In a panic, the passengers threw themselves on the floors of the cars and tried to hide behind the seats. Above the cracking of rifle shots could be heard the screams of the wounded and frightened passengers, mingled with the exultant shouts of "Viva Cristo Rey" and "Viva Nuestra Señora de Guadalupe." The train guards soon exhausted their small store of ammunition, and the rebels closed in to kill every government soldier. When all resistance had ceased, the Cristeros entered the coaches and ordered the passengers into the pullman car. Then they poured oil on the coaches and burned that section of the train and the passengers and soldiers who were too severely wounded to be moved. As they left, the rebels took 150,000 pesos from the mail car and all baggage. Eduardo Mestre was a passenger on the train. He was not injured, however, and he was able to come to Mexico City, where he gave the newspapers a stark account of the Cristero assault.

Reports from the rebel camp confirmed later that the attack had been led by two priests. The rebels had torn up the tracks and then waited in the dark for the train to be wrecked before making their assault. The stated reason for the attack on the train and its passengers was that it was in retaliation for the government troops' cruel treatment of villagers in the Altos district of Jalisco. In trying to put down the rebellion in that area, federal soldiers had ruthlessly destroyed homes and fields of any persons suspected of aiding the Cristeros. During the attack on the train,

more than fifty passengers were killed, in addition to the guard of
52 men.[37]

This was not a large-scale action, and the destruction of one train
did little to further the cause of the Catholic rebels. But the government seized upon the occasion to dramatize the rebels' wanton
cruelty and, above all, to demonstrate that the clergy played a leading role in the revolt. José Álvarez gave the Mexico City newspapers
an official statement on the incident with orders to publish it ver-
batim and without comment in columns seven and eight of the first
page. On April 21 *El Universal* carried a bold headline: "A gang of
bandits, organized by the Catholic episcopate and directed personally by the priests Vega, Pedraza, and Angula, assaulted the train
that left Guadalajara day before yesterday evening for Mexico City.
They burned all the cars and killed with knives most of the second-
class passengers, many of whom were burned alive in the coaches
of the train." Because of rigid government censorship, the Church
spokesmen could not publish statements refuting Álvarez' charges.
Only newspapers outside Mexico carried the bishops' answer. The
government was resolved to punish the Church leaders for their
alleged complicity in the attack. On April 21 six of the prelates in
the capital, including the archbishops of Mexico and Morelia, were
summarily arrested and ordered to leave the country. A few days
later Archbishop Vera y Zuria of Puebla and Manríquez y Zárate of
Huejutla were also expelled to the United States. On his arrival in
San Antonio, Ruiz y Flores told the American press that Álvarez'
charges had no foundation. In Mexico, where the newspapers could
carry only the government version of the affair, the public was told
that the prelates had left Mexico "voluntarily" when confronted
with "incontrovertible proof" of their guilt.[38]

During the rest of the month of April and in May Calles' government stepped up its campaign of harassment against clergy and
laymen. Many scores of Catholics were arbitrarily arrested and sent,
without trial, to the penal colony in the Tres Marías Islands. And
the government troops in Jalisco and in other areas of rebellion took
even more stringent measures against the Cristeros. By the end of
June 1927 the situation looked so favorable for the government that
Calles proposed to free all the prisoners held on charges of sedition
at the Tres Marías prison. He told reporters that he wanted to be
"magnanimous with those defeated in rebellion."[39]

The war was not over yet, however, for hundreds of rebels still held out in the mountains of the West. The remaining months of 1927 saw several attempts by Americans and Mexicans to resolve the issues, some by reviving the Cristero's moribund cause, others by ending the revolution and bringing the priests back to the churches through peaceful means.

In San Antonio the exiled bishops, leaderless, isolated from Díaz, from Washington, and from the Vatican, found themselves caught up in the factional wrangling that had plagued the Mexican émigrés for nearly a year. Various reactionary exiles or representatives of the Liga Nacional sought to gain the prelates' support for this or that bizarre plan. In July Alberto María Carreño, sent by the League's Executive Committee to explore new avenues for obtaining money in the United States, told the bishops that he and other League representatives could get loans from American bankers if the Mexican hierarchy would agree to mortgage Church properties. Gerardo Anaya, the new secretary of the Episcopal Committee, replied that the bishops did not have the power to do so without the prior consent of the Holy See. Besides, it was well known, Anaya said, that the properties of the Church had been seized by the government many years earlier. Nevertheless, Carreño went ahead with plans for a proposed coalition government in Mexico when (or if) the Cristero revolution was successful. He told Pascual Díaz in New York that a regime that was not patently Catholic stood a better chance of gaining the support and approbation of the American Department of State. Carreño proposed a new political alignment, based on the Liga Nacional, that would reestablish the Constitution of 1857, where it did not conflict with the bishops' Memorial of July 1926. The new party would accept social reforms to improve the conditions of the working classes and would respect the rights of foreign and native capital and of rural property owners. In Havana the quixotic Capistrán Garza published similar plans for his own coalition government when Calles should be defeated.[40]

On June 25 Obregón made the long-expected announcement that he was a presidential candidate. In a carefully worded statement he took pains to support the religious policies of Calles. But he left the door open for a peaceful solution of the crisis by promising freedom for the Church, while at the same time demanding of the clergy "absolute respect for the regulations that our laws established." Soon after he released his statement, Obregón received a request for an interview from Ignacio P. Gaxiola, then in New York.

The two met in Los Angeles, and Gaxiola asked Obregón to declare publicly that he was not an "enemy of the Church." Obregón, still hoping to get the problem out of the way while Calles was president, replied that he would not find it "inconvenient" to "receive and exchange impressions" with a representative of the Mexican clergy. As a result of this preliminary conversation, an American priest, Richard H. Burke, met Obregón in Sonora, and, with Gaxiola as an interpreter, the two conferred on means to arrive at a satisfactory settlement. Burke insisted that Obregón conclude an agreement with the Church before taking power. In turn, the American priest said, the clergy in Mexico would give him support in his campaign. Obregón replied that he could make no agreement, for the conflict had been started by the published statement of Mora y del Río. He said that the Mexican clergy should deal with Calles and that he could give no promises that infringed on the law.[41]

Father Burke asked Obregón what difficulties the representatives of the Church might expect if he was in power. Obregón said: "They will have all the difficulties they want to have. If they do not want difficulties, they will encounter not a single one, for the basis of complete harmony rests on those who dedicate themselves to their religious mission exclusively and renounce their interference in the politics of the country." He said that the leaders of the Church in Mexico could not point to a single instance in which he had taken the initiative to molest them or to hinder their operations. Obregón wanted a settlement, but one that would see the prelates binding themselves to obey the laws. As for the political support of the bishops, he had no need for that. He could win the election, whatever they chose to do.[42]

Nonetheless, Obregón and his partisans continued to interest themselves in a solution—a solution, that is, based on their own terms, not those of the Church. Some Obregonistas feared that Calles might use the civil war as a pretext to postpone elections and keep himself in power. Moreover, Obregón wanted peace in Mexico, so that his administration could begin to implement the social revolution promised in 1917 at Querétaro. He was well aware that there had been no peaceful transfer of power in Mexico since the Revolution of 1910. In early August, Obregón told a Canadian banker that the religious question would soon be settled, that arrangements would be made by which all the expelled priests could return to Mexico. He added that services would then begin again in the churches. To facilitate a settlement Obregón sent his campaign manager, Aarón Sáenz, to San Antonio to confer with the exiled prelates. Sáenz tried to keep his mission secret, traveling to the United States incognito. But the Mexican consul general in San Antonio, who had advance notice of his arrival, released the news to the press. Sáenz denied vehemently that he had come to San Antonio to see the bishops. He was only on "private business," he said. Despite his denials, he did, in fact, come to confer with the bishops. Through Mestre, Sáenz met a representative of the prelates to learn under what conditions the priests would consent to return. Mestre drew up a proposed compromise by which Calles would state that the registration of the clergy was a purely administrative matter, while the bishops promised that the Church would not mix in politics or obstruct the work of the government. The bishops added one modifying statement: "The government, convinced of the respect of the episcopacy for the lawfully constituted authorities, gives it all facilities and guarantees for devoting itself to its mission." So certain did the restoration of peace seem, that Valdespino y Díaz in San Antonio asked his family to prepare his house for his immediate return.[43]

An agreement proved to be impossible, however, for the bishops continued to insist that they must obtain approval from the Vatican, while Obregón refused to accept the modification, which seemed an apology on the part of the government. He told Mestre that the bishops must make their own decisions and that the Mexican government would never treat with Rome. Mestre telegraphed Obregón's message to Díaz in New York, who replied that he was leaving for Italy the following day. He promised that he would cable an answer from Rome. But Díaz and Ruiz y Flores released a statement to the press denying that the Church sought an accommodation with the Mexican government or would make "concessions of any sort." Mestre heard nothing further from Díaz. The Vatican wanted a government representative to offer guarantees to Rome before a peace could be sanctioned.[44]

Despite Díaz' public truculence, he brought recommendations from Fumasoni-Biondi and the American heirarchy that the Mexican bishops must adapt themselves to a compromise settlement. He told Gasparri that Archbishop González Valencia was a troublemaker, whose belligerence would only prolong hostilities and harm the Church. The papal Secretary of State called in the three

prelates who formed the Episcopal Committee in Rome and accused them of giving the Holy See false information about the
Mexican situation. He said that it was the Holy Father's wish that
they dissolve their committee and leave Italy. The pope made clear
that the bishop of Tabasco would be the sole intermediary between
the Holy See and the Mexican episcopate. Thereafter, the policy
followed by the Vatican reflected the views of Pascual Díaz and the
American hierarchy that some means of peaceful accommodation
must be found, though Rome continued to insist that the Mexican
laws be modified and that Mexico send an accredited agent to the
Vatican before the priests could end their strike. On his return to
the United States, Díaz wrote Bustos that the Liga Nacional must
give up its military and political activities and devote itself "purely
and simply" to Catholic Action.[45]

Alarmed by the persistent reports that the bishops would accept
a peaceful compromise, the leaders of the Liga Nacional in Mexico
City bombarded the Vatican with protests, insisting that the Cristero movement was growing stronger. And without episcopal counsel to temper their militancy, some League members became increasingly violent. Young Catholics plotted to strike at the
government through Obregón. Luis Segura Vilchis, an engineer for
the Mexican Power and Light Company, conceived the plan of as-
sassinating the presidential candidate to highlight the terroristic
methods used by the government against the Catholics of Mexico.
Segura, as a member of the ACJM, had been active earlier in distributing the boycott pamphlets of the Liga Nacional. After the
Cristero rebellion broke out, he was named chief of the League's
War Committee. When he brought his plan to the Central Committee of the League, its members refused to accept responsibility for
a political murder, but they did not attempt to dissuade him from
perpetrating the act. On Sunday, November 13, working with two
accomplices, Juan Tirado and Lamberto Ruiz, Segura followed
Obregón's car through Mexico City in his own Essex. As the young
Catholics pulled abreast of the other automobile they tossed a dyna-
mite bomb and then raced off under a rain of bullets from
Obregón's guard. The candidate was unharmed. In their attempt to
flee, the would-be assassins ran their Essex into another car and
were forced to continue on foot. The police captured Tirado and
Ruiz, though Segura managed to escape.

The following day the police traced the car to Humberto Pro

Juárez, a regional delegate for the Liga Nacional in the Federal District. One of the prisoners revealed the name of Segura to the police before he died (both prisoners were tortured and killed while in custody of the police), and Segura was arrested. He had bought the car a few days earlier from Pro, he said, but he insisted that he had been at the bullfights on the afternoon of the attack. He showed the police the ticket stubs, which he still retained. Satisfied with Segura's alibi, the chief of police, Roberto Cruz, released him, but ordered the arrest of Humberto Pro and his brother. Miguel Pro Juárez, a Jesuit priest, had returned from Europe during the previous year, after studying social reform in Belgium. The police had long sought him for holding religious services in private homes in violation of Ortega's decree of February 2.

News of the arrest of the Pro brothers dismayed Segura, for he had not intended to implicate others in his crime. He returned to police headquarters to confess that he alone was responsible for the attempt on Obregón's life. The Pros were completely innocent, he insisted. Cruz refused to believe Segura, however. To make an example of the priest and the other young Catholics, he ordered their immediate execution. None had a trial. There was no opportunity for an *amparo* to secure their release. The crime committed by Segura, and with which the Pros were charged, was not a capital offense. Nevertheless, they died before a firing squad by the order of Roberto Cruz and with Calles' approval. To impress the Mexican Catholics with the consequences of such assassination attempts, General Cruz had photographs taken of the executions, including the administration of the coups de grace. The police then released the pictures to the public. Father Pro was shown with his arms outstretched in the attitude of Christ on the Cross, as the bullets tore through his breast. Another photograph showed him crumpled on the ground, an officer bending over with a pistol at the priest's head. The burial of Miguel Pro produced a spontaneous outpouring of grief mixed with piety and superstition. Thousands of sorrowing Catholics joined the funeral procession, many pushing and jostling for an opporutnity to touch his coffin—and to rub off and transfer to themselves the miracle-producing powers of the martyred priest's body.

The brutality of the police and the atmosphere in which the executions were carried out only served to demonstrate the barbarism of the Calles government, and Catholic sentiment was so outraged

by Father Pro's death that there was no possibility in the remaining
weeks of 1927 for a settlement on any grounds. And since Obregón
could not make a commitment without the approval of Calles, it was
clear that the anticlerical president must be made a party to any
settlement, if it were to come before the end of 1928. It was to this
difficult task that the new American ambassador to Mexico dedicated himself in the early months of the new year.[46]

8

A Modus Vivendi

On October 27, 1927, Dwight W. Morrow presented Calles his credentials as American ambassador to Mexico. The two men were a study in contrasts. The diminutive Morrow was an experienced corporation lawyer, a highly successful man of business with an international reputation. Yet he radiated an almost boyish charm and an enthusiasm that compelled all those he met to accept immediately the proffered hand of friendship. The tough, solidly built Plutarco Elías Calles had achieved the presidency of Mexico against the enemies of the Revolution and in the bloody arena of national politics. He regarded his fellowmen, Mexicans and foreigners alike, with well-deserved suspicion. Calvin Coolidge's appointment of his Amherst College classmate, a Wall Street lawyer and an associate of J. P. Morgan, raised fears in Mexico of military intervention to collect the debts owed to American capitalists—"After Morrow the marines!" shouted the alarmists.

Yet the Mexican president's forebodings came to naught, for few American representatives in the long history of relations between the two countries proved to be as understanding, as willing to see and appreciate the Mexican side of a dispute, as Dwight Morrow. He read Mexican history and studied the origins of problems that divided the two neighboring countries. He embraced Mexican culture, particularly the folk arts, demonstrating a genuine interest, unusual for an American diplomat, in pottery, baskets, and serapes. He visited the handicraft markets. He bought a house in Cuernavaca as a hideaway from the busy life of the capital, and filled it with Mexican furnishings. He gazed with wonder at Mexico's ancient monuments. "Here," said his biographer, Harold Nicolson, "was a North American who neither patronized nor sneered."[1]

An undiplomatic diplomat, Morrow succeeded in Mexico precisely because he eschewed the traditional niceties, as well as the deviousness, of correct diplomatic behavior. He was completely honest and open in his dealings with the Mexicans. He avoided confrontations and took great pains to find solutions that would satisfy all parties. No side should feel defeated or lose face, he felt. He spent his own money lavishly in his diplomatic career, traveling about Mexico and back to the United States in a private train and running up astronomical telephone bills to communicate with the Department of State more directly and quickly. He scorned secrecy and ignored warnings from Washington that his telephone wires were tapped and that all he said was immediately known by the Mexican government. "If we spend our time feeling that the main object of the Embassy is secrecy, we will become the slaves of our suspicions, instead of the servants of our governments," he said. Morrow soon became a warm, personal friend of Plutarco Elías Calles, overcoming the Mexican's initial doubts, and he was able to bypass the punctilious Foreign Relations Office by taking important matters directly to the president. In turn Calles came to trust and esteem the American representative. Within a fortnight the two, so dissimilar in origin, careers, and temperament, representing countries long at loggerheads, were able to find a satisfactory solution to the vexing and dangerous petroleum controversy.[2]

Two days after his first official visit, Morrow returned to the presidential palace at Chapultepec to see Calles. Though he spoke no Spanish, the American ambassador went alone. He wanted to lay the groundwork of confidence and understanding before he took up any touchy diplomatic business with the Mexican president, and he let Calles use his own interpreter, James Smithers, an American business associate. Four days later Morrow accepted an invitation to visit Calles' Santa Barbara ranch about fifteen miles from Mexico City, where the two breakfasted—at dawn—on ham and eggs. Again Morrow came alone, without a translator. And he still avoided the petroleum question. Instead he talked enthusiastically of cattle and farming and of Calles' interest in irrigation projects. On November 9 Morrow came to the presidential palace once more. He had prepared his case well, for before leaving the United States he had studied the oil problem intensively. He believed ardently that the threat of force no longer suited relations between great powers and the weaker developing nations. At the same time he felt that the legitimate rights of private property should be protected. He proposed to Calles a compromise, a face-saving device for both countries, whereby the issue would be resolved on the basis of Mexico's own constitution, which, he found, banned retroactive legislation. Nine days later Calles' pliant Supreme Court declared the petroleum law unconstitutional, finding that those companies that had exploited their holdings with "positive acts" could not be forced to exchange their titles for long-term leases. Having settled the petroleum question so expeditiously, Morrow then turned to the much more thorny problem of Church-State relations.[3]

Before taking up his post in Mexico, Morrow had met John J. Burke, of the National Catholic Welfare Conference, to talk about Mexico's religious situation. Monsignor Burke, at the request of Patrick Cardinal Hayes, archbishop of New York, asked the new ambassador to use his good offices to bring representatives of the Mexican government and the Catholic Church together. Morrow's initial concern in Mexico was to deal with the diplomatic question raised by the petroleum legislation, however, and he realized that the Church question, because it was an internal problem, required much more tact. He did not broach the matter in his first conversations with Calles, but he began to study the backgrounds of the Church strike to prepare the way for a possible settlement. On November 29 Morrow breakfasted with Calles at the president's ranch. In an expansive mood, Calles began, of his own accord, to talk of the religious dispute. He told Morrow that the Catholic Church had held back the development of Mexico by keeping the people in ignorance and poverty. The Revolution, he said, had at last awakened the nation to the need for reform. Though he had been forced into the conflict by the belligerence of the Church, he said, he was confident that he and his government would win in the end. The Cristero rebellions would be stamped out within a month, he believed. Morrow held his counsel, for he was not ready to make concrete proposals, but on the following day he wrote to R. E. Olds, the Under Secretary of State, that "until some better modus vivendi than the present is reached, the very existence of the controversy will hamper efforts for a permanent reform."[4]

Morrow continued to work tirelessly to improve relations between Mexico and the United States. In the first week of December

he toured northern Mexico with Calles to inspect irrigation projects. Before he left he was asked by Manuel J. Sierra, chief of the
diplomatic department of the Mexican Foreign Office, to take up
with President Calles "certain phases of the religious question and
particularly the injurious effects the executions of civilians would
cause in the United States." Sierra stressed that the "negotiations
now progressing so favorably between the two countries might be
seriously jeopardized by adverse public opinion." The ambassador
took with him a number of prominent Americans, including the
homespun humorist, Will Rogers. "Morrow has learned five words
of Spanish and is eating chili!" reported Rogers in a telegram to the
New York *Times*.[5]

Because the trip followed so soon after the funeral of Miguel Pro,
Morrow received a number of anonymous letters from angry Mexican Catholics, attacking his close contacts with the president. And
Morrow wrote the State Department that he went "with reluctance,
because it might be considered by some as an endorsement of the
acts of the Government." But it was then too late to back out, he
explained. Though he did not discuss Pro's execution directly with
Calles, he did take the opportunity "to talk with him in a personal
way about the importance to Mexico of not affronting the feelings
of large numbers of devout Catholics in the world and especially
America." Calles insisted, however, that the Church was in open
rebellion against his government, and that he was determined to
complete the pacification of the country.[6]

Kellogg proved to be less concerned than Morrow about the
deleterious effects of his association with Calles. "I think you are
entirely right about taking the trip with the president," he said. "I
do not worry at all about it creating an unfavorable impression
among the Catholics." The Secretary of State told Morrow that
while the United States could not intervene to help Catholics in
Mexico or even to protest acts against Mexican citizens, "You may
find the opportunity . . . to informally discuss the matter with
the president and perhaps influence his action in the right direction. . . ."[7]

If Morrow lost public favor in Mexico by going north with Calles,
he soon retrieved it by inviting Colonel Charles A. Lindbergh to fly
to Mexico City in the Spirit of St. Louis. The Lone Eagle's visit to
Mexico—he spent two weeks in the country—was an unqualified
triumph. Thousands greeted him with great emotion at the Mexico

City airport, after several anxious hours in the hot sun, because the American flyer became lost in a thick fog between Tampico and the Mexican capital. More thousands lined the streets of Mexico City, cheering hoarsely and tossing flowers to the tall, slim, unprepossessing hero. Calles presented Lindbergh with the keys to the city. The young flyer stayed with Morrow and his family at the American embassy and toured Mexico's historic sites during the Christmas week. (A year and a half later Lindbergh married Morrow's second daughter, Anne.)[8]

As the year ended, Calles and the ambassador had become close friends, and Morrow felt that the time was ripe to work on the obdurate Mexican president, to persuade him to negotiate with representatives of the Church and bring the strike to an end. Morrow wrote Under Secretary Olds: "It is greatly to the interests of Mexico that this fierce religious controversy should not go on. I think it would be possible for the Church to deal with President Calles. He will not, in my opinion, give up his principle. It would seem to me, however, not impossible that a modus vivendi could be worked out, without loss of dignity to either side, if there were any method by which a liberal Catholic of the type of Father Burke . . . were dealing directly with President Calles."[9] As yet he said nothing to Calles, and the president maintained in public his hostile attitude toward the Church. In his New Year's Day address to the Mexican people, he made clear that neither the opposition of the clergy nor the attacks of the Cristero rebels had caused any change in his government's position. He would not tolerate a "state within a state," and he would require all Mexicans to respect the country's laws.[10] Through the month of January the government stepped up its campaign against Catholic priests and laymen, arresting many, fining some, and sending others to the federal prison on Tres Marías Islands.[11]

Outside Mexico Catholics began to call openly for an end to Church-State strife. The Catholic journal *Commonweal*, speaking for Church moderates, said on January 4: "Having faith in Ambassador Morrow, we therefore confidently await the announcement not only that the question of American property rights in Mexico will be satisfactorily adjusted, but that also the religious issue will be met and solved. . . . No settlement which does not take into account the religious problem can be a just or lasting one."[12] And on January 16 Pascual Díaz, backed by Burke's National Catholic Welfare Conference, appealed to the Mexican government to find a solution to the religious controversy. But he insisted that the Church would not surrender its principles. "You must admit," he wrote Calles, "that it is not impossible for the law to be incompatible with the conscience of a citizen."[13]

In Rome, Vatican officials, perturbed by the failure of the Mexican Church strike and by the inability of the exiled bishops to find any common program, began to consider the possibility of outside intercession. On January 6 Cardinal Gasparri told Sir Odo Russell, British minister to the Holy See, that he was at his "wits' end." The Vatican had sought, unsuccessfully, Gasparri said, to secure the assistance of several foreign governments, including Spain. But Spain proved to be a "broken reed," he said with disgust. Gasparri asked Sir Odo if his government might help, but the British diplomat demurred, insisting that foreign intervention was "useless." When word reached the Vatican that Morrow might be willing to act as a mediator, Gasparri told Russell that he had instructed Fumasoni-Biondi to consult with the American ambassador. The Holy See, he said, "would leave no stone unturned to improve the lot of the sufferers in Mexico." Like Díaz, however, the papal Secretary of State was not ready to capitulate. He saw Morrow, not as an arbiter, but as a "champion" of the Catholic Church. And the Vatican continued to insist that Mexico's religious laws be changed, before any peace terms could be approved.[14]

Meanwhile, Morrow went to Cuba as one of the American representatives at the Sixth International Conference of the American States. Burke came down from Washington to confer with Morrow once more. He told the ambassador that he was willing to visit Mexico, if invited, to begin talks with Calles. But Morrow knew Calles well enough to realize that he would never take the first step, and that he was not likely to invite Burke. He asked the priest if he were willing to request an interview, with the understanding that the request, if made, would be granted. Burke replied that he was. From the beginning of his mediation efforts Morrow sought to assure that no party felt put upon, that each would be satisfied with the position of the other. And he made certain that no proposal would be made unless he had a prior commitment that it would be accepted. In effect, he took the negotiations into his own hands, as confidently as though he were arranging a financial matter on Wall Street, ultimately deciding what the position of each party must be, based on what he knew the other party would stand for and insist upon. For good or for bad, the peace, when it was finally concluded, was almost completely the work of Dwight W. Morrow.[15]

On his return to Mexico Morrow talked to Calles about his conversations with Monsignor Burke. He assured the president that he was speaking as a personal friend and as a friend of Mexico. All plans for the economic recovery of Mexico, he said, which concerned both countries, must be based on peaceful conditions. This meant that a solution to the Church problem was essential. Calles readily agreed and said that he would be glad to meet Burke in Mexico. Morrow had hoped to keep the negotiations secret, for he knew that Calles would not publicly back away from the strong position he had maintained since the strike began. Unfortunately, the American priest was less discreet. On February 6 he met Luis G. Bustos and two other representatives of the Liga Nacional in New York City to tell them of his and Morrow's plans. Bustos replied angrily that any settlement made independently of his group would not be acceptable. The only solution, he insisted, was to restore civil rights to Mexico's Catholics. And it would be foolish to trust Calles, he said. The sole true guarantee must be a strong Catholic party in Mexico to maintain the Church's rights. He demanded that the Liga Nacional participate in any settlement made by Morrow. Burke sought to placate the Mexican Catholics, pointing out that Morrow would only use his good offices to help find a solution. The final settlement would be worked out with Calles by church authorities and with the approval of the Holy See. In the end Bustos withdrew his demands, but Burke feared that the opposition of the Catholic laymen could be a serious impediment to a settlement.[16]

Burke was correct. On February 9 the New York *Herald-Tribune*, in a story probably given out by Bustos, revealed Burke's plan to visit Mexico to confer with Calles, as well as Morrow's role as an intermediary. Reporters in Mexico were rebuffed when they asked the American embassy to confirm the story, but Morrow had a lengthy long-distance conversation with Olds in Washington about the article—a fact also duly reported in the *Herald-Tribune*. The leaking of the story infuriated the Mexican president. Calles told Morrow that because of the publicity an interview between him and Burke would now be "of little value."[17]

Bustos' militant stand drew support from several of the prelates still in Mexico. Leopoldo Lara y Torres, bishop of Tacámbaro,

telegraphed the League representatives in New York his "approbation." And Orozco y Jiménez, "from a place in the archbishopric of
Guadalajara," cabled the pope to ask that the Liga Nacional be
permitted to continue its armed struggle against Calles' persecution. González Valencia, still in Europe, protested the "fatal" policies of conciliation, which he attributed to Pascual Díaz. And Lara
y Torres, in a letter to Díaz, challenged the designation of Burke as
a representative of the Mexican clergy. "I fear that the time has
passed to enter into a deal with a government that has demonstrated
such intransigence . . . and whose word no one can prudently
trust . . . ," he wrote. The bishop of Tacámbaro wanted to hold out
until the Calles government agreed to restore relations with the
Vatican, hoping thereby to protect the rights of the Church.[18]

Morrow was not content to let the matter drop, however. He had
worked intensively for several days, gathering materials on religious
problems, not only in Mexico, but also in various European countries, relying chiefly on the *Cambridge Modern History* and the *Ency-
clopaedia Britannica.* On February 15 he had breakfast with Calles, as
so often before, at the Santa Barbara ranch. He sought to placate
the Mexican president, assuring him that the Vatican would be more
disposed to a moderate course than the bishops of Mexico. His
studies had shown him, he said, that two provisions of the Mexican
legal code might, in the end, destroy the identity of the Church—
the law requiring priests to register, which could lead to their "control and discipline" by the civil government, and the section of
Article 130 that allowed states to fix the number of priests. Calles
said that he had no desire to control the spiritual life of the Church.
He would continue to enforce the laws and the constitution, but
only in a "reasonable manner." Convinced by Morrow's arguments,
Calles again agreed to meet Burke, though only in the utmost
secrecy. The road to peace was strewn with rocks, however, and
Morrow realized that he had taken just one small step. He wrote to
Olds: "The president is a proud man, ready to go down on a question of principle, rather than to yield."[19]

With Morrow and Burke taking the lead in seeking a settlement
the Mexican bishops, like puppets on a string, played little part in
determining their own destiny. The hierarchy was shattered and
leaderless, dispersed through two continents. In early 1928 only
nine prelates remained in Mexico, most in hiding or completely
inactive. Thirteen resided in the United States, two in Los Angeles,

two in San Francisco, one in El Paso, one in New York (Díaz), one in Washington (Ruiz y Flores), and the rest in San Antonio. Two lived in France, two in Italy, and three, including the Mexican primate, Mora y del Río, in Havana. Morrow worked through the American Under Secretary of State Olds and Monsignor Burke, and only Díaz, Ruiz y Flores, and the apostolic delegate in Washington, Fumasoni-Biondi, were apprised of his plans or consulted. Morrow and Olds agreed that no settlement was feasible on the principles involved, for the excessive claims of both parties left no room for compromise. All that was possible, as Olds wrote to the ambassador on March 9, was a "common-sense adjustment on the basis of the actual facts of the situation." Olds told Burke in Washington that Calles could not be "expected to modify his position that the constitution and laws must be enforced" and that the only question to be agreed upon was "the degree or kind of enforcement." Burke indicated his willingness to accept a modus vivendi, rather than hold out for a complete settlement of the issues. Olds suggested that, since the Vatican must make the final decision for the Mexican Church, Gasparri consider appointing a Mexican as apostolic delegate to carry out the concluding negotiations with Calles. Burke agreed to take up the matter with Fumasoni-Biondi, and Olds' proposal was subsequently relayed to Gasparri and implemented in the following year.[20]

Morrow's position was bolstered by the American journalist, Walter Lippmann, in a private conversation with the Mexican president. Lippmann raised the two points that had bothered Burke—the registration of the clergy and the fixing of quotas by the states. Calles told Lippmann that the churches in Mexico were the property of the nation and that they had been for over a generation. They had been given to the clergy in trust to be used for religious purposes. For that reason, he said, it was necessary to have an official record of those priests entrusted with national property. When Lippmann asked the president if the civil authorities had the power to refuse to register any priest designated by his bishop, Calles said, "Absolutely no." The law was merely statistical, he said, and was not designed to interfere in any way with the internal discipline of the Church. As for the state quotas, he assured Lippmann that his government could compel the states to conform to a national policy.[21]

Ernest Lagarde, on his way to France, gave Burke the same advice. The French chargé d'affaires, soon to assume new duties as chief of the American section at the Quai d'Orsay, had stopped off in Washington, at Morrow's request, to give Olds his frank views on the religious situation in Mexico. Like Olds, he told Burke that Calles would never retreat from his position that the laws would be enforced. But he also assured the American priest that clerical registration could be interpreted as a statistical device. Burke held himself in readiness to leave for Mexico at any time, and he came to the State Department almost daily to ascertain if there were news from Morrow.[22]

In Mexico City the ambassador continued to prepare the basis for a meeting between Calles and Burke and, subsequently, direct negotiations between the president and a representative of the Mexican Church. On March 13 he sent the State Department the text of a letter ostensibly from Msgr. Burke to the American ambassador. Morrow told Kellogg that he had tried, wherever possible, to use the language and ideas of previous communications between the Church and the Mexican government, notably a letter from Cardinal Gasparri to Obregón's Secretary of Foreign Relations in 1924, and Ruiz y Flores' and Díaz' letter to Calles in August 1926. He also took into account, as evidence of the desire of the Church for peace, the *Commonweal* editorial of January 4, 1928, which Burke had shown him in Havana. Morrow sought to avoid a promise that the Mexican clergy would keep out of politics, because such a promise could be seen as "an admission that they had been involved in politics heretofore." Nonetheless, he made clear that such an "implied promise" must be part of any settlement.

Burke's letter, which he signed on March 29 and returned to Morrow, stated that he had learned that Calles had said "it was never his purpose to destroy the identity of the Church or to interfere with its spiritual functions." For their part, the Mexican bishops were "desirous to have a true and lasting peace," if they could find some toleration "within the law." He asked Calles if he could "find it in full accordance with his constitutional duties" to make a declaration that it was "not the purpose of the constitution and the laws, or his purpose, to destroy the identity of the Church. . . ." And he asked if Calles' government "would be willing to confer from time to time with the head of the Church in Mexico." If so, the Mexican clergy would "resume forthwith their spiritual offices." Morrow showed the letter to Calles before he sent it to Washington and

obtained from the Mexican president a promise that he would meet
Burke during the first week of April in Veracruz. Morrow also provided Calles with a letter replying to Burke's requests. Morrow
proposed to keep both letters until Calles and Burke had worked
out a satisfactory agreement.[23]

Each year during Easter week Mexican official business ceases, as
public servants, high and low, take vacations, usually in the warmer
climes, at a beach or a spa. Calles used the opportunity to visit the
port of Veracruz, where, in complete privacy and with no publicity,
he could meet Burke. Mexico's newspapers noted only that the
president was spending the holidays at the island fortress of San
Juan de Ulúa to "rest from his official duties." Though *El Universal*
reported that Morrow had come from Mexico City with Calles and
that the two had conferred for ten hours, there was no mention of
Burke or of his companion, William F. Montavon, director of the
Legal Department of the National Catholic Welfare Conference. In
the dingy old fortress Calles and Burke explored the basis for a
modus vivendi.[24]

John Joseph Burke, a Paulist priest, was born in New York City
in 1857 of Irish-American parentage. After a short tour as a missionary, he joined the staff of *The Catholic World* in 1901 and three years
later became its editor, a post he held until 1922. In 1919 he was
named general-secretary of the newly founded National Catholic
Welfare Conference, which worked to give some semblance of coor-
dination to the activities of the several dioceses and archdioceses in
the United States. In 1927 the Sacred Congregation of Seminaries
and Universities of the Holy See conferred upon Burke a doctorate
of sacred theology for "exceptional service" to the Catholic Church.
An eminently successful priest, Burke was also a partiotic citizen,
imbued with the ideals of democracy. Thoroughly American in his
outlook, he believed that the Catholic Church in the United States
enjoyed liberties unequaled in other, less enlightened countries. He
hoped to introduce into Mexico the benefits of American religious
toleration and concord between Church and government.

The fifty-three-year-old Burke was tall, taller than most other men
he met by half a head or more. He towered over the diminutive
Morrow, and even the bulky Calles was much shorter. Burke's hand-
some, Irish, masculine face radiated good humor. An accomplished
raconteur and mimic, he loved a good joke. His eyes betrayed a
gentle, yet compelling, spirit. A friend wrote of Burke later:

"Beneath his humor and side by side with his scholarship, he was a man of the firmest convictions. No one could be in doubt as to which side of the fence John was on. . . . We argued sometimes against his ideas, but no one who debated with John retained any animosity against him." And Montavon wrote: "He was never intolerant of his opponent. His desire and his whole effort was to help his opponent to analyze, reach an understanding of his own attitude, and in attaining that understanding discover for himself the flaws and weaknesses [to produce] that meeting of minds between him and his opponent that is the indispensable characteristic of every lasting conciliation." It is not surprising that Calles' obduracy disappeared before the compelling arguments and the Gaelic charm of Msgr. John J. Burke.[25]

Burke opened the meeting with a short statement concerning his reasons for coming to Mexico. He had done so at the request of Fumasoni-Biondi, he said, "with no power to promise, with no final authority, and with no power to accept anything." But he hoped to make clear to Calles the wishes of the Holy Father for peace and to see if the laws might be interpreted in such a way that the Mexican Church, "with preservation of her own organization and dignity," might accept them and restore public worship. He told the president that the Holy See should not be judged by the acts of some Mexican bishops.

After Smithers had translated Burke's statement, Calles launched a lengthy and bitter attack on the evils of the Catholic Church in Mexico. He insisted that he had never wanted to destroy the Church, but only to enforce the country's laws. He could not accept a papal nuncio, Calles said, though if the pope wished to send a private representative, who did not officiate in public ceremonies, he could talk with members of the government about religious matters. Calles then handed Burke an answer to his letter of March 29. "I am advised of the desire of the Mexican bishops to renew public worship," he wrote, "and I take advantage of the opportunity to declare with all clearness, as I have on other occasions, that it is not the purpose of the constitution, nor the laws, nor my own purpose to destroy the identity of any church, nor to interfere in any form in its spiritual functions." His sole aim was to see that the law was applied "in a state of reasonableness and without any prejudice." As the two parted, Calles told Burke: "I hope your visit means a new era for the life and people of Mexico." On his return to

Mexico City, Morrow talked with the British minister about the negotiations. Everything depended, he said, "on the attitude of the Vatican."[26] Both Burke and Morrow knew that the conference at Veracruz was but the starting point, that peace would come only when Calles met a representative of the Mexican Church, empowered by the Holy See to negotiate with the Mexican president.

For the Vatican, however, Mexico might as well have been the other side of the moon. With the bishops scattered and no apostolic delegate in the country, direct contact with the Mexican Church had been lost, and news, much of it contradictory, came from many sources in various parts of Europe and North America. When the British minister, Sir Odo Russell, asked Cardinal Gasparri about reports of negotiations between Calles and an American "prelate," the papal Secretary of State denied all knowledge of the matter. In any event, said Gasparri, without an "explanation" by the Mexican government of the outrages against priests, any agreement was "impossible." And the "explanation must precede negotiations," he insisted. The Mexican government appeared to want a settlement, he said, only because it needed to float a loan in the United States. Gasparri's hostility toward Mexico was mirrored in a series of articles in *Osservatore Romano* that attacked the barbarism of Calles' government. The semiofficial Vatican organ charged that Mexico had "lost control, not only of the situation, but of itself."[27]

On his return to Washington Msgr. Burke, who was ill for several days after his stay in Mexico, submitted copies of the two letters to Fumasoni-Biondi for the Vatican's approval. The apostolic delegate preferred, however, to get the approbation of the Mexican bishops —not for the letters, because these and Burke's negotiations remained secret, but for the principle of negotiation. Several Mexican prelates living in the United States had scheduled a meeting during April in San Antonio, and Fumasoni-Biondi asked Ruiz y Flores to attend the conference and sound out his colleagues. The bishops readily agreed to accept any decision made by the Holy See, but they asked that the negotiations include the questions of restoring the religious buildings confiscated by the government and of a general amnesty for Catholic rebels and exiles. As a result, Burke composed a second letter to Calles, taking into account the bishops' request. When he showed it to Olds and Fumasoni-Biondi, however, both told him that it was too specific. "I did not like the draft and said so," wrote the Under Secretary to Morrow. "I cannot help feeling that they have not handled the meeting at San Antonio as well as they might have done." Both advised Burke to remove the reference to an amnesty. He then rewrote the letter, and it was telegraphed to Morrow for delivery to the Mexican president. He asked Calles to give further assurance concerning the registration requirements and the legality of religious education—in a public statement, if possible, by the president's office.[28]

Morrow believed that the time seemed appropriate for a major breakthrough in the negotiations. In April Mora y del Río, whom Calles held chiefly responsible for the bitter religious conflict died, and though the Vatican made no move to replace him as primate of Mexico, the moderate and conciliatory Ruiz y Flores assumed his role as the country's senior prelate. In a long-distance telephone call to Olds, Morrow suggested that Burke return to Mexico and bring the archbishop of Morelia with him. But when the American ambassador made his proposal to Calles, the Mexican president opposed the plan vigorously. He said that Ruiz y Flores could not come to Mexico without getting into discussions with the other prelates and the Catholic laymen, and the resulting publicity would once more jeopardize the peace negotiations. He told Morrow that there was a "small but powerful party" in Mexico that worked stead-fastly against any adjustment and would "welcome the opportunity to impede the work Burke was trying to do." Calles preferred to deal with Morrow and Burke and to see if the strike could be ended on the basis of his letter of April 4 to the American priest. Morrow used all his persuasive powers, however, and ultimately he brought the reluctant Calles, against his better judgment, to meet Ruiz y Flores.[29]

The American priest and the Mexican archbishop arrived by train at Tacuba, a small town on the outskirts of Mexico City, on the morning of May 17. From Tacuba they were taken by motor car to the home of Captain McBride, Morrow's naval attache. Like Burke's first meeting with Calles, this trip was kept secret, and no one recognized Burke or Ruiz y Flores at the station or during the discussions in the capital. They talked with no one except the president and the ambassador. There was no publicity in the Mexican or foreign newspapers. At McBride's home Ruiz y Flores told Morrow that he had instructions to ask Calles if the public schools might be used at certain hours for religious classes. The ambassador told him that there was no hope of this, and that he should take great care in broaching the subject with the president.

Late the same afternoon Ruiz y Flores and Burke came to the Chapultepec Castle, Calles' official residence. As Morrow had predicted, Calles turned down Ruiz y Flores' request to use the public school buildings for religious instruction, but he said they could teach as much as they liked in the churches. "What else were the churches for?" he asked. Ruiz y Flores then referred to a speech made the previous month by J. M. Puig Casauranc, in which Calles' Secretary of Public Education denied that his government aimed to destroy religion in Mexico. The archbishop asked the president if he agreed with the conciliatory sentiments of Puig Casauranc. When Calles assented, Ruiz y Flores said that he would accept the positions outlined in the Veracruz letters. He wrote a letter to Calles, signed it, and asked Morrow to send a copy to Washington for transmission to Rome. Morrow had requested Olds to remain all night in his office so the message could be given immediately to Fumasoni-Biondi. If the expected approval from the Vatican arrived promptly, Ruiz y Flores planned to exchange letters officially with Calles and to make public a brief statement: "In the light of the attached two letters the Holy See has authorized the resumption of religious worship in Mexico." He seemed optimistic that the churches could be opened in time to hold services on the following Sunday, which was the Feast of the Pentecost.[30]

Vatican officials, with the view of millennia behind and of eternity ahead, exhibited no such sense of urgency. When the British minister asked Gasparri on the following day about the conflict in Mexico, he replied that he had no reports "or any other sign" of a change in the situation. He told Sir Odo that the pope was "only too willing to listen to any new overtures likely to lead to an improvement in the unfortunate conditions now prevailing in Mexico." Moreover, the question of a settlement was complicated by the need to select a successor to Mora y del Río as archbishop of Mexico. When Ruiz y Flores' message arrived at the Vatican, Gasparri cabled the archbishop, through Fumasoni-Biondi, asking the Mexican prelate and Burke to come to Rome. Burke misinterpreted the Holy See's procrastination, and took an unwarrantedly optimisitic view of the turn of events. On May 19 he told Calles that the trip to Rome meant an "expeditious conclusion" to the church conflict. The apostolic delegate decided subsequently, however, that Burke should remain in Washington, while Ruiz y Flores took the pope the terms negotiated with Calles. On May 26 the archbishop of Morelia sailed from New York aboard the Leviathan. The decision to accept or to reject the terms agreed to in Mexico now lay with Gasparri and the pope.[31]

The more militant representatives of the Mexican Church and the leaders of the Liga Nacional, at odds with Díaz and Ruiz y Flores, stepped up their campaign against a peaceful settlement. In late April the nine prelates who remained in Mexico appointed a new subcommittee, composed of José Othón Núñez, archbishop of Oaxaca, and Miguel M. de la Mora, bishop of San Luis Potosí, to bypass Díaz and Ruiz y Flores, and to deal directly with Rome. Manríquez y Zárate, exiled in Los Angeles, wrote to de la Mora: "Who named Monsignor Ruiz as the representative of the bishops before the Vatican?" Lara y Torres, still in Mexico, concurred: "Because Monsignor Ruiz and Monsignor Díaz are still president and secretary respectively of the Episcopal Committee is no reason to consider them as representatives of the opinion of each and every one of the members of the committee."

On the day Ruiz y Flores left New York Rafael Ceniceros y Villarreal telegraphed Gasparri, stressing the League's support for the new subcommittee, and asking the Vatican to consult Núñez and de la Mora before sanctioning any agreement with Calles' government. He asked for the "greatest respect" toward the new subcommittee's view, for it represented the sentiments of those still fighting in Mexico for a just solution. Núñez and de la Mora, he said, were still in "intimate contact" with the situation in their country, unlike Díaz and Ruiz y Flores, who, in exile, had lost touch with Mexican Catholics. And on May 31 the leaders of the Liga Nacional. Catholic Youth, and the Knights of Columbus joined to send a lengthy memorial to the pope. Accepting an accord with the government would be tantamount, they said, "to seeing the Church subjected to a law that it had already condemned" and to forcing the surrender of those who had fought "for the sacred right of legitimate defense," had "opposed tyranny," and had "resisted with arms in their hands."[32]

Ruiz y Flores arrived in Paris on June 1, where he was met by American reporters. Without Burke with him to counsel restraint, the archbishop talked at length to the representatives of the press. He had come to Europe, he said, to ask the pope to use his influence

in bringing the Mexican dispute to an end. "I am going to explain
to the Holy Father just how matters are. . . ." he said. "In a comparatively short time President Obregón will assume the reins of government. President Calles has himself seen the trouble which has followed our exile, and we have reason to believe he favors
reconciliation. The new president, we know, wants peace, because
he needs the support of the Catholic Church to carry out his policies. The only remedy, of course, is the suspension of the present
laws prohibiting the Church from holding public services and from
performing the rites of baptism and marriage without government
consent. . . . But we believe the Holy Father can bring this about.
That is why I have come abroad. The bishops and priests I represent
want to know just what they should do."[33]

Through subsequent articles in American and even Mexico City
newspapers, Morrow's role in the new secret negotiations was revealed. The ambassador, in the United States on vacation, refused
to comment to reporters, and the Mexican consul-general in New
York City, Arturo M. Elías, denied that Calles had been a party to
any negotiations with Morrow and representatives of the Church.
The National Catholic Welfare Conference released a statement to
the press in Washington, maintaining that Ruiz y Flores had been
misquoted. But the damage caused by the archbishop's garrulous-
ness could not be undone. Calles was furious, as the British minister, Sir Edmond Ovey, put it, that his agreement to negotiate had
been seen as a "climb down." Calles proposed to make a public
statement, denying the reports, but Morrow advised him, through
embassy officials in Mexico City, that the best course was to say
nothing. The news of Ruiz y Flores' trip to Rome caused the intran-
sigent Mexican Catholics to redouble their efforts to prevent a settlement. Orozco y Jiménez, de la Mora, and Lara y Torres, in joint
letters to the Holy See, denied that the armed struggle had failed.
Rather, they insisted, it had gained a "precious victory" and would
continue to grow as a movement "of the people." They praised
"this admirable resistance to the greatest of tyrannies." "Of what
purpose are such sacrifices," they asked, "if in the end we Catholics
must remain slaves?" The three prelates stressed that the only solution must be the "revocation and reform" of the offending laws.[34]

On his arrival in Rome Ruiz y Flores conferred at length with
Gasparri and the papal Under Secretary of State for Extraordinary
Affairs, Msgr. Gorgoncini-Duca, and then talked for an hour and a

half with the pope. In contrast to his earlier openness with the press, Ruiz remained incommunicado after his conferences, and Vatican spokesmen also refused to discuss the contents of the proposal he brought from Mexico. But the New York *Times* reporter sensed a mood of "genuine optimism." Ruiz y Flores wrote to Burke that he expected an "amicable adjustment," though the Holy See felt "that for the sake of such peace, no particular body of citizens should, so to speak, be left out in the cold; that it would be helpful if some way could be taken by the government of Mexico to give public expression of its desire for a reconciliation of all citizens—even for those who had borne arms against the government, provided of course they would lay down their arms and follow the way of peace." And the Vatican also expected, he said, "more explicit guarantees for the liberty of the Church in exercising her spiritual functions. . . ."[35]

The Vatican was still in no hurry to effect a settlement, especially on the terms brought by Ruiz y Flores. Gasparri referred the matter to the Congregation on Ecclesiastical Affairs for careful study and for recommendations of the "minimum conditions" that the Mexican government should grant before the Holy See approved the resumption of services. He told Sir Odo Russell that the situation "remained unchanged." As the Mexican prelate "came with no definite mandate, with no definite suggestions, and with no authority," said Gasparri, "his visit could lead to no result." The papal Secretary of State repeated "with considerable emphasis" that the Holy See desired a settlement. But no settlement was possible, he said, "without guarantees for the future and without some show at least of contrition for all the grievous wrongs which have been done to the Church." And the Vatican withheld its approval, hoping to force Calles to send a representative to Rome or else to wait for Obregón's accession to the presidency—presumably the new president would be more amenable to a compromise and more acceptable to the Church. When the British minister to Mexico saw Sir Odo's account of his conversation with Gasparri, he told the Foreign Office: "I cannot think that the Vatican are being very clever in the matter. . . ." He said that it was useless to expect Calles to "mend his ways" and to admit that he persecuted the Church. The Vatican in 1928 lived in a dream world, believing that the head of a secular state would still heed the words of the pope. The plain fact was that Calles would never deal with the Vatican. He was no Henry IV; he could not be compelled to come to Canossa.[36]

On July 1, 1928, Obregón was elected president of Mexico, the Congress having finally yielded to Calles' demands to amend the constitution. Though he ran unopposed, the campaign was bitter and at times violent. Calles' Minister of Industry, Commerce, and Labor, Luis Morones, also leader of the Labor Party, attacked the official candidate in fiery and intemperate speeches, and in April there was an attempt on Obregón's life in Orizaba, Veracruz. But Obregón had the strong support of Calles. In turn, Obregón stressed his association with the president's policies, especially on the religious question. In an interview in June he called upon the Catholic clergy to "support rather than obstruct" Mexico's revolutionary government. On July 15 Obregón came to Mexico City from his home in Sonora and paid an immediate call upon the president in the National Palace. Despite Morones' animus toward Obregón, all public signs indicated that Calles would transfer power peacefully to the newly elected chief executive. On the following day General Obregón told reporters that as far as he could see, there would be no change in the government's attitude toward the Church when he took power four and a half months later.[37]

In early July Morrow returned to his post in Mexico City. On the morning of July 7 he conferred for an hour and a half with Calles to review once more the state of the negotiations. He told Calles that he had no doubt that considerable pressure was being brought upon the Vatican "to make no adjustment" until Obregón came in or unless more definite assurances could be given. Calles praised Burke and his efforts toward peace, but he said that he "never expected a favorable outcome," after he heard that the American priest was not going to Rome with Ruiz y Flores. Since it was certain that Calles would not retreat, Obregón seemed the only hope. On the day after Obregón's arrival in Mexico City, his campaign manager, Aarón Sáenz, came to the embassy to arrange a meeting between Morrow and the president-elect. The next morning Sáenz returned to the embassy and talked with Morrow at great length about the religious question. He told the ambassador that Calles and Obregón had consulted fully about the proposed settlement, and that Obregón hoped that a modus vivendi might be worked out as soon as possible, that the new president looked for an "era of peace" during his administration. Sáenz left to attend a luncheon in honor of Obregón at La Bombilla, a restaurant on the outskirts of the capital. Morrow never met Obregón. The general died at La

Bombilla, the victim of an assassin's bullets. And with Obregón died also the Catholics' flickering hopes for a more equitable settlement.[38]

Police took the young assailant into custody immediately. He refused to identify himself, however, despite police torture, or to give any motive for the slaying, and suspicion fell at once upon Luis Morones. Though he proved to be innocent of any complicity in the crime, Morones and many of his henchmen went into hiding, because they feared reprisals at the hands of the dead general's associates. Police investigators soon showed that the assassin was a twenty-six-year-old art teacher, José de León Toral, a staunch Catholic and long-time friend of Humberto Pro Juárez. The police also implicated a Catholic nun, Mother María Concepción Acevedo y de la Llata, in the plot and charged her with counseling Toral to kill Obregón. At La Bombilla Toral had pretended to be making a sketch of the general. As he approached the speaker's table, he pulled out his pistol and fired five times at Obregón from close quarters. The general died immediately. Later, in prison, Toral wrote to his jailer, Felipe Islas, to explain his motivations in the slaying: "I had always heard that Obregón was an enemy of religion, that he was responsible for the persecuting articles of the Constitution of 1917. . . . The idea circulated that he was going to settle the religious question, but no news ever came, official or serious, and while the constitution was reformed in other parts, at his initiative, nothing was done about the religious question, despite public anxiety." Toral was condemned to death before a firing squad. Mother Concepción was convicted in the same trial and received a long prison term.[39]

Calles' first response to Obregón's slaying was an intemperate attack upon the Mexican Church. He announced to the press that "clerical action was directly implicated" in the assassination. In Rome Ruiz y Flores told reporters that Obregón's death could help negotiations between State and Church in Mexico. "Unhappily, it is but natural that the newly elected president should perish by violence," he said. "He caused so many people's death that sooner or later the friends of those whose blood he shed would have killed him." The archbishop had not as yet heard that Obregón had been slain by a Catholic, and he thought that the assassination was a political act. He added that the president "probably desires peace more anxiously than before. He is tired of bloodshed. Besides, the federal finances are in a parlous state. Calles needs money, and it won't be forthcoming until a settlement between the Catholics and the liberals is reached." Pascual Díaz reacted in a more conciliatory manner. When reporters in New York told him of the assassination, he said: "No good can come from such violent measures. . . . Peace must come from love, not from hate." He assured the reporters that the Mexican Church had "absolutely no connection" with the slaying.[40]

Calles' statement seemed to Burke so patently inflammatory that he proposed to publish a reply, refuting the Mexican president's charges. But A. B. Lane, chief of the Mexican desk in the State Department, persuaded him to wait while Morrow sought to get the president to retract his accusation against the Church. As a result of Morrow's intervention, Calles told reporters that "one cannot honestly accuse the entire Mexican clergy, nor extend the responsibility for the awful crime to all Catholics." But he continued to insist that "legal investigations" showed that there were "definite responsibilities on the part of individual Catholics and members of the Catholic clergy." Mollified by Calles' partial retraction, Burke proposed to Morrow that he and Ruiz y Flores return to Mexico to meet the president once more in an attempt to break the stalemate. On August 9 Morrow had another early-morning conference at Calles' ranch. For most of the four hours Calles talked of the situation in Mexico as a result of Obregón's death. He said that he would not continue in office after November and that he would suggest that Congress select an interim president until national elections could be held in the following year. Calles expressed his irritation at Ruiz y Flores' statements in Rome that it was "very natural" that Obregón had been killed, and that the president wanted to settle the religious question because his government needed money. He told Morrow that he would not permit the archbishop to return to Mexico. The religious situation was a "closed incident," he said. Morrow knew that it would be useless to raise with him the question of a new mission by Burke and Ruiz y Flores, so he said nothing of Burke's suggestion.[41]

Almost twelve months had passed since Morrow had interested himself in the religious question, and the contending parties were no nearer an agreement. Calles and the Vatican officials maintained their entrenched positions, with Burke, Ruiz y Flores, and the moderates among the Mexican clergy caught in the middle. Calles continued to insist that his statement to Burke in April was his ultimate concession, and he would not budge. Gasparri still believed that at some time the Mexican government would be moved to send a representative to Rome to treat directly with the Vatican. In August *Osservatore Romano* began a new series of articles on Mexico's religious crisis. The Vatican newspaper vilified Calles, likening him to Nero and Diocletian in his persecution of the Catholic Church. The only good to come from Calles' rule, said the editor, was the purification and unification of Mexican Catholics under the lash of tyranny and suffering. Burke told an American official in Washington that the articles were "irresponsible," and Morrow said that someone in Rome had "gone out of his mind." In a telephone conversation with Lane, he said that "much of the trouble in Mexico" had been caused by a "disorganized lot of women" who had been "wildly accusing President Calles and others, without knowing the facts or without realizing the harm their remarks are doing."[42]

Though Bishop Fulcheri of Zamora telegraphed to Ruiz y Flores in Rome his disapproval of *Osservatore Romano*'s slurs against the Mexican president, Gasparri showed no signs of altering the Vatican's firm stand. In September he told A. W. G. Randall, of the British legation to the Vatican, that the "Mexican government had so far put forward no proposals for settlement which were even worth serious examination by the Holy See. . . ." It was true, he said, that the suggestions made in April, May, and June had "aroused some hope in the Vatican." But the "halfheartedness and vagueness of the official Mexican attitude caused suspicion and dampened any optimism that might have been raised." Gasparri insisted that Calles had to give guarantees for the future, and his "declaration," when actually received, "was shown to declare nothing." The cardinal said that the Mexican government had demanded the "entire and unconditional spiritual subjugation of the Catholic Church and the Catholic religion to the Mexican State."[43]

If Morrow seemed to have reached a dead end, others tried to induce the Vatican to modify its stand during Calles' last weeks in office. Agustín Legoretta, president of Mexico's Banco Nacional, went to Rome in September to talk to Gasparri. At the same time Under Secretary of State Olds, on a trip to Europe, worked through the American embassy in Paris and Ernest Lagarde in the Quai d'Orsay to obtain an interview with the papal Secretary of State. But Gasparri told the American diplomat that "without new facts or proposals," his coming to Rome could accomplish nothing. Of these and other like attempts to influence the Vatican, Gasparri told Randall that none of the proposals could give the Church the freedom that the Holy See considered "essential" to fulfill its mission in Mexico. There must be an "absolute certainty" that the religious laws would not be applied again. As for Morrow's reports that the Mexican economic situation had improved substantially, Gasparri insisted that the Americans' interest in Mexico was solely pecuniary —they only wanted to "enrich themselves." In November Morrow made one last approach to Calles, suggesting that Burke and Ruiz y Flores might come to Mexico again with new proposals. And Rafael Guízar Valencia, bishop of Veracruz, who hinted to Mexican officials that he expected to be named the next archbishop of Mexico, offered his services to Calles' government. He intimated that he would compromise the Church's position, that only a "slight modification" of the registration law would be needed. But Calles said that it was too late to reopen the question with either Guízar Valencia or Burke. It would be especially unwise, he felt, during the trial of José de León Toral.[44]

On November 30, 1928, Emilio Portes Gil, Calles' Minister of Gobernación, assumed his duties as provisional president. During his first weeks in office, negotiations on the Church question languished. The Vatican continued to insist that no agreement could be approved unless Mexico sent a representative to Rome with authority to offer changes in the religious laws. Burke in Washington maintained his willingness to come again to Mexico to confer with the new president. Portes Gil told Morrow that the situation was unchanged, that he stood by the terms stated by Calles in his letter of the previous April. The Cristeros fought small skirmishes in the West under a new leader, Jesús Degollado Guízar, who took command of the rebel forces when Gorostieta was killed in battle. Federal troops contained the rebel movement, but made no attempt to destroy it. Pascual Díaz remained in New York with little to do or say about the religious situation in his own country. Ruiz y Flores returned to the United States from Rome with an admonition to the Mexican prelates in California and Texas to keep quiet and to accept any terms sanctioned by the Vatican. No progress seemed possible until the Mexican government or the Church officials in Rome backed away from their extreme positions. A break in the deadlock came in February 1929, however, under the most unlikely circumstances—the execution of Obregón's assassin, José de León Toral.

On the morning of February 9, 1929, Toral went to his death before a firing squad. That afternoon he was buried in Mexico City. Thousands of sorrowing Catholics followed his funeral cortege, appearing to honor him, like Miguel Pro, as a martyr to his faith. The government made no attempt to interfere with the funeral or with the burial procession. On the following day, as Portes Gil returned to Mexico City, a bomb wrecked the presidential train. Portes Gil was unhurt, however, and he published a statement attributing the attack to religious fanatics. He condemned the excesses of some Catholic leaders, whom he labeled "frankly subversive," and he promised to punish those who broke the law. But he did not attack the Church or accuse the hierarchy of complicity in the attack. Felipe Canales, the Minister of Gobernación, announced that "because of the subversive conduct adopted by a part of the higher clergy, he was ordering each priest in the Republic to register his place of residence. Those who did not would be considered "accomplices of the rebel Catholics. . . ."

Despite the new public attack on the clergy, the leaders of the Church did not choose to challenge the government. Most of the priests and prelates registered; only a few, including de la Mora and Navarrete did not. De la Mora, speaking for the episcopal subcommittee, denied that the bishops or the clergy were subversive. The government had no legal right, he said, "to compel priests to register or to indicate their residence." But several of the moderate bishops in Mexico, such as Nicolás Corona of Papantla, Antonio Guízar Valencia of Chihuahua, Fulcheri of Zamora, and Francisco Banegas of Querétaro, condemned the attack on the president, and the spirit of good will shown by these churchmen was matched by Portes Gil's own moderate view of Church-State relations. The provisional president, though beholden to Calles for his position and unable to act in complete freedom, nevertheless did not share his predecessor's anticlericalism, and he intimated to Morrow that he would now be willing to meet representatives of the Church.[45]

Negotiations were once more delayed, however, when a potentially dangerous armed rebellion broke out against Portes Gil's government in March. The rebel commander, José Gonzalo Escobar, hoping to draw wide backing for his movement, declared his sympathy with the Catholic Church. Though the revolution had little success, Portes Gil took no chances. He named Calles Minister of

War to lead the campaign against Escobar's forces. The American government announced its full support for Portes Gil's regime and offered weapons, supplies, and munitions. Within a month Mexican federal troops had broken the back of the rebellion, and the leaders were either dead or in exile. With peace restored, Portes Gil finally turned to the question of a religious settlement.[46]

Ruiz y Flores also took a more pacific course. On May 2 he told reporters in Washington that there were no problems in Mexico that could not be corrected "by men of sincere good will." He praised Portes Gil's conciliatory attitudes: "The Church and its ministers are prepared to cooperate with him in every just and moral effort to aid the Mexican people." "In Mexico," he said, "the Catholic Church asks no privileges. She asks only that, on the basis of an amicable separation of Church and State, she be allowed that liberty which is indispensable to the well-being and happiness of the nation. The Catholic citizens of my country, whose faith and patriotism can never be doubted, will accept sincerely any agreement reached between the Church and the government."[47]

When reporters in the Mexican capital brought the archbishop's statements to the attention of Portes Gil, the president responded that if Ruiz y Flores "should desire to discuss with me the method of securing the cooperation in the moral effort for the betterment of the Mexican people, which he desires, I shall have no objection to conferring with him on the subject." His government would always, he said, "exchange views with ministers of the Catholic Church or have conversations with ecclesiastical dignitaries on the laws applying to the clergy."[48] Rome too made one slight concession to the Mexican government. Gasparri, after reading Portes Gil's statement, relayed a suggestion to the president, through the British legation in Mexico City, that conversations with a Vatican representative might take place in Washington, if it were not "convenient" for a Mexican to travel to Rome. In private, however, Gasparri gave vent to his anger against both the Mexican and American governments. Walter Lippmann, who was visiting Rome, wrote to Morrow that he was "compelled to listen to a long and bitter harangue in bad French against our government for its favoritism for the enemies of the Church." Even the Vatican had come after three years to see that the strike was a lost cause.[49]

On May 16 Fumasoni-Biondi returned from Rome bringing the appointment of Ruiz y Flores as apostolic delegate to Mexico. Thus

Gasparri hoped to avoid the problems caused by the earlier appointments of Filippi, Cimino, and Caruana. Because Ruiz y Flores was a Mexican citizen, the laws banning foreign priests could not be used against him. Gasparri expected that the archbishop could confer in Washington with an agent of the Mexican government and report back to the Holy See the results of his negotiations. The Vatican still planned to make the final decision on whether to accept or reject any agreement made by the negotiators.[50]

For weeks Morrow had stressed in his dispatches to the State Department that the negotiations must take place in Mexico and solely with the president, that Portes Gil, like Calles, would not treat directly with Rome. Nor had Burke and Fumasoni-Biondi any illusions on this score. Both advised Ruiz y Flores to seek permission to return to Mexico. On May 18 the archbishop called on the Mexican ambassador, Manuel Téllez, to apprise the government of his appointment as apostolic delegate. Ruiz y Flores indicated that he would be glad to conduct any negotiations for a religious settlement with Portes Gil. On receipt of approval from his government, Téllez immediately granted passports to Ruiz y Flores and any others that would accompany him to Mexico City.

Morrow, who had returned to the United States for the marriage of his daughter Anne to Colonel Lindbergh, met the archbishop in Washington. He told Ruiz y Flores that although he was on vacation, he would be glad to return to Mexico if he would be needed. The archbishop said that the pope still hoped to see the Mexican laws changed as a price for a settlement. But Morrow replied that this course of action could not succeed and that it would be "useless for him to lend his good offices" to the negotiations. Though Burke was willing to go with Ruiz y Flores, the archbishop preferred to take only Pascual Díaz. The settlement, if reached, would be between Mexican citizens. Morrow lent the two prelates his private railway car for the trip to Mexico. Concerned that they might still need an impartial mediator, he decided to cut his vacation short in order to be in the Mexican capital during the negotiations.[51]

The two prelates arrived in Mexico City on the evening of June 8. Their train was met by Edmund Walsh, vice-president of Georgetown University, and they were taken to the house of Agustín Legoretta. Though there was no undue attempt at secrecy, and their presence in the capital became known almost immediately, they remained in seclusion, refusing to meet the many Mexican Catholics, including leaders of the Liga Nacional and Bishop de la Mora, who wished to protest the negotiations with Portes Gil. Walsh, a Jesuit priest, had come to Mexico more than a month earlier, ostensibly to plan a student exchange program with officials of the National University. But his real purpose was to make an independent try at effecting a peace settlement. Working with his friend, Miguel Cruchaga, a Chilean diplomat, Walsh had been asked by Gasparri to study the religious question and report his findings to Rome. He had no authority, however, to negotiate a final settlement with the Mexican government. Morrow had advised Walsh in May to coordinate his efforts with those of Burke and Fumasoni-Biondi, but both the Jesuit priest and Cruchaga preferred to hold themselves aloof from the previous negotiations, which had proved fruitless. Now, however, with Ruiz y Flores and Díaz in Mexico City, the two allied themselves with the Mexican prelates, in a sense to make the negotiations their own cause. Walsh acted as an intermediary between the American embassy and the two prelates. Neither Cruchaga nor Walsh saw Portes Gil, and the Chilean's actual participation in the talks was limited to the furnishing of diplomatic facilities to transmit secret messages between Mexico City and the Vatican.[52]

On the evening of June 10 Father Walsh came to the American embassy to discuss the negotiations with Morrow. He informed the ambassador that Ruiz y Flores and Díaz had not prepared a definite proposal as yet. He said that, in his opinion, it was possible to interpret the religious laws in such a way as to favor the position of the Church. Morrow told the Jesuit priest that such devious arguments would only serve to irritate Portes Gil and perhaps imperil the success of the negotiations. On the following day Walsh returned to the embassy with the news that the prelates had decided to go back to the original letters of Burke and Calles and to seek an adjustment on a general assurance by Portes Gil that it was not the purpose of the constitution, laws, or government to destroy the identity of the Church or to interfere with its spiritual functions. Nor would they insist upon specific guarantees by the president. Morrow believed that the way was now cleared for a speedy conclusion to the negotiations and an end to the long Church strike.[53]

At noon on June 12 Ruiz y Flores and Díaz met Portes Gil at the presidential palace to begin their discussions in an atmosphere of cordiality and good will. The president told the prelates that he was prepared to offer the same assurances as Calles—no more, no less.

Ruiz y Flores and Díaz indicated their willingness to accept his
assurances. Both sides agreed to draft statements, which if subsequently accepted and submitted to the Vatican for the pope's approval, would be published simultaneously. Morrow, who had taken
no part in the negotiations to this point, had reason for optimism,
as he saw the imminent success of his yearlong efforts to bring about
a peaceful solution to the religious strife. He wrote Reuben Clark,
the Under Secretary of State, that the two prelates had "carried
themselves with admirable discretion." They would not insist, he
said, upon alterations in the constitution and the laws as a price for
peace.

Morrow's hopes plummeted the next day, however, when the
negotiators met for the second time. Portes Gil submitted a statement almost identical to the letter Calles had handed Burke at
Veracruz more than a year earlier. The prelates had prepared no
letter, for they wanted to see the president's statement first. Evidently they believed that Portes Gil would take a more conciliatory
position. They told Walsh that the president's statement was "un-
necessarily brusque" and his attitude during the second discussion
"hard and cold." Morrow, who had hoped to remain aloof, saw that
there was every likelihood that the negotiations would break down
unless he interjected himself into the discussions. The only solution, he felt, was to secure the consent of both parties to the exact
wording of an agreement before they next met. With great care he
prepared two new statements, based upon Burke's letter to Calles
and the former president's reply.[54]

Morrow agreed with the prelates that Portes Gil's statement,
while substantially the same as Calles' letter, seemed couched in
needlessly abrupt language. Moreover, he said, it was not sufficiently explicit in its guarantees to the Church. He therefore wrote
new statements (in English) and asked for an appointment to see the
president on the afternoon of June 15. To make sure he was on safe
ground he showed the proposed statements to Calles before he met
Portes Gil. Calles said that they contained nothing that he would
have been unwilling to say at the time of his conference with Msgr.
Burke. In his meeting with the provisional president, Morrow
pointed out that Calles' statement had been in reply to Burke's
letter and that, read together, both formed a "courteous and intelli-
gible statement of an agreement upon a modus vivendi." Portes Gil
replied that he would have the statement that was attributed to him

translated and then study it. Later the same day, Morrow conferred
with the two churchmen and readily obtained their approbation.
They made only one minor change in the wording. Using the code
of the Chilean embassy, they telegraphed their proposed statement
to Gasparri for the Vatican's approval. Portes Gil also indicated his
acceptance—with a few insignificant changes. Morrow and the prelates awaited uneasily the reply from the Vatican, afraid that militant
opponents of a peaceful settlement, who continued to bombard the
pope with protests, might persuade Gasparri to reject it.[55]

Edmund Walsh brought Gasparri's cablegram to the American
embassy on the morning of June 20. The Holy Father was "most
anxious" for a peaceful solution, said the papal Secretary of State.
But he placed three conditions on any agreement. The president
must guarantee a complete amnesty to the bishops, priests, and
laymen who had opposed the government. All residences of priests
and bishops and seminaries, seized by Calles, must be restored. And
free relations between the Vatican and the Mexican Church must be
assured. "Only on those understandings may you close, if you think
proper before God," he warned. Morrow told Walsh that this cablegram represented a "grave change" in the situation, that it failed to
authorize the terms agreed to by Portes Gil and the Mexican prelates. He said that the conditions would be unacceptable to the
president and that Gasparri's message meant an end to the negotiations.

After lunch Walsh returned to the embassy to tell Morrow that he
brought "good news." Ruiz y Flores had not been "disturbed" by
the cablegram, for, as apostolic delegate, he had sufficient authority
to give "wide interpretation" to the agreement. In effect, the leaders
of the Mexican Church, tired of the fruitless struggle, ignored the
conditions imposed by Rome and settled on the only terms possible,
those prepared by the American ambassador, agreed to by Burke
and Calles, and now accepted in face-to-face negotiations with
Portes Gil. It is not surprising that Morrow, though he had provided
a settlement acceptable to both sides, was subsequently criticized
harshly by Mexican Catholics, who charged that he had betrayed the
best interests of the Church and sold out the loyal members of the
Liga Nacional and the Cristero soldiers who had fought bravely and
long to preserve their religious liberties.[56]

The final meeting between Portes Gil and the two prelates took
place at 1:30 P.M. on June 21, in which the declarations were signed

and released to the press. In that moment the long and bitter religious conflict, which had erupted nearly three years earlier, came to an end. Portes Gil agreed that the enforcement of the registration law did not mean that his government could register priests who had not been designated by their hierarchical superiors, that the laws regarding religious education did not prevent the teaching of children and adults within church confines, and that the constitution, as well as the laws of the land, guaranteed to all citizens the right to petition the appropriate authorities for the reform, repeal, or passage of any law. In turn, the apostolic delegate announced that the Mexican clergy would restore religious services "in accordance with the existing laws." He expressed the hope that the resumption of the Masses and sacraments might lead the Mexican people, "animated by a spirit of mutual good will," to cooperate in "all moral efforts made for the benefit of all the people of our Fatherland."[57]

Though he made no further public guarantees, Portes Gil acceded in private to the request of the Vatican for an amnesty and the return of the church residences that had been seized by the government. At the same time he told Ruiz y Flores that he intended to exile the bishop of Huejutla and the archbishops of Guadalajara and Durango. The apostolic delegate protested, but with no effect. He knew that he was in no position to bargain further with the Mexican president. Portes Gil said, smiling: "I believe that the absence of these gentlemen will be necessary for quite some time." Subsequently, the Mexican government also excluded from the country the principal leaders of the Liga Nacional, René Capistrán Garza, Juan Lainé, Luis G. Bustos, and Father David G. Ramírez.[58]

The conference concluded at about 2 o'clock in the afternoon, and the two prelates drove to Tepeyac, to the basilica of Guadalupe. Among the many pilgrims, some lame or infirm, some looking for miraculous cures, some merely penitent, no one recognized the two princes of the Church, kneeling in silent prayer before the great altar, for they wore civilian clothes. As yet few Mexicans were aware that these two had committed the Catholic Church to a new and perhaps dangerous course—the acceptance of the Revolution as an accomplished fact and the determination to give Mexico a viable religious life within the framework of the anticlerical laws. No longer could the Mexican Church aspire to dominate State and nation. No longer would creole aristocratic families determine the shape of the Mexican hierarchy. The future belonged to middle- and lower-class clerics, to mestizos and even Indians such as Pascual Díaz, to the people of the dark Virgin of Guadalupe. The Vatican was determined to change the complexion of the Mexican Church, to bring able and ambitious priests from the non-elite classes into places of leadership. Ruiz y Flores, the pope's personal representative, turned to Díaz, at the altar rail beside him. "I must tell you," he whispered, "that you are the archbishop of Mexico." Humbly and with some show of surprise, Díaz said only: "Hombre! Que barbaridad!"[59]

In the succeeding days priests throughout the Republic began to register with the local authorities. Portes Gil's government then gave its approval to the resumption of religious ceremonies. On the morning of June 30, the Feast of St. Peter the Apostle, clergymen said the first public Sunday Masses in almost three years. The night before, Ambassador and Mrs. Morrow had retired to Cuernavaca to seek the quiet and seclusion of their little house. At dawn they were jarred awake by the clanging of all of the town's church bells. "Betty," he said. "Do you hear that? I have opened the churches of Mexico!" As the bells continued and fireworks explosions added to the early morning din, Morrow asked his wife dryly: "Would you now like me to close the churches in Mexico?"[60]

And so the strike had ended with a modus vivendi, an agreement to disagree peacefully. The Church would register the priests, as the government had demanded, and in return would be allowed the opportunity to impart religious education to children inside the churches. Though Catholics prepared new petitions, the anticlerical laws were never changed and continued to pose a threat that they could someday be enforced by a revolutionary government to destroy the identity of the Catholic Church in Mexico. Despite Portes Gil's promise of amnesty, several hundred Cristeros, who surrendered to federal forces, were summarily shot. Yet the Church made every effort to live within the restricting laws. Ruiz y Flores, backed by the Vatican, ordered the rebel armies to dissolve and required the Liga Nacional to change its name and abandon its "secondary and accidental" activities in order to dedicate itself to nonpolitical activities. He warned Catholics against criticizing the accord: "Once the pope has sanctioned the terms of reconciliation, within the limits of the Catholic conscience, it is not right for any Catholic to rebel and constitute himself a judge of the supreme authority of his

Church, for obedience to the Church is not limited to dogma, but reaches to the fullest extent to administrative discipline. . . . Now is not the time to discuss, but to obey. . . ." The settlement, seen as an abject surrender by the militant Catholics, left rancorous sores that troubled the Church for years. And even in the United States the achievement of peace caused vexations and jealousies among the successful peacemakers. Reports of the modus vivendi in the Washington *Post* stressed the role of the Jesuit, Edmund Walsh, in facilitating the negotiations, ignoring completely the long and arduous labors of Msgr. John J. Burke.[61]

Time heals many wounds, and revolutionary enthusiasms wane with the passage of the years. Calles, though he had maneuvered the formation of a new official party in 1929 and the election of General Pascual Ortiz Rubio as president, continued to dominate Mexican politics as Jefe Máximo. In the early 1930s Calles' anticlericalism fixed relations between Church and government. Local legislatures passed new and more stringent laws limiting the number of priests who could function in their states. In 1931 the president expelled Ruiz y Flores as a "pernicious foreigner," because Catholics had celebrated too ostentatiously the four hundredth anniversary of the Virgin of Guadalupe. Three years later, the constitution was amended to require that all education be, not only secular, but "socialistic." A brief, but bitter, conflict ensued between the Church and the government, in which many Mexicans lost their lives. But in 1934 General Lázaro Cárdenas became president, and though he was no friend of the Church, he did not share Calles' rabid anticlerical views. He restored the modus vivendi with a gentlemen's agreement that the laws would remain, but that they need not be enforced, if the Church kept to its own sphere and did not attack the Revolution.

Since then church schools have operated—with the fiction that they are private and secular. If the Church restricts its public ceremonies, priests and nuns do appear outside the churches in their religious garb, without challenge from the government. Religious orders, Jesuits, Franciscans, Dominicans, and Carmelites, among many, do function openly, if illegally. And an important political group, the National Action Party, is known to be Catholic, in fact though not in name.

If the Revolution by the 1970s had banked its fires, the Church too had grown increasingly complacent with social conditions in

Mexico. The Catholic Social Action movement continued, but without the enthusiasm of the pre-1926 days. In May 1969 members of the hierarchy praised separation of Church and State, insisting that the constitutional arrangement was in the "best interests" of Mexico's Catholics. The Mexican Church was among the least progressive in the Latin American countries, for, like the Revolution, it too had become "institutionalized." The agreement worked out by Morrow in 1929 brought peace, it is true, but at a high price to the Church. It meant that the Catholic religion could probably never play a significant role in effecting social change in Mexico.

Bibliographical Note

THE CONFLICT BETWEEN the Church and the Mexican revolutionary government has drawn the attention of writers both inside and outside Mexico for more than a half-century, in fact, from the earliest days of the Revolution. But almost all the Mexicans have been partisans of either the Church or the State, and their writings must be read with considerable care. Though I have used some of the books in this study, wherever possible I have relied upon other sources—archival materials, private papers, newspapers, and pamphlet collections. My dissertation (Harvard University, 1951) contains a lengthy list of books, especially for the period of the 1920s. Two recent writers, however, Alicia Olivera Sendano in *Aspectos del conflicto religioso de 1926 a 1929* and Antonio Rius Facius, have applied more modern scholarly methods to their accounts of the conflict. Though Rius Facius, a Catholic, is by no means impartial, his *Méjico cristero* and *De don Porfirio a Plutarco*, a history of the Catholic Youth movement, come as close as one probably can in Mexico to an accurate reconstruction of the events. Two other books proved to be equally indispensable, Bishop Emeterio Valverde Téllez' *Bio-bibliografía eclesiástica mexicana*, for the lives of leading prelates and priests, and the *Diario de los debates del Congreso Constituyente, 1916-1917*, for the history of Mexico's Constitution of 1917.

The late Canon Jesús García Gutiérrez accumulated during his lifetime the most extensive library on the Mexican church conflict available anywhere. With unmatched courtesy and hospitality, he permitted me complete access to his collection, even when he went to Spain for several weeks in the 1950 Marian Year. His library consisted of hundreds of books, ecclesiastical journals, pastoral letters, pamphlets, and other religious publications. He also talked to me at great length about his own participation in the historical events. At that time, as I worked on my dissertation, I had hoped to use the "Cristero" archives of Miguel Palomar y Vizcarra, but I had no success. Nor was I granted access to the official Church archives. Nearly two decades later, after Palomar y Vizcarra's death, I was able to go through his collection, which is now available on microfilm in the library of the Museum of Anthropology and Archaeology in Mexico City.

The National Archives in Washington provided another important source on the religious conflict. Now purchasable on microfilm, these materials are in the State Department 812.404 files. American diplomats gave outside assessments of the happenings in Mexico that the Mexicans themselves were often too busy to record accurately or at any length. The diplomats also sent back copies of significant documents with their dispatches. The most valuable single item in these files was a report by the French chargé d'affaires, Ernest Lagarde, to his superiors at the Quai d'Orsay on the state of the Mexican Church in 1926. This document was translated and then made available to the American State Department by Ambassador Dwight W. Morrow. British diplomats too reported on the Church conflict. Their dispatches can be found among the Foreign Office Papers in London's Public Record Office. Because the British government maintained diplomatic relations with the Holy See, these papers also contain firsthand information on the Vatican's attitudes toward the conflict in Mexico.

The story of Morrow's negotiation efforts was reconstructed principally through the large collection of his papers at Amherst College and the State Department 812.404 files. Morrow's secretary at the Mexico City embassy, George Rublee, wrote a summary of the religious conflict, based on Morrow's dispatches, which is also to be found in the Amherst library. Two other minor collections in the United States proved to be helpful, the William F. Buckley Papers in the University of Texas library and the José de León Toral Papers in Indiana University's Lilly Library. From previous studies I had made on Mexican-American relations, I was able to extract letters of President Woodrow Wilson from the Wilson Papers at the Library of Congress.

Many Mexican newspapers and periodicals for the years of the conflict can be found in the Biblioteca de México, in Washington's Library of Congress, and at the University of Texas. But the most complete holdings are those of the Hemeroteca Nacional in Mexico City. The employees there were invariably helpful and friendly. Particularly important were the files of *La Nación,* the Catholic newspaper of the Madero period, and obscure newspapers for cities other than the national capital. Finally, I must note the value of the New York *Times* with its admirable index. The *Times* could report on events freely when Mexican newspapers were under a tight censorship. And because the index furnished the dates of events in Mexico, it made much easier the finding of articles in the Mexican periodicals.

Notes

Chapter 1

1. For a well-written, firsthand account of Mexican religious practices, see Anita Brenner, *Idols behind Altars* (New York, 1929); also Frank Tannenbaum, *Mexico, the Struggle for Peace and Bread* (New York, 1950), 123-126; Ernest Gruening, *Mexico and its Heritage* (New York, 1928), 238–239; and Oscar Lewis, *The Children of Sánchez* (New York, 1961), xiv, xxvii, 20–21, 489.

2. Charles M. Flandrau, *Viva México!* (Urbana, 1964), 46-50, 76-77, 124, 204-207.

3. For an excellent study of this important period in Mexican history, see Charles A. Hale, *Mexican Liberalism in the Age of Mora, 1821–1853* (New Haven, 1968).

4. For the Reform period, see Walter V. Scholes, *Mexican Politics during the Juárez Regime, 1855–1872* (Columbia, 1957).

5. John A. Ryan and Francis J. Boland, *Catholic Principles of Politics* (New York, 1940).

6. A. M. Crofts, *Catholic Social Action* (St. Louis, 1936); Daniel A. O'Connor, *Catholic Social Doctrine* (Westminster, 1956); Emmet John Hughes, *The Church and the Liberal Society* (Princeton, 1949); John F. Cronin, *Catholic Social Action* (Milwaukee, 1948); Georges Hoog, *Histoire de Catholicisme Social en France, 1871–1931* (Paris, 1946); Henry Somerville, *Studies in the Catholic Social Movement* (London, 1933); *Idées Social et Faits Sociaux* (Paris, 1903).

7. Karl Schmitt, "Evolution of Mexican Thought on Church-State Relations, 1876–1911" (Ph.D. dissertation, University of Pennsylvania, 1954).

8. Carlos Septién García, "Avanzada Social," *Mañana*, October 27, 1951, 10–11; Antonio Rius Facius, *De don Porfirio a Plutarco* (México, 1958), 4–8; Genaro María González, *Catolicismo y revolución* (México, 1961), 313–314, 327–328; Emeterio Valverde Téllez, *Bio-bibliografía eclesiástica mexicana* (3 vols., México, 1949), II, 121–125, 129; Pedro de Alba, "El Episcopado Mexicano y el Problema Agrario," *El Globo*, March 20, 1925, 5:7–8.

9. Stanley R. Ross, *Francisco I. Madero, Apostle of Mexican Democracy* (New York, 1955).

Chapter 2

1. Valverde Téllez, *Bio-bibliografía*, III, 280; *El Universal*, December 27, 1924, 3:7, 9:7.

2. *La Nación*, November 29, 1912, 5:1.

3. José Mora y del Río, *Carta pastoral colectiva* (Zamora, 1913), 4–5.

4. Joaquín Márquez Montiel, *La doctrina social de la iglesia y legislación obrera mexicana* (México, 1939), 46; Septién García, "Avanzada Social."

5. Mora y del Río, *Carta pastoral* (Zamora), 4; *Memoria de la Segunda Gran Dieta de los Círculos Católicos de Obreros* (Zamora, 1913), 41.

6. Mora y del Río, *Carta pastoral colectiva* (México, 1914), 12–15.

7. Eduardo Correa, "La XXV [*sic*] Legislatura," *El Sol de Puebla*, October 27, 1955, 4:6–8; Francisco Banegas, *El porqué del Partido Católico Nacional* (México, 1960), 49–54.

8. *La Nación*, June 1, 1912, 3:4–5; March 23, 1913, 6:4–5.

9. Quoted in *La Nación*, January 14, 1913, 1:1, 7:1; *La Nueva Era*, January 4, 1913, 4:6; *La Nación*, January 9, 1913, 3:1–4; *El País*, January 22, 1913, 3:1–4.

10. Banegas, *El porqué*, 52–53.

11. *La Nación*, June 5, 1912, 4:4; Mora y del Río, *Carta pastoral* (México), 10.

12. *La Nación*, August 6, 1912, 5:7.

13. Wilfred H. Callcott, *Liberalism in Mexico, 1857–1929* (Stanford, 1931), 217; Miguel M. de la Mora, *Quinta carta pastoral* (Zacatecas, 1912), 11.

14. *Ibid.*, 4–7; *La Nación*, June 5, 1912, 4:5–6.

15. Callcott, *Liberalism*, 218; *La Nación*, February 7, 1913, 3:1–4; October 9, 1912, 1:1; *El País*, January 4, 1913, 1:4.

16. *El Estado de Jalisco*, LXXII (1913), 255, 323–327; Callcott, *Liberalism*, 235.

17. Personal conversation with Canon Jesús García Gutiérrez, 1950.

18. *El País*, February 20, 1913, 3:2–5.

19. *Ibid.*, February 23, 1913, 1:1–2; February 25, 1913, 3:2–5; Michael Meyer, *Huerta* (Lincoln, 1972), 69–82.

20. *El País*, February 20, 1913, 1:5–7; *La Nación*, February 22, 1913, 1:1; Meyer, *Huerta*, 83.

21. *La Nación*, February 25, 1913, 3:1–4; *Mexican Herald*, February 26, 1913, 8:4; *El País*, February 27, 1913, 3:2–5.

22. *La Nación*, February 27, 1913, 1:4–5; *Mexican Herald*, March 3, 1913, 8:4; René Capistrán Garza, "La Iglesia y la Revolución Mexicana," *Mañana*, XXXVI (April 1, 1950), 23; Mora y del Río, *Carta pastoral* (México), 4; Aquiles P. Moctezuma (pseudonym for Joaquín Cardoso), *El conflicto religioso de 1926* (México, 1929), 212–213.

Chapter 3

1. Much of the material here on the political history of the period comes from my *Mexican Revolution, 1914–1915* (Bloomington, 1960). See also John Womack, Jr., *Zapata and the Mexican Revolution* (New York, 1969); Luis Fernando Amaya C., *La Soberana Convención Revolucionaria, 1914–1916* (México, 1966); Michael Meyer, *Mexican Rebel* (Lincoln, 1967); Kenneth J. Grieb, *The United States and Huerta* (Lincoln, 1969); and Charles C. Cumberland, *Mexican Revolution: the Constitutionalist Years* (Austin, 1972).

2. *La Nación*, April 13, 1913, 3:1–4.

3. Banegas Galván, *El porqué*, 70.

4. For the American occupation of Veracruz see my *Affair of Honor* (Lexington, 1962).

5. Luis Liceaga, *Félix Díaz* (México, 1958), 270, 294–295; *La Tribuna*, April 25, 1913, 1:6–7; *La Nación*, April 8, 1913, 1:5; April 25, 1913, 1:2–6.

6. *Mexican Herald*, July 9, 1913, 1:5; Eduardo J. Correa, "La XXVI Legislatura," *Diario de Yucatán*, January 8, 1956, 3:3–5; Liceaga, *Félix Díaz*, 302; *La Nación*, July 9, 1913, 1:1–2: July 18, 1913, 1:1.

7. *Mexican Herald*, August 7, 1913, 1:2; Banegas, *El porqué*, 62.

8. Liceaga, *Félix Díaz*, 306–307; *Mexican Herald*, September 3, 1913, 1:6; September 5, 1913, 1:3; September 25, 1913, 1:6.

9. Liceaga, *Félix Díaz*, 307–309.

10. Howard F. Cline, *The United States and Mexico* (Cambridge, 1953), 146–147; *La Nación*, September 22, 1913, 1:4; September 25, 1913, 1:3–5; *Mexican Herald*, September 19, 1913, 1:4; September 23, 1913, 1:1.

11. *Ibid.*, September 25, 1913, 1:6–7; *La Nación*, September 26, 1913, 1:2–4; Cline, *United States*, 147.

12. *La Nación*, September 19, 1913, 1:1–2; *Mexican Herald*, September 20, 1913, 1:6–7; September 21, 1913, 1:7–8; Eduardo J. Correa, "La XXVI Legislatura," *Diario de Yucatán*, December 18, 1955, 3:7–8.

13. *Mexican Herald*, October 10, 1913, 1:6–7; October 11, 1913, 1:7–8; Banegas, *El porqué*, 63; *La Nación*, October 11, 1913, 1:1–2; Meyer, *Huerta*, 136–138, 145–149.

14. *La Nación*, October 24, 1913, 1:1–2; Cline, *United States*, 47; *Mexican Herald*, October 19, 1913, 1:3.

15. *Ibid.*, October 19, 1913, 1:1; October 23, 1913, 1:1; October 24, 1913, 1:1–3; October 26, 1913, 1:4; October 29, 1913, 1:6–7; Liceaga, *Félix Díaz*, 313–321.

16. *La Nación*, October 28, 1913, 1:3–4; *Mexican Herald*, October 27, 1913, 1:6–7; Cline, *United States*, 147; "National Catholic Party," State Department Files of the National Archives, Washington, D.C., 812.404/22. Unless otherwise indicated all correspondence of the Department of State will be from the 812.404 files and will be identified only by the slash number. Other citations will carry the full file number.

17. New York *Times*, May 13, 1914, 2:5; May 20, 1914, 2:1.

18. Marion T. Letcher to Secretary of State, January 26, 1915/52; Report of Eber C. Byam, November 15, 1919, Buckley Papers, University of Texas Library, Folder 145.

19. Letcher to Secretary of State, January 26, 1915/52.

20. Jules Jusserand to Secretary of State, June 20, 1914, 312.51/44; Byam, Buckley Papers, 145.

21. William P. Blocker to Secretary of State, January 19, 1915/43.

22. Byam, Buckley Papers, 145; Silliman to Secretary of State, July 27, 1914/3.

23. Silliman to Secretary of State, July 27, 1914/3; New York *Times*, July 28, 1914, 3:5; Byam, Buckley Papers, 145.

24. Silliman to Secretary of State, July 24, 1914, 312.51/68.

25. Hanna to Secretary of State, June 27, 1914, 312.51/46; *ibid.*, July 11, 1914/4; Silliman to Secretary of State, July 27, 1914/3; Leon J. Canova to Secretary of State, July 29, 1914/5; Silliman to Secretary of State, August 1, 1914/2.

26. Byam, Buckley Papers, 145; Canova to Secretary of State, August 3, 1914, 312.51/80.

27. Canova to Secretary of State, August 4, 1914, 812.00/12826; *ibid.*, August 7, 1914/6; J. M. Cardoso de Oliveira to Secretary of State, July 9, 1914, 312.12/24; Hanna to Secretary of State, July 31, 1914, 312.-51/77.

28. Richard M. Stadden to Secretary of State, January 18, 1915/49; "Religious Persecution in Guadalajara," no date/22; Byam, Buckley Papers, 145.

29. Gaston Schmutz to Secretary of State, January 20, 1915/44; Byam, Buckley Papers, 145; William C. Canada to Secretary of State, September 25, 1914/16.

30. Maria Elisa Thierry to Archbishop James H. Blenk, November 4, 1914, Buckley Papers, 145.

31. New York *Times*, December 18, 1914, 7:3.

32. Miguel M. de la Mora to James Cardinal Gibbons, August 14, 1914/8; John Tracy Ellis, *The Life of James Cardinal Gibbons* (2 vols., Milwaukee, 1952), II, 206–207, 209–210; Gibbons to Woodrow Wilson, August 18, 1914, Wilson Papers, Library of Congress, VI, 61; Gibbons to Secretary of State, August 18, 1914/8; Gibbons to Wilson, August 18, 1914/8; Bryan to Gibbons, August 20, 1914/8.

33. Wilson to Gibbons, August 21, 1914/134.

34. Quirk, *Affair of Honor*, 156–171; New York *Times*, September 20, 1914, II, 10:1; Anthony Matre to Secretary of State, November 21, 1914/24; New York *Times*, November 14, 1914, 1:3; November 20, 1914, 4:6; Bryan to R. H. Tierney, November 27, 1914/22.

35. Ellis, *Gibbons*, II, 210; New York *Times*, October 1, 1914, 5:4; Robert Lansing to American Federation of Catholic Societies, October 6, 1914/13.

36. Ellis, *Gibbons*, II, 212; R. H. Tierney to Secretary of State, October 17, 1914/22; New York *Times*, November 16, 1914, 5:1; November 19, 1914, 5:6.

37. The almost prurient interest of priests and other males in alleged

assaults upon nuns is a phenomenon worth noting and easily explained by Freudian psychology or even by common sense.

38. Francis C. Kelley, *The Bishop Jots It Down* (New York, 1948), 190.

39. Theodore Roosevelt, "Our Responsibility in Mexico," New York *Times*, December 6, 1914, VI, 1:1–5.

40. Ellis, *Gibbons*, II, 212–215.

41. Bryan to James P. Maher, January 21, 1915/30; Silliman to Secretary of State, January 22, 1915/41; "Statement of Antonio Paredes," January 22, 1915/123; see statements to Secretary of State from Thomas Bevan, Thomas D. Edwards, Jesse H. Johnson, Willis B. Davis, Calvin M. Hitch, Homer C. Coen, and William W. Canada, all consular agents in Mexico, 812.404/45, 47, 51, 76, 82, 87, 128.

42. Kelley to Dudley Field Malone, February 26, 1915, Buckley Papers, 145; "Statement of Archbishop of Mexico," no date/97; Bryan to Cardoso de Oliveira, February 24, 1915/73a; Cardoso de Oliveira to Secretary of State, February 26, 1915/74; Silliman to Secretary of State, January 1, 1916/109.

43. Kelley to Wilson, February 23, 1915/85.

44. Bryan to Kelley, March 20, 1915/85.

45. Kelley to Bryan, April 19, 1915/112.

46. New York *Times*, March 25, 1915, 7:2; Ellis, *Gibbons*, II, 215–216.

47. *El Monitor*, April 22, 1915, 1:6–7, 2:3.

48. *Ibid.*, May 8, 1915, 2:3, 3:2; May 9, 1915, 1:1, 2:3; *La Convención*, May 10, 1915, 1:1–2.

49. *El Pueblo*, December 22, 1914, 4:3; January 7, 1915, 1:2–6; Julio Cuadros Caldas, *Catecismo Agrario* (Puebla, 1923), 17–26; *Documentos de la Revolución* (México, 1945), 76–82.

50. Antonio Bahamonde, *México, es así* (México, 1940), 107; Eyler N. Simpson, *The Ejido, Mexico's Way Out* (Chapel Hill, 1937), 78; *El Pueblo*, June 12, 1915, 3:1–4.

51. *Ibid.*, January 21, 1915, 5:1; February 10, 1915, 5:1–5; September 3, 1916, 1:1–4.

52. *Ibid.*, January 23, 1916, 6:2; February 14, 1916, 1:1,4; February 18, 1916, 3:1–4.

53. Antonio Manero, *¿Qué es la Revolución?* (Veracruz, 1915), lx–lxii; Luis Cabrera, et al., "The Purposes and Ideals of the Mexican Revolution," *Supplement* to the *Annals of the American Academy of Political and Social Science* (Philadelphia, 1917), 6; *El Pueblo*, June 19, 1915, 3:3–4; José Mora y del Río, *Carta pastoral colectiva* (Havana, 1914), 4; New York *Times*, March 22, 1916, 2:2; March 23, 1916, 2:4; March 26, 1916, I, 2:8; *El Pueblo*, June 2, 1915, 3:1–4; February 6, 1915, 3:1–4; March 22, 1916, 1:3; March 24, 1916, 1:3–4.

54. Francisco Ramírez Plancarte, *La Ciudad de México durante la revolución constitucionalista* (México, 1941), 325; *Mexican Herald*, February 13, 1915, 1:2.

55. *El Pueblo*, February 15, 1915, 1:4; February 21, 1915, 1:3–4; *Efemérides Galván* (México, 1926), 588–589; *Mexican Herald*, February 16, 1915, 1:5;

February 20, 1915, 1:1; *La Prensa*, February 19, 1915, 1:4; *Mexican Herald*, February 21, 1915, 1:1–2; February 22, 1915, 1:1.

56. Bryan to Silliman, February 20, 1915/65.

57. From a personal conversation with Canon Jesús García Gutiérrez, 1950. See also Buckley Papers, 145; New York *Times*, March 7, 1915, II, 10:3; Silliman to Secretary of State, March 19, 1915/80.

58. Eliseo Arredondo to Secretary of State, October 8, 1915/101.

59. New York *Times*, October 2, 1915, 4:2; November 29, 1915, 5:2–3; December 3, 1915, 8:2; December 9, 1915, 16:1; Francis Kelley to Secretary of State, December 30, 1915/110.

60. Kelley to L. W. Reilly, June 9, 1916; Kelley to R. H.Tierney, December 24, 1915, Papers of Francis C. Kelley, Center for Christian Renewal, Oklahoma City.

Chapter 4

1. *El Pueblo*, January 25, 1915, 1:1–2; March 13, 1915, 1:1–2; Félix F. Palavicini, *Nuevo congreso constituyente* (Veracruz, 1915), 62.

2. Gruening, *Mexico*, 99; *El Pueblo*, September 17, 1916, 3:1–4; September 20, 1916, 1:4, 2:5–7; *Diario de los debates del Congreso Constituyente. 1916–1917* (2 vols., México, 1960), 16.

3. For the backgrounds to the Constituent Congress see my dissertation, "The Mexican Revolution and the Catholic Church, 1910–1929: An Ideological Study" (Harvard University, 1951), Chapter VI; and Cumberland, *Mexican Revolution*, 212–274.

4. *El Pueblo*, September 14, 1915, 1:2; Armando de María y Campos, *Múgica, crónica biográfica* (México, 1939), 102; "El General Francisco J. Múgica, Hombre de ideología vertical," *Revista Militar de México* (April 1954), 6–7; Gabriel Ferrer Mendiolea, "Francisco J. Múgica," *El Nacional*, April 9, 1958, 3:4–6; César Martino, "Francisco J. Múgica, Personaje de la Historia," *Hoy*, May 8, 1954, 15–17.

5. Ferrer Mendiolea, "Múgica."

6. Miguel Castro Ruiz, "José Natividad Macías, Constituyente y Universitario," *La Nación*, August 27, 1951, 12–13; *El Pueblo*, December 6, 1916, 1:1–2.

7. Quirk, Dissertation, Chapter VI.

8. Félix F. Palavicini, *Historia de la Constitución de 1917* (2 vols., México, 1938), I, 221; A. D. Melgarejo Randolph, *El Congreso Constituyente de 1916 y 1917* (México, 1917), 348; *Diario de los debates*, I, 530–531.

9. *El Pueblo*, November 23, 1916, 1:4–5; November 24, 1916, 1:2–6; November 26, 1916, 1:4–6; December 2, 1916, 6:5; *Diario de los debates*, I, 49.

10. *Ibid.*, I, 385–388; Jesús Romero Flores, "Mis Recuerdos del Constituyente de Querétaro," *El Nacional*, February 19, 1957, 3:4–6; *El Pueblo*, December 2, 1916, 5:2–3.

11. *Ibid.*, December 3, 1916, 3:1–4.

12. *Diario de los debates,* I, 492, 503; *El Pueblo,* December 5, 1916, 2:1; December 6, 1916, 6:3–4; December 7, 1916, 1:5.

13. *Diario de los debates,* I, 503; Jesús García Gutiérrez, "La Iglesia Mexicana y los Constituyentes," *Todo,* September 9, 1954, 30; Gabriel Ferrer Mendiolea, "Luis G. Monzón," *El Nacional,* November 12, 1958, 3:4–6; Omar Gómez Mañana, "La Herencia de Monzón," *Diario del Sureste,* June 12, 1942, 3:1–4; Juan Jerónimo Beltrán, "Luis G. Monzón," *El Popular,* June 10, 1942, 5:6–8.

14. *El Pueblo,* December 12, 1916, 1:6–7, 2:1–4; *Diario de los debates,* I, 541–543.

15. *Ibid.,* I, 641; *El Pueblo,* December 14, 1916, 6:2–7.

16. Diego Arenas Guzmán, "Luis Manuel Rojas," *El Nacional,* March 2, 1949, 5:6–8, 7:1–2; *Diario de los debates,* I, 643–655.

17. *Ibid.,* I, 657–665; Gabriel Ferrer Mendiolea, "Alfonso Cravioto," *El Nacional,* October 1, 1958, 3:3–6.

18. *Diario de los debates,* I, 667–712.

19. *Ibid.,* I, 732–774; *El Pueblo,* December 17, 1916, 1:4, 4:3.

20. Andrés Molina Enríquez, *Esbozo de la historia de los primeros diez años de la revolución agraria de México* (México, 1937), 172–174; *El Pueblo,* December 17, 1916, 3:5; *Diario de los debates,* I, 18.

21. *El Demócrata,* December 16, 1916, 3:1–4.

22. *El Pueblo,* December 14, 1916, 3:1–4.

23. *Diario de los debates,* II, 1031–1040.

24. *El Pueblo,* December 17, 1916, 5:6; *Diario de los debates,* II, 1042, 1216; "Religious Clauses of the Mexican Constitution," *Current History,* XXIV (1926), 503–504.

25. *Diario de los debates,* II, 1044–1061; *El Pueblo,* January 29, 1917, 7:5, 8:7.

26. *Diario de los debates,* II, 1174–1175.

27. *El Pueblo,* January 18, 1917, 7:3; Miguel A. Quintana, "La Primer Oposición al Artículo 3," *El Nacional,* November 9, 1945, 3:4–6.

28. Mora y del Río, *Protesta con ocasión de la Constitución* (Acordada, Texas, 1917), 1–7; "Protesta que hacen los prelados mexicanos," February 27, 1917/152.

29. Mora y del Río, *Instrucción pastoral* (México, 1917), 4–6; Asociación Nacional de Padres de Familia, *Estatutos generales* (México, 1917), 14–15; Pope Benedict XV, *Carta a los arzobispos y obispos de los Estados Unidos Mexicanos* (Rome, 1917), 1; García Gutiérrez, "La Iglesia Mexicana y los Constituyentes," *Todo,* September 23, 1954, 20.

30. Pope Benedict XV to Woodrow Wilson, January 26, 1917/132½; Robert Lansing to Joseph Tumulty, January 27, 1917, Woodrow Wilson Papers, Library of Congress, VI, 459; New York *Times,* January 29, 1917, 4:5; *El Pueblo,* November 1, 1917, 1:6–7; Ellis, *Gibbons,* II, 219; *Investigation of Mexican Affairs,* 66th Congress (1919), Senate Documents 7665–7666.

31. V. Blasco Ibáñez, *Mexico in Revolution* (New York, 1920), 128.

32. *El Pueblo,* October 7, 1918, 1:5; Eyler Simpson, *The Ejido,* 78–79; for

congressional debates see *El Pueblo,* issues of September 1918; Rosendo Salazar and J. G. Escobedo, *La pugna de la gleba 1907–1922* (México, 1923), 68–69.

33. *El Pueblo,* March 25, 1917, 3:1–2; *La educación pública en México a través de los mensajes presidenciales* (México, 1926), 183, 425–426; *El Pueblo,* December 24, 1917, 2:7; November 20, 1918, 5:4–5; Bernardino Mena Brito, *Carranza, sus amigos, sus enemigos* (México, 1935), 73.

34. *El Pueblo,* September 25, 1918, 1:7; October 3, 1918, 2:6–7.

35. *Ibid.,* May 11, 1919, 1:7; May 15, 1919, 1:3–4; *Educación pública en México, 1926,* 201.

36. Kelley, *Bishop Jots,* 198; García Gutiérrez, "Calumnia. Que Algo Queda," *Todo,* January 17, 1946, 40.

37. Francisco Orozco y Jiménez, *Memoir* (Chicago, 1918), 5–6; Kelley, *Bishop Jots,* 199–200.

38. Orozco y Jiménez, *Memoir,* 12, 14, 36; Silliman to Secretary of State, July 17, 1917/145; *ibid.,* July 19, 1917/146; T. J. Walsh to Secretary of State, July 29, 1917/149; Silliman to Secretary of State, July 31, 1917/150; *ibid.,* August 8, 1917/152; *El Occidente* (Guadalajara), August 8, 1917, 1:1–2.

39. Silliman to Secretary of State, February 13, 1918/117.

40. J. Ignacio Dávila Garibi, *Colección de documentos relativos a la cuestión religiosa en Jalisco, 1918–1919* (2 vols., Guadalajara, 1920), I, 384; *El Estado de Jalisco* (Guadalajara, 1919), 571; *ibid.,* (1918), 453; *El Universal,* July 6, 1918, 2:3.

41. *Estado de Jalisco* (1919), 572.

42. Orozco y Jiménez, *Memoir,* 29; *El Occidental,* July 7, 1918, 1:3–5; *El Universal,* July 9, 1918, 1:6–7; *El Demócrata,* July 8, 1918, 1:3.

43. Orozco y Jiménez, *Memoir,* 34; *El Demócrata,* July 17, 1918, 1:6; Claude I. Dawson to Secretary of State, July 11, 1918, 312.12/425; Kelley, *Bishop Jots,* 200–201; Kelley to Woodrow Wilson, July 14, 1918, Wilson Papers, VI, 91.

44. Rius Facius, *De don Porfirio,* 104; *El Universal,* July 10, 1918, 1:1; Silliman to Secretary of State, July 11, 1918, 312.12/429; *ibid.,* July 17, 1918/181; *El Demócrata,* August 3, 1918, 5:5; August 4, 1918, 5:7; Silliman to Secretary of State, July 31, 1918/186; *ibid.,* August 6, 1918/187.

45. Silliman to Secretary of State, August 3, 1918/192; *ibid.,* August 8, 1918/191; *ibid.,* August 12, 1918/197; *ibid.,* November 18, 1918/209; *ibid.,* December 11, 1918/213; *ibid.,* December 21, 1918/216.

46. *El Estado de Jalisco* (1919), 355–356, 541; Edward L. Antletz to Secretary of State, February 7, 1919/217; *Excélsior,* February 17, 1919, 4:5; Rius Facius, *De don Porfirio,* 112.

Chapter 5

1. John W. F. Dulles, *Yesterday in Mexico* (Austin, 1961), 86; Rius Facius, *De don Porfirio,* 152, 156; *Omega* (Mexico City), July 14, 1920, 1:1–6; Jesús

Degollado Guízar, *Memorias* (México, 1957), 9; Eber Byam to Wallace Thompson, Buckley Papers, 145.

2. Charles W. Hackett, *The Mexican Revolution and the United States* (Boston, 1926), 352; Cline, *The United States*, 203–208.

3. Cline, *United States*, 207–208.

4. Francisco de Sales Sarrión, "Figuras de la Raza," *La Raza*, May 27, 1922.

5. Manuel Gamio, *Hacia un México nuevo* (México, 1935), 5; José Vasconcelos and Manuel Gamio, *Aspects of Mexican Civilization* (Chicago, 1926), 95; Moisés Sáenz and Herbert I. Priestley, *Some Mexican Problems* (Chicago, 1926), 72.

6. José Vasconcelos, *Proyecto de ley para la creación de una Secretaría de Educación Pública* (México, 1921), 11; Vasconcelos, *El Desastre* (México, 1938), 24, 169; *Boletín de educación pública* (México, 1923), 177.

7. *Boletín de educación pública* (México, 1922), 54; Verna Carleton Millán, *Mexico Reborn* (Boston, 1939), 43–44; Richard B. Phillips, "José Vasconcelos and the Mexican Revolution of 1910" (Ph.D. dissertation, Stanford University, 1953), 124–125.

8. *Boletín de educación pública*, 1923, 395–396; Tannenbaum, *Mexico*, 161; *Escuela Rural*, I (May 1926), 101.

9. Gruening, *Mexico*, 221; *Mexico* (New Haven, 1926), 24; New York *Times*, April 11, 1926, 7:2.

10. Gruening, *Mexico*, 220.

11. Simpson, *Ejido*, 82–83, 219, 318; Tannenbaum, *Mexico*, 65.

12. Leopoldo Ruiz y Flores, *Instrucción pastoral sobre la repartición de tierras* (Morelia, 1920), 9–12; Gruening, *Mexico*, 215–219.

13. *Manual de las cooperativas en México* (México, 1925).

14. *Constitución de la Confederación Regional Obrera Mexicana* (México, 1933), 3; Ausencio López Arce, "La Doctrina de la CROM ante la Representación Nacional," *CROM*, I (November, 1925), 56–57; *CROM*, I, 1.

15. Marjorie Clark, *Organized Labor in Mexico* (Chapel Hill, 1934), 89–91; *CROM*, I, 35, 49.

16. *Semana Social en Puebla* (Puebla, 1919), 54, 134, 151, 155.

17. Ruiz y Flores, *El socialismo. Instrucción pastoral* (Morelia, 1921), 4–10; Mora y del Río, *Carta pastoral sobre la Acción Social Católica* (México, 1920), 4.

18. Francisco Orozco y Jiménez, "Excitativa a los Agricultores, Industriales, Comerciantes y Propietarios," *Revista Eclesiástica*, Año II, II (December 1920), 826; "Deberes de los Ricos y de los Pobres—Instrucciones," *ibid.*, Año III, I (April 1921), 274.

19. *Revista Eclesiástica*, Año III, II (July–August 1920), 544–545, 555–556; Orozco y Jiménez, "Círculo Número 33," *ibid.*, Año III, I (May 1921), 348.

20. Márquez Montiel, *Doctrina social*, 49–50; *Acción y Fe*, II (April 1923), 234–236; *La Dama Católica*, I (September 1, 1920), 2, 16–19.

21. *Excélsior*, April 23, 1922, 1:6, 4:4.

22. *El Universal,* April 25, 1922, 1:1; *Revista Eclesiástica,* Año IV, II (May 1922), 303–305; González, *Catolicismo,* 316.

23. Alfredo Méndez Medina, "La Cuestión Social en México—Orientaciones," *Cuestiones Actuales,* I (January 1923), 10.

24. *El Universal,* October 7, 1924, 1:7.

25. *Ibid.,* February 13, 1921, 3:6.

26. *Ibid.,* February 21, 1921, 5:4–7.

27. Moctezuma, *Conflicto,* 224; *Efemérides Galván,* 648; *Revista Eclesiástica,* Año III, II (July 1921), 64–65.

28. Rius Facius, *De don Porfirio,* 217; *Revista Eclesiástica,* Año IV, I (May 1922), 298–302; Salazar and Escobedo, *Las pugnas,* 156.

29. Carlos Septién García, "Sindicalismo Libre," *Mañana,* November 3, 1951, 10–11; *Revista Eclesiástica,* Año III, II (December 1921), 530; *ibid.,* Año V, I (June 1923), 280.

30. Mora y del Río, *Carta pastoral colectiva con la ocasión del monumento nacional al Sagrado Corazón de Jesús* (México, 1921), 5.

31. *Ibid.,* 10.

32. Mora y del Río, *Instrucción pastoral en la fiesta de Cristo Rey* (México, 1926), 1.

33. *El Universal,* January 11, 1923, 1:4; José Franco Ponce, "El Monumento Nacional al Sagrado Corazón de Jesús," *Revista Eclesiástica,* Año V, I (January 1923), 45; New York *Times,* January 12, 1923, 4:4.

34. *El Universal,* January 12, 1923, 1:3, 8:4; January 14, 1923, 1:1–2; Gruening, *Mexico,* 224.

35. New York *Times,* January 15, 1923, 14:8.

36. *El Universal,* January 24, 1923, 1:4–5, 5:4–6; New York *Times,* January 17, 1923, 3:3.

37. From *El Universal,* February 2, 1923, cited in 812.404/238; New York *Times,* February 2, 1923, 4:5; *El Universal,* November 7, 1926, 11:3; Inman, *Journal of Religion,* 404.

38. From *El Universal,* February 7, 1923, cited in 812.404/239.

39. *Revista Eclesiástica,* Año V, II (December 1923), 417; *Acción y Fe,* II (April 1923), 232.

40. Ernest Lagarde, "The Religious Crisis in Mexico," confidential memorandum by the French chargé d'affaires in Mexico, 812.404/867½; Walter Lippmann, "Church and State in Mexico: The American Mediation," *Foreign Affairs,* VIII (1930), 186–207; British Legation to Holy See to the Foreign Office, December 18, 1924, FO 204, 1925, Foreign Office Papers, Public Record Office, London. Hereafter all Foreign Office dispatches will be listed by names and dates only.

41. *El Universal,* October 11, 1924, 1:7; October 12, 1924, 13:6–7; New York *Times,* October 11, 1924, 18:4.

42. Lagarde, "Religious Crisis."

43. Dulles, *Yesterday,* 232, 286.

44. *CROM,* September 15, 1925, 1; Cline, *United States,* 210; *El Universal,* December 7, 1925, 1:6; December 11, 1925, 1:1; December 31, 1925, 1:8;

January 1, 1926, 1:1; *Diario de los debates de la Cámara de Senadores*, December 29, 1925, 1–2, 26.

45. L. Ethan Ellis, "Frank B. Kellogg," in Norman A. Graebner (ed.), *An Uncertain Tradition* (New York, 1961), 158.

46. *El Universal*, February 6, 1926, 8:5; New York *Times*, November 1, 1925, 29:2; November 3, 1925, 22:2.

47. "Alleged Schismatic Movement in the Roman Catholic Church in Mexico," 812.404/257; L. F. Bustamante, "Existe en México un Papa Cismático," *Jueves de Excélsior*, July 6, 1944 (no pagination); New York *Times*, February 24, 1925, 21:6.

48. "Alleged Schismatic Movement"; New York *Times*, March 15, 1925, I, 4:5; March 22, 1925, 3:6; Callcott, *Liberalism*, 376.

49. Rius Facius, *De don Porfirio*, 312–313, 317–318; Conflicto Religioso, Roll 10 (Microfilms of the archive of Miguel Palomar y Vizcarra in the library of the Museum of Anthropology and Archaeology in Mexico City. Hereafter cited as Conflicto Religioso); Miguel Palomar y Vizcarra, *El caso ejemplar mexicano* (México, 1966), 143–146.

50. Lippmann, "Church and State," 186–207; Norman King to Foreign Office, April 4, 1925; *ibid.*, May 27, 1925.

51. Gruening, *Mexico*, 658–659.

52. *El Universal*, December 15, 1925, 1:3; Rius Facius, *Méjico cristero* (Mexico, 1960), 21–22.

Chapter 6

1. Lagarde, "Religious Crisis in Mexico," gives the French chargé d'affaires' sometimes unflattering impressions of the bishops and archbishops. For biographical data see Valverde Téllez, *Bio-bibliografía*.

2. *El Universal*, December 30, 1925, 1:7; January 19, 1926, 1:5; January 25, 1926, 1:6.

3. *Ibid.*, January 27, 1926, 1:6; January 29, 1926, 1:3.

4. New York *Times*, April 20, 1926, 4:2; *El Universal*, January 1, 1926, 1:7–8.

5. *Ibid.*, February 4, 1926, 1:2; Ernest Gruening, *Mexico*, 275.

6. *El Universal*, February 5, 1926, 1:5; February 6, 1926, 1:1, 3:3–6; February 7, 1926, 1:1.

7. *Ibid.*, February 9, 1926, 10:6–7; February 11, 1926, 12:3; James R. Sheffield to Secretary of State, February 9, 1926/280; New York *Times*, February 12, 1926, 1:6.

8. *El Universal*, February 12, 1926, 1:2–3; Alexander Weddell to Secretary of State, February 1 [*sic*], 1926/371; Alicia and María Luisa Huerta, "Historia del Conflicto Religioso," *El Mundo*, August 30, 1951, 34–35; *El Universal*, February 13, 1926, 1:6; February 14, 1926, 1:6; Esmond Ovey to Foreign Office, February 15, 1926.

9. Huerta, *El Mundo*, August 30, 1951, 31; Calles to state governors, February 24, 1926/327; *El Universal*, February 14, 1926, 1:7; Sheffield to

Secretary of State, February 15, 1926/275; *El Universal,* February 16, 1926, 5:4; February 18, 1926, 1:5; February 21, 1926, 1:8; February 24, 1926, 1:3; "Statement of Minister of Gobernación, Adalberto Tejeda," February 23, 1926/327.

10. Huerta, *El Mundo,* September 13, 1951, 28–32; *El Universal,* February 24, 1926, 1:7–8; New York *Times,* February 24, 1926, 1:4–5; February 25, 1926, 3:5.

11. Rius Facius, *Méjico cristero,* 37; New York *Times,* February 26, 1926, 5:2; *El Universal,* February 25, 1926, 3:3–6.

12. *Ibid.,* March 6, 1926, 5:4.

13. *Ibid.;* Rius Facius, *Méjico cristero,* 38–44.

14. *El Universal,* March 14, 1926, 1:2; March 17, 1926, 1:6–7; March 28, 1926, 1:3; April 6, 1926, 1:6; New York *Times,* March 15, 1926, 11:7; March 20, 1926, 12:6; Leopoldo Lara y Torres, *Documentos para la historia de la persecución religiosa en México* (México, 1954), 91–131.

15. Rius Facius, *Méjico cristero,* 48–50; Gruening, *Mexico,* 276; Conflicto Religioso, roll 10.

16. *El Universal,* April 14, 1926, 1:7; April 17, 1926, 1:8; New York *Times,* April 18, 1926, I, 2:6; April 22, 1926, 8:2; *El Universal,* April 23, 1926, 1:7–8; May 12, 1926, 1:6.

17. Rius Facius, *Méjico cristero,* 50–52; *El Universal,* May 25, 1926, 1:8; Sheffield to Secretary of State, May 26, 1926/484; New York *Times,* May 23, 1926, I, 3:2; Valverde Téllez, *Bio-bibliografía,* II, 62.

18. Weddell to Secretary of State, June 3, 1926/493; *El Universal,* May 29, 1926, 1:7; June 3, 1926, 1:3; Sheffield to Secretary of State, June 3, 1926/490; New York *Times,* June 4, 1926, 5:2.

19. Lagarde, "Religious Crisis in Mexico"; Weddell to Secretary of State, February 1 [*sic*], 1926/371.

20. Odo Russell to Foreign Office, April 9, 1926; George Caruana to Secretary of State, June 4, 1926, 312.1124; *El Universal,* March 13, 1926, 1:2; Weddell to Secretary of State, March 1 [*sic*], 1926/416; New York *Times,* March 16, 1926, 11:2; May 17, 1926, 5:3.

21. *El Universal,* April 7, 1926, 1:8; April 13, 1926, 1:7–8; Sheffield to Secretary of State, May 22, 1926/482; Huerta, *El Mundo,* September 20, 1951, 46.

22. Alberto María Carreño, *El Arzobispo de México Pascual Díaz y el conflicto religioso* (2nd ed., México, 1943), 16–17; *El Universal,* May 11, 1926, 1:7; María Elena Sodi de Pallares, "Historia del Último Conflicto Religioso," *Jueves de Excélsior,* March 6, 1952, 6–7.

23. Frank Tannenbaum, *Mexico,* 132–133; Tannenbaum to author, December 12, 1961.

24. New York *Times,* May 16, 1926, 27:5; *El Universal,* May 17, 1926, 1:7–8; May 19, 1926, 1:8, 8:5; New York *Times,* May 20, 1926, 52:3; Sheffield to Secretary of State, June 22, 1926, 312.1124.

25. *Catholic Universe-Bulletin* (Cleveland), May 28, 1926, 1:6.

26. New York *Times,* February 18, 1926, 3:6; February 20, 1926, 1:6.

27. *Ibid.,* February 19, 1926, 12:2; March 1, 1926, 19:1.

28. R. C. T. to Franklin M. Gunther, March 8, 1926/340; New York *Times*, March 17, 1926, 3:2; March 31, 1926, 7:1.

29. New York *Times*, April 1, 1926, 8:1.

30. *Ibid.*, April 11, 1926, 7:2; American bishops and archbishops to Calvin Coolidge, April 15, 1926/413.

31. "Memorandum of interview of Father Burke and Secretary Kellogg," April 21, 1926/502; Gunther to Secretary of State, May 1, 1926/462; *ibid.*, May 14, 1926/464; John J. Burke to Secretary of State, May 18, 1926/466.

32. New York *Times*, April 25, 1926, 23:3; Sheffield to Secretary of State, May 7, 1926/448; *ibid.*, May 19, 1926/480.

33. *El Universal*, April 21, 1926, 1:7–8, 6:1–6; William F. Montavon, *The Facts Concerning the Mexican Problem* (Washington, D.C., 1926), 57; Gruening, *Mexico*, 276.

34. Sheffield to Secretary of State, April 30, 1926/477; *El Universal*, April 30, 1926, 1:8; New York *Times*, May 2, 1926, II, 3:4.

35. *Ibid.*, May 3, 1926, 5:3; *El Universal*, May 12, 1926, 1:2; May 19, 1926, 1:2; May 20, 1926, 1:1; New York *Times*, June 9, 1926, 4:3; *El Universal*, June 10, 1926, 1:5; Francisco Orozco y Jiménez, "Apologia pro Vita Sua," Archive of Archdiocese of Los Angeles (edited by Francis J. Weber); Huerta, *El Mundo*, August 30, 1951, 27; Chicago *Tribune*, June 19, 1926, 3:5–6.

36. *El Universal*, July 3, 1926, 1:3; *Diario Oficial*, January 30, 1926, 1; July 2, 1926, 1; Conflicto Religioso, roll 10.

37. *Diario Oficial*, July 2, 1926, 1.

38. *El Universal*, July 4, 1926, 1:1; New York *Times*, July 5, 1926, 1:4; Rius Facius, *Méjico cristero*, 63–64; James W. Wilkie and Edna Monzón de Wilkie, *Mexico visto en el siglo XX* (Mexico, 1969), 442 (interview with Miguel Palomar y Vizcarra).

39. Sodi de Pallares, *Jueves*, March 20, 1952, 10–11; Miguel Palomar y Vizcarra and Jorge Núñez, "Ahora nosotros," *Excélsior*, September 11, 1943, 4:7–8; Orozco y Jiménez, "Apologia."

40. Lagarde, "Religious Crisis in Mexico."

41. Sodi de Pallares, *Jueves*, March 6, 1952, 7; Palomar y Vizcarra and Núñez, *Excélsior*, September 11, 1943, 4:7–8.

42. *El Universal*, July 16, 1926, 1:3; July 17, 1926, 1:6–7; July 23, 1926, 1:3; Rius Facius, *Méjico cristero*, 65–66; Sheffield to Secretary of State, July 16, 1926/510; New York *Times*, July 22, 1926, 5:2; *Diario Oficial*, July 28, 1926, 7–8; Sheffield to Secretary of State, July 24, 1926/532.

43. Sheffield to Secretary of State, July 20, 1926/519.

44. *El Universal*, July 22, 1926, 1:5, 6:3; July 23, 1926, 1:7–8; July 24, 1926, 1:8; New York *Times*, July 25, 1926, 12:3–6; July 26, 1926, 2:1; Conflicto Religioso, roll 10.

45. Sheffield to Secretary of State, July 20, 1926/518; *ibid.*, July 21, 1926/523; *ibid.*, July 21, 1926/525; Arthur Bliss Lane to Secretary of State, July 29, 1926/544; Ovey to Foreign Office, July 27, 1926.

46. "Collective Pastoral Letter," July 24, 1926/535, 539; Rius Facius, *Méjico cristero*, 66; New York *Times*, July 26, 1926, 2:2; *El Universal*, July 25, 1926, 1:7–8, 4:4–6; Conflicto Religioso, roll 10.

47. New York *Times*, July 24, 1926, 12:1–2; *El Universal*, July 26, 1926, 1:4; July 28, 1926, 1:5.

48. New York *Times*, July 29, 1926, 2:4, 2:7; *El Universal*, July 30, 1926, 1:2–3.

49. New York *Times*, July 25, 1926, 2:5.

50. *Ibid.*, July 30, 1926, 1:1, 3:5–6.

51. *Ibid.*, July 26, 1926, 1:8, 2:1, 2:3; July 27, 1926, 1:1, 3:5; July 31, 1926, 1:8, 2:1, 2:3; August 1, 1926, 1:5; *El Universal*, July 31, 1926, 1:4–5; Sheffield to Secretary of State, July 28, 1926/541.

52. For descriptions of the first days of the strike see dispatches of Dudley Dwyre in Guadalajara/459, 560, 631; Bartley F. Yost in Torreón/540, 573, 580; Henry C. A. Damm in Nogales/563; William P. Blocker in Mazatlán/581, 679; Thomas A. Horn in Saltillo/589; Henry G. Krause in San Luis Potosí/596; Willys A. Myers in Veracruz/640; David J. D. Myers in Durango/645; Drew Linard in Piedras Negras /647; Frank Bohr in Mexicali/653; and Peter H. A. Flood in Tampico/667; British Vice-consul to Esmond Ovey, August 27, 1926.

53. Weddell to Secretary of State, August 2, 1926/553; New York *Times*, August 1, 1926, VIII, 15:2.

54. New York *Times*, August 2, 1926, 1:6–7, 2:1; Sheffield to Secretary of State, August 2, 1926/555.

55. Sheffield to Secretary of State, August 3, 1926/554.

56. New York *Times*, August 3, 1926, 1:6; August 4, 1926, 1:8; August 5, 1926, 1:2, 3:4; August 11, 1926, 2:3; Palomar y Vizcarra and Núñez, *Excélsior*, September 11, 1943, 4:7–8.

57. Mora y del Río, "Memorial de los Prelados Mejicanos al Señor Presidente," México, August 16, 1926; *El Universal*, August 20, 1926, 1:3–4; New York *Times*, August 19, 1926, 1:4, 3:4.

58. *Ibid.*, August 20, 1926, 1:1; *El Universal*, August 21, 1926, 1:3.

59. *Ibid.*, August 22, 1926, 1:5–6; August 23, 1926, 1:7–8; August 24, 1926, 7:3–4; New York *Times*, August 22, 1926, I, 1:1; August 23, 1926, 1:7, 2:3.

60. Lagarde, "Religious Crisis in Mexico."

61. Palomar y Vizcarra and Núñez, *Excélsior*, September 11, 1943, 4:7–8; New York *Times*, August 24, 1926, 1:1, 2:2; August 28, 1926, 12:2.

62. *El Universal*, September 2, 1926, 5:2, 10:7–8; September 7, 1926, 1:4; New York *Times*, September 3, 1926, 19:1.

63. *Ibid.*, September 8, 1926, 1:5.

64. *Ibid.*, September 23, 1926, 10:5; September 25, 1926, 10:1; *El Universal*, September 23, 1926, 1:8, 6:3; September 24, 1926, 1:8.

65. James A. Flaherty to Coolidge, August 6, 1926/565; New York *Times*, August 6, 1926, 1:8.

66. *Mexico* (New Haven, 1926).

67. Kellogg to Flaherty, August 12, 1926/565; Kellogg to Coolidge, August 26, 1926/638; New York *Times*, August 17, 1926, 1:1.

68. *Pastoral Letter of the Catholic Episcopate of the United States on the Religious Situation in Mexico* (New York, 1926), 8–9.

69. *The Congregationalist,* August 12, 1926, 195–196; H. W. Evans to Secretary of State, September 17, 1926/652.

70. New York *Times,* October 3, 1926, 24:1; October 13, 1926, 6:1; October 17, 1926, 17:1; *El Universal,* October 16, 1926, 1:8; November 26, 1926, 1:8; H. F. Arthur Schoenfeld to Secretary of State, November 6, 926/701; *ibid.,* November 26, 1926/713.

71. Rius Facius, *Méjico cristero,* 169; Orozco y Jiménez, "Apologia"; Vilkie and Wilkie, *México,* 451, 460.

Chapter 7

1. Orozco y Jiménez, Apologia pro Vita Sua; McDonough to Secretary f State, November 17, 1926/708; Conflicto Religioso, microfilm rolls 15– 1, contains battle reports from the Cristero commanders; for a scholarly ationalization of the rebellion see James W. Wilkie, "The Meaning of the Cristero Religious War against the Mexican Revolution," *Church and State,* VIII (Spring 1966), 214–233; "Memorandum for the Ambassador," May 6, 1928, Morrow Papers, Amherst College.

2. Degollado Guízar, *Memorias,* 43, 55, 91.

3. Rius Facius, *Méjico cristero,* 123; Dulles, *Yesterday,* 311; Liceaga, *Félix Díaz,* 800–801.

4. Degollado Guízar, *Memorias,* 135; Dulles, *Yesterday,* 311; J. Andrés Lara, *Prisionero de callistas y cristeros* (México, 1954); Spectator (pseud.), *Los cristeros del Volcán de Colima* (México, 1961); Silvano Barba González, *La Rebelión de los cristeros* (México, 1967); Morrow to Kellogg, July 16, 1928, 312.00/29215½.

5. Degollado Guízar, *Memorias,* 22, 45; Sodi de Pallares, *Jueves,* March 13, 1950, 10–11.

6. Rius Facius, *Méjico cristero,* 123–124; René Capistrán Garza, *Andanzas de un periodista* (México, 1959), 150; Jesús Guisa y Azevedo, *Los católicos y la política. El caso de Capistrán Garza* (México, 1952), 12.

7. Rius Facius, *Méjico cristero,* 125, 137–138

8. *Ibid.,* 138–139.

9. *Ibid.,* 140–142.

10. *El Universal,* November 7, 1926, 1:4; New York *Times,* November 10, 1926, 13:2.

11. Jesús García Gutiérrez, "Peor esta que estaba," *Todo,* October 14, 1954, 37; British Legation to Holy See to Foreign Office, August 12, 1926; A. Randall to Foreign Office, August 19, 1926; New York *Times,* November 21, 1926, I, 2:3; November 24, 1926, 11:4.

12. New York *Times,* November 26, 1926, 5:6; *El Universal,* December 28, 1926, 1:2, 1:8; December 31, 1926, 1:8; January 1, 1927, 1:5, 11:4.

13. Sheffield to Secretary of State, January 20, 1927/742; Weddell to Secretary of State, January 25, 1927/752; *El Universal,* January 1, 1927, 1:7–8.

14. Rius Facius, *Méjico cristero,* 153–155.

15. Weddell to Secretary of State, December 7, 1926/727; Sheffield to Secretary of State, December 10, 1926, 812.00/28126; Rius Facius, *Méjico cristero,* 164.

16. *Ibid.,* 163; New York *Times,* December 5, 1926, 17:1–2; December 11, 1926, 8:2; Capistrán Garza, *Andanzas,* 150.

17. Rius Facius, *Méjico cristero,* 166.

18. *Ibid.,* 167.

19. Liceaga, *Félix Díaz,* 815–822.

20. Alberto María Carreño, *Pascual Díaz y el conflicto religioso* (México, 1934), 264–265; New York *Times,* October 6, 1958, 33:1; March 28, 1930, 18:2–5; Capistrán Garza, *Andanzas,* 151.

21. *El Universal,* January 4, 1927, 1:1, 1:5; January 6, 1927, 1:6; January 11, 1927, 1:3; Rius Facius, *Méjico cristero,* 156.

22. *El Universal,* January 17, 1927, 1:6.

23. *Ibid.,* January 18, 1927, 1:2, 5:5; Dudley G. Dwyre to Secretary of State, February 3, 1927/754; New York *Times,* February 1, 1927, 4:2; February 4, 1927, 2:6; *El Universal,* February 3, 1927, 1:1; Huerta, *El Mundo,* October 25, 1951, 37.

24. Sheffield to Secretary of State, January 18, 1927/747; Huerta, *El Mundo,* October 25, 1951, 39; New York *Times,* January 10, 1927, 1:5; January 18, 1927, 2:5; January 22, 1927, 2:4; Carreño, *Pascual Díaz y Barreto* (México, 1936), 16–17.

25. John A. Ryan to Norman Thomas, in Francis L. Broderick, "Liberalism and the Mexican Crisis of 1927," *Catholic Historical Review,* XL (October 1959), 316.

26. New York *Times,* February 6, 1927, 18:1; February 7, 1927, 4:2.

27. Rius Facius, *Méjico cristero,* 235–236; Carreño, *Pastorales, edictos y otros documentos del Exmo. y Rvmo. Dr. D. Pascual Díaz, Arzobispo de México* (México, 1938), 299, 322–323, 336; Wilkie and Wilkie, *México,* 458.

28. Orozco y Jiménez, Apologia pro Vita Sua; Valverde Téllez, *Bio-bibliografía,* I, 354–358; Rius Facius, *Méjico cristero,* 159.

29. Walter Lippmann, "Church and State," 197; Gruening, *Mexico,* 280; Rius Facius, *Méjico cristero,* 156–157.

30. *Ibid.,* 236–238; Antonio López Ortega, "Aclaraciones a lo dicho por don Alberto María Carreño," *Excélsior,* December 6, 1943, 4:1–3; Wilkie and Wilkie, *México,* 464.

31. Rius Facius, *Méjico cristero,* 238.

32. *Ibid.,* 239; Carreño, *Pastorales,* 301–302, 304.

33. *Ibid.,* 298, 311; Conflicto Religioso, roll 15.

34. *El Universal,* March 25, 1927, 1:1; March 26, 1927, 1:1, 12:5; Rius Facius, *Méjico cristero,* 244.

35. New York *Times,* March 27, 1927, 14:1–3.

36. Gruening, *Mexico,* 276; Huerta, *El Mundo,* November 1, 1951, 32; Dulles, *Yesterday,* 310; *El Universal,* March 21, 1927, 1:1–2.

37. *El Universal,* April 22, 1927, 1:5; Dwyre to Secretary of State, April 20, 1927, 812.00/28341; *ibid.,* April 21, 1927, 812.00/28363; *ibid.,* April 23, 1927, 812.00/28370.

38. *El Universal,* April 21, 1927, 1:4; Sheffield to Secretary of State, April 29, 1927/780; *ibid.,* April 23, 1927, 812.00/28345; *ibid.,* April 23, 1927/775; New York *Times,* April 23, 1927, 1:3; Genaro M. González, "Hombre y Estilo," *Excélsior,* February 4, 1948, 6:4–6; New York *Times,* May 1, 1927, 1:2.

39. Sheffield to Secretary of State, May 3, 1927/782; *El Universal,* May 26, 1927, II, 1; Dwyre to Secretary of State, May 26, 1927, 812.00/28444; *ibid.,* May 26, 1927/795; Sheffield to Secretary of State, May 27, 1927, 812.00/28445; H. F. Arthur Schoenfeld to Secretary of State, June 14, 1927/807; *El Universal,* June 14, 1927, 1:2–3; New York *Times,* July 16, 1927, 14:5.

40. Rius Facius, *Méjico cristero,* 248–249; Conflicto Religioso, roll 15; Díaz to [?], May 30, 1928, Conflicto Religiso, roll 17.

41. New York *Times,* June 27, 1927, 2:6; *El Universal,* June 26, 1927, 1:7–8, 7:3; Celso García Bracho, "El General Álvaro Obregón y la cuestión religiosa," *El Nacional,* October 25, 1931, 3:3–5; Schoenfeld to Secretary of State, January 11, 1928/846.

42. García Bracho, "El General Álvaro Obregón," *El Nacional,* October 25, 1931, 8:1–3.

43. Schoenfeld to Secretary of State, August 2, 1927, 812.00/28613; *ibid.,* August 2, 1927, 812.00/28613; *ibid.,* August 8, 1927/820; *ibid.,* August 15, 1927/824; *ibid.,* August 15, 1927/825; *El Universal,* August 9, 1927, 1:8; Harry B. Ott to Secretary of State, August 11, 1927/822; Eduardo Mestre, Statement to Dwight W. Morrow, October 8, 1927, Morrow Papers; Mestre to Aarón Sáenz [September 1927 (?)], Morrow Papers.

44. Mestre, Statement, Morrow Papers; Conflicto Religioso, roll 15.

45. Rius Facius, *Méjico cristero,* 250; Carreño, *Pascual Díaz y el conflicto religioso,* 46–52; Conflicto Religioso, rolls 16 and 21; Pascual Díaz to Luis G. Bustos, January 17, 1928, 812.404/896; Díaz to Morrow, July 24, 1928, Morrow Papers.

46. Rius Facius, *Méjico cristero,* 315–319; New York *Times,* November 22, 1927, 1:4; Morrow to Secretary of State, December 9, 1927/845½; Morrow to R. E. Olds, December 9, 1927, Morrow Papers; Wilkie and Wilkie, *México,* 451–452; Conflicto Religioso, rolls 15 and 16.

Chapter 8

1. Walter Davenport, "With Morrow in Mexico," *Collier's,* 86 (November 1, 1930), 7–9; Harold Nicolson, *Dwight Morrow* (New York, 1935), 309–310.

2. *Ibid.,* 258, 323.

3. Davenport, "With Morrow," 7–9; Nicolson, *Morrow,* 315–316, 328; Stanley R. Ross, "Dwight Morrow and the Mexican Revolution," *Hispanic American Historical Review,* XXXVIII (November 1958), 509–515.

4. Nicolson, *Morrow,* 341; Morrow to Secretary of State, July 23, 1928/895 2/9; Morrow, "Memorandum," November 29, 1927, Morrow

Papers; Morrow, "Confidential Memorandum for Mr. Olds," November 30, 1927, Morrow Papers.

5. *El Universal,* December 2, 1927, 1:1; Arthur Bliss Lane to R. E. Olds, December 13, 1927/845 3/4; New York *Times,* December 7, 1927, 31:7.

6. Morrow, "Memorandum to R. E. Olds," December 9, 1927, Morrow Papers.

7. Kellogg to Morrow, December 17, 1927, Morrow Papers.

8. Nicolson, *Morrow,* 310; New York *Times,* December 15, 1927, 1:7–8.

9. Morrow to Olds, December 9, 1927, Morrow Papers.

10. *El Universal,* December 31, 1927, 1:7–8.

11. *Ibid.,* January 28, 1928, 1:1; February 7, 1928, 1:2; February 8, 1928, 1:2; New York *Times,* January 29, 1928, 3:4; February 7, 1928, 5:4.

12. *Commonweal,* VII (January 4, 1928), 883–884.

13. New York *Times,* January 17, 1928, 44:5.

14. Odo Russell to Foreign Office, January 6, 1928; *ibid.,* January 27, 1928.

15. Morrow to Olds, February 21, 1928, Morrow Papers; Morrow to Secretary of State, July 23, 1928/895 2/9; Nicolson, *Morrow,* 341.

16. John J. Burke to Olds, February 6, 1928, Morrow Papers.

17. Morrow to Olds, February 21, 1928, Morrow Papers; New York *Herald-Tribune,* February 10, 1928 (clipping in Morrow Papers); New York *Times,* February 10, 1928, 4:6.

18. Conflicto Religioso, roll 16; Leopoldo Lara y Torres, *Documentos,* 239–246.

19. Morrow to Olds, February 21, 1928, Morrow Papers.

20. Olds to Morrow, March 9, 1928, Morrow Papers; *ibid.,* March 20, 1928, Morrow Papers.

21. Walter Lippmann to Burke, March 7, 1928, Morrow Papers.

22. Olds to Myron T. Herrick, March 10, 1928/873A; Olds to Morrow, March 9, 1928, Morrow Papers.

23. The original signed papers, which were never delivered, are in the Morrow Papers at Amherst College. Morrow to Secretary of State, March 13, 1928/872; Olds to Morrow, March 23, 1928, Morrow Papers; Morrow to Olds, March 27, 1928/874; Olds to Morrow, March 29, 1928/872; Nicolson, *Morrow,* 342.

24. Carreño, *Páginas de la historia mexicana* (México, 1936), 60; *El Universal,* April 4, 1928, 1:6; April 6, 1928, 1:4.

25. *Catholic World,* XVIII (December 15, 1926). The entire issue of this official NCWC organ was devoted to Burke's life and career.

26. George Rublee, "Religious Conflict," Morrow Papers; Olds to Morrow, April 18, 1928, Morrow Papers; Morrow to Clark, October 19, 1928/931 6/12; Plutarco Elías Calles to Burke, April 4, 1928/931 1/12; Morrow to Secretary of State, April 6, 1928/877; Ovey to Foreign Office, April 10, 1928; Nicolson, *Morrow,* 342.

27. Russell to Foreign Office, April 27, 1928; *ibid.,* May 4, 1928.

28. Rublee, "Religious Conflict"; Olds to Morrow, April 25, 1928, Morrow Papers; *ibid.,* April 25, 1928, Morrow Papers; *ibid.,* May 9, 1928, Mor-

row Papers; Kellogg to Morrow, May 9, 1928/882b; Pedro J. Sánchez, *Episodios eclesiásticos de México* (México, 1948), 562; *El Universal,* April 23, 1928, 1:1.

29. Rublee, "Religious Conflict"; Morrow to Kellogg, July 23, 1928/895 2/9; Nicolson, *Morrow,* 343.

30. Morrow to Secretary of State, May 17, 1928/884; Morrow to Agustín Legorreta, July 16, 1928, Morrow Papers; Morrow to Secretary of State, May 17, 1928/805; Morrow to Olds, May 17, 1928, Morrow Papers; Ovey to Foreign Office, May 24, 1928; Rublee, "Religious Conflict"; Morrow to Secretary of State, July 23, 1928/895 2/9.

31. Russell to Foreign Office, May 18, 1928; Ovey to Foreign Office, May 24, 1928; Rublee, "Religious Conflict"; Burke to Calles, May 19, 1928/931 2/12; Morrow to Secretary of State, July 23, 1928/895 2/9.

32. J. M. González Valencia to Díaz, April 28, 1928, Conflicto Religioso, roll 16; Rius Facius, *Méjico cristero,* 392–393; Rafael Ceniceros y Villarreal to Cardinal Gasparri, May 26, 1928, Conflicto Religioso, roll 16; "Memorial suscrito por la LNDLR, etc.," Conflicto Religioso, roll 17.

33. New York *Times,* June 2, 1928, 8:3.

34. *Ibid.,* June 7, 1928, 1:4; Schoenfeld to Secretary of State, June 6, 1928/889; *El Universal,* June 8, 1928, 1:7–8, 5:3; Schoenfeld to Secretary of State, June 8, 1928/891; *El Universal,* June 11, 1928, 1:7–8; Rublee, "Religious Conflict"; Ovey to Foreign Office, June 13, 1928; Morrow to Secretary of State, July 23, 1928/895 2/9; Palomar y Vizcarra, *El Caso,* 192–193; Palomar y Vizcarra and Núñez, *Excélsior,* September 11, 1943, 8:7–8; Lara y Torres, *Documentos,* 270; Orozco y Jiménez and de la Mora to the pope, June 22, 1928, Conflicto Religioso, roll 19; New York *World,* July 10, 1928, 1:1.

35. New York *Times,* June 8, 1928, 1:3; Warren D. Robbins to Secretary of State, June 15, 1928/893; Burke to Morrow, June 29, 1928, Morrow Papers.

36. New York *Times,* June 9, 1928, 3:1; June 14, 1928, 10:3; Russell to Foreign Office, June 15, 1928; Ovey to Foreign Office, August 7, 1928; *ibid.,* August 17, 1928.

37. Dulles, *Yesterday,* 335–361; New York *Times,* July 17, 1928, 1:4.

38. Morrow to Secretary of State, July 23, 1928/895 2/9; Dulles, *Yesterday,* 366.

39. *Ibid.,* 366–372; *El Universal,* July 18, 1928, 1:6–8; February 9, 1929, 1:7–8; Morrow to Secretary of State, July 18, 1928, 812.00/29215; *ibid.,* July 22, 1928, 812.00/29221; José de León Toral to Felipe Islas, November 22, 1928, Mendel Collection, Indiana University; *El jurado de Toral y la Madre Conchita* (2 vols., México, n.d.).

40. New York *World,* July 18, 1928, 2:2–3; July 19, 1928, 1:6–7.

41. Lane to Morrow, July 19, 1928/895 3/9; Morrow to Secretary of State, July 20, 1928, 812.00/29218; *El Universal,* August 4, 1928, 1:1; Lane to Morrow, July 25, 1928, Morrow Papers; Morrow to Secretary of State, August 14, 1928/895 8/9; Lane, "Memorandum of telephone conversation with Morrow," August 9, 1928/895 7/9.

42. *Osservatore Romano, passim;* Lane, "Memorandum of a telephone conversation with Morrow," August 7, 1928/903 3/5; *ibid.,* August 14, 1928/903 3/5.

43. Lane, "Memorandum of a telephone conversation with Morrow," August 29, 1928/908 ½; A. W. G. Randall to Foreign Office, September 26, 1928.

44. A. L. Negrete to Legorreta, September 1, 1928, Morrow Papers; Norman Armour to Secretary of State, September 17, 1928/915; Randall to Foreign Office, October 28, 1928; *ibid.,* December 3, 1928; Rublee, "Religious Conflict."

45. *Ibid.; El Universal,* February 11, 1929, 1:7–8; February 12, 1929, 1:5–6, 1:7–8; Morrow to Secretary of State, February 12, 1929/950; Nicolás Corona to Felipe Canales, February 21, 1929/974 3/17.

46. Dulles, *Yesterday,* 438–449; New York *Times,* March 22, 1929, 4:5; James G. Powell to Secretary of State, March 12, 1929/962.

47. *El Universal,* May 3, 1929, 1:5; New York *Times,* May 3, 1929, 2:5.

48. *El Universal,* May 8, 1929, 1:7–8; Lippmann, "Church and State," 204; Morrow to Secretary of State, May 8, 1929/977.

49. "Memorandum from the British legation in Mexico City," May 16, 1929, Morrow Papers; Lippmann to Morrow, May 3, 1929, Morrow Papers.

50. Rius Facius, *Méjico cristero,* 435; New York *Times,* June 1, 1929, 14:1; Valverde Téllez, *Bio-bibliografía,* II, 274.

51. Morrow to Clark, March 19, 1929, Morrow Papers; Lane, "Memorandum," May 23, 1929/974 12/17; *ibid.,* May 28, 1929/974 14/17; Lippmann to Morrow, May 3, 1929, Morrow Papers; Palomar y Vizcarra and Núñez, *Excélsior,* July 23, 1943, 4:3–4; Rublee, "Religious Conflict"; Nicolson, *Morrow,* 345.

52. Rius Facius, *Méjico cristero,* 436–437; Morrow to Legorreta, July 16, 1929, Morrow Papers; Morrow, "Memorandum," May 9, 1929/974 8/17; Lane, "Memorandum," May 9, 1929/974 5/17; Morrow to Clark, May 10, 1929/974 8/17; Gasparri to Legorreta, May 13, 1929, Morrow Papers; Miguel Cruchaga Tocornal, "El Conflicto Religioso Mexicano," *Revista chilena de historia y geografía,* 113 (January–June 1949), 216–255; Rublee, "Religious Conflict."

53. *Ibid.*

54. *Ibid.;* Morrow to Clark, June 13, 1929/997; Morrow to Secretary of State, June 14, 1929/998; Morrow to Cotton, June 15, 1929/1000; Rius Facius, *Méjico cristero,* 438.

55. Rublee, "Religious Conflict"; Morrow to Clark, June 15, 1929/1001; Rius Facius, *Méjico cristero,* 438; Morrow to Cotton, June 18, 1929/1003; "Memorandum of Palomar y Vizcarra," October 4, 1939, Conflicto Religioso, roll 20.

56. Rublee, "Religious Conflict"; "Summary by Fr. Walsh of a telegram received from the Holy See," June 20, 1929, Morrow Papers; Rius Facius, *Méjico cristero,* 439.

57. *El Universal,* June 22, 1929, 1:7–8; Rublee, "Religious Conflict"; Emilio Portes Gil, *Quince años de política mexicana* (México, 1941), 315–316;

Morrow to Clark, June 17, 1929/1002; *ibid.*, June 19, 1929/1004; *ibid.*, June 19, 1929/1005.

58. Rius Facius, *Méjico cristero*, 439–440; Orozco y Jiménez, Apologia pro Vita Sua; Carreño, *El Arzobispo*, 66, 72; Conflicto Religioso, roll 21.

59. Rius Facius, *Méjico cristero*, 440; Carreño, *Pascual Díaz y Barreto* (México, 1936), 22; New York *Times*, June 23, 1929, 22:2.

60. Orozco y Jiménez, Apologia; Nicolson, *Morrow*, 347.

61. *Ibid.*, 347; Ruiz y Flores to Ramón Villa and José Tello, August 4, 1929, Conflicto Religioso, roll 20; New York *Times*, September 23, 1930, 7:3; Wilkie and Wilkie, *Mexico visto*, 441, 444, 446; Eduardo Correa, "Dos Libros Muertos en su Cama," *Excélsior*, May 19, 1943, 4:5–6; Datos proporcionados por el Sr. Miguel Palomar y Vizcarra, no date, Conflicto Religioso, roll 20; Carreño, *El Arzobispo*, 66; New York *Times*, July 18, 1929, 18:4; Lane to Morrow, July 5, 1929, Morrow Papers.

Index